Henry Boynton

History of the Nineteenth Century in the United States and Europe

Period I: During the Triumphs of Napoleon's Empire

Henry Boynton

History of the Nineteenth Century in the United States and Europe
Period I: During the Triumphs of Napoleon's Empire

ISBN/EAN: 9783337274177

Printed in Europe, USA, Canada, Australia, Japan

Cover: Foto ©ninafisch / pixelio.de

More available books at **www.hansebooks.com**

HISTORY OF THE

NINETEENTH CENTURY

IN THE

UNITED STATES

AND

EUROPE

ILLUSTRATED

Period I
During the Triumphs of Napoleon's Empire

By HENRY BOYNTON
Author of "THE WORLD'S GREATEST CONFLICT"

PRESS CO., PUBLISHERS
AUGUSTA, ME.

INDEX OF ILLUSTRATIONS.

PAGE.
- 1 Napoleon's Empire at its Height in 1810.
- 2 Central North America in 1806.
- 3 Costumes in 1799; A Marriage. From Kammerer's Painting.
- 4 James Watt's First Lesson in Steam. Painted by David Neal.
- 10 Relative Populations of Countries.
- 16 Alpenmarchen. Painted by K. Dielitz.
- 24 Governor W. H. Harrison treating with Indians.
- 64 William Pitt. By Hoppner. Charles J. Fox. By Opie.
- 80 Kremlin, Moscow Royal Palace, Madrid.
- 104 Napoleon and his Son and War. By Steuben and Sartain.
- 109 Relative Forces in the Ulm Campaign.
- 112 Battle of Trafalgar.
- 120 Lord Nelson and Wreck of the Indomptable.
- 151 Napoleon's System of Line of Battle.
- 160 Palace of Fontainbleau.
- 184 One-Sixth of Jefferson's Effective Navy, 1806-9.
- 192 Jefferson Opposing Washington in the First Cabinet.
- 224 The Cavalry Charge. From Detaille's Painting.
- 240 Battle of Eylau in a Fierce Snow Storm.
- 256 Empress Josephine. The Beautiful Luise of Prussia and her Sister, Honoring Soldier's Graves.
- 296 Napoleon's Palaces and Prisons. Tuileries and Louvre and a Jail.
- 328 Duke of Wellington. Painted by Lawrence, the Figure by Evans.
- 400 Made a Blind Beggar by Walcheren.

PUBLISHER'S NOTICE.

THIS is a new, independent history, written from the American standpoint, teeming with important facts, some of which are new to most American and British readers, all of which are tersely written, and it strongly presents the great story of the real people and their rulers.

The author has given profound study to this period of history. He has twice visited Europe to obtain material from records, State papers, and other original documents not accessible in America.

Differing from all those writers who palliate the offenses of their favorites, he describes the greatest scenes of one of the most eventful periods of all history, without excusing the crimes of any one because of high rank or dazzling deeds. Only from books thus written without favoritism may we learn the true lessons which real history teaches, and avoid admiring false heroes.

UNITED STATES AND EUROPE.

Wurtemburg after 1805,	1,100,000
Bavaria after 1805,	3,250,000
Austria before Presburg treaty,	27,000,000
Austria after Presburg treaty,	25,000,000
Russia,	36,000,000
Prussia,	9,500,000
Great Britain, Ireland not included,	11,000,000
United States of America,	6,000,000
France,	27,000,000
Napoleon's Empire, not including his vassal states,	49,000,000
Spain,	9,000,000*

*Not very certain.

Relative population in 1804 is shown approximately by the above figures and by the length of the lines.

UNITED STATES AND EUROPE.

RULERS IN 1804.

Great Britain and Ireland, George III, king; limited; William Pitt, premier.
France, Napoleon Bonaparte, emperor; almost absolute. Talleyrand, premier.
Austria, Francis I, emperor; absolute; Stadion, premier.
Prussia, Frederick William, king; absolute; Haugwitz. premier.
Russia, Alexander I, czar; absolute.
Spain, Charles IV, king; absolute; Godoy, premier.
Sweden, Gustavus IV, king; absolute.
Denmark, Christian VII, king (insane); Bernsdorff, premier; Prince Frederick was regent. It held Norway.
Portugal, Marie, queen (insane); Prince Joam was regent.
Holland, "the Batavian Republic," controlled by Napoleon.
Belgium was a part of France.
Brunswick-Mecklinberg, Bavaria, Wurtemberg, Saxony Baden, Hesse-Cassel, Oldenberg, were under absolute electors.
Hanover, George III of England was its "elector." "
Switzerland, called "The Helvetian Republic," was controlled by Napoleon as "protector."
Kingdom of Italy (north). Napoleon Bonaparte, king; almost absolute; Eugene Beauharnais, viceroy.
Rome, Pius VII, pope. Held by Napoleon; absolute.
Naples and Sicily, Ferdinand, king; absolute.
Turkey, Selim III, sultan; almost absolute.
Poland, divided between Russia, Prussia and Austria.
United States of America, Thomas Jefferson was president from March 4, 1801, to March 4, 1809. James Madison was Secretary of State.
Brazil was held by Portugal.
Except Guiana all the rest of South America and all Mexico, Central America and Cuba, were held by Spain.
Great Britain had great possessions in India and America.

SOME OF THE WORKS AND AUTHORS CONSULTED.

Abrantes, Duchess d', Memoirs de.
Adams, John, Works of.
Adams, John Q., Works of.
Alison's History of Europe.
Americana Cyclopedia.
Annual Register.
Appleton's Cyclopedia.
Badeker's Maps.
Bain's France.
Baldwin's Party Leaders.
Bancroft's History of the U. S.
Belsheon's Geo. III.
Bignon's Memoirs of Napoleon.
Blaine's Twenty Years in Congress.
Blair's Annals of America.
Botta's Italy.
Bourrienne, Memoirs de.
Boytelin.
Bradbury, James W., Speech on French Claims.
Britannica Encyclopedia.
British Museum Historical Papers.
British State Papers.
Burt, Paul.
Butler's Settlers of Kentucky.
Calhoun, John C., Life of, by Jenkins.
Canning, George. State Papers.
Caulaincourt,   "   "
Census Reports of Several Nations.
Chambers' Cyclopedia.
Christie's History of Canada.
Clark, Edson C., Races of Turkey.
Clay, Henry, Speeches and State Papers.
Cobb, T. R., Slavery.

Cobbett, William.
Collingwood, Life of, by his Nephew.
Congress, Acts of.
" Debates of.
Cooper's Naval History.
Coote's Modern Europe.
Crowe's History of France.
Denmark, History of.
Diplomacy, "
" American.
Duffy, Gavan, Young Ireland.
Edinburgh Review, 1802-16.
Engineers, The Great, by Smiles.
Fouché, Memoirs de.
Fox, Charles J., Speeches.
Garneau's History of Canada.
Gay-Bryant History of U. S.
Giddings' Florida Exiles.
Goodrich's History of U. S.
Grattan, Irish Speeches.
Green, J. R., History of England.
Greeley, Horace, Life of Clay.
Guizot's History of France.
Hale, Salma, History of U. S.
Hardenberg, State Papers.
Harrison, William H., Life of, by Montgomery
Hildreth's History of U. S.
Hugo Victor.
Indian Empire, History of the.
Irving's Life of Columbus.
James' Naval History.
Jefferson, Thomas. State Papers and Works.
Johnston's Cyclopedia.
Johnston's Maps.
Kendall's Notes of Travel 1807 — Wm. B. Lapham.
Knight, Charles, History of England.

Koch-Schoell, Revolution in Europe.
Lalor's Political Science.
Lanfrey's Napoleon.
Las Casas.
Law Reports.
Lossing's U. S.
Macaulay, T. B., Life of Pitt.
Mackenzie's 19th Century.
Maister, Stephen d', on Russia.
Madison, James. State Papers.
Malthus.
Martineau's England.
Martin's History of France.
McCarty, Justin H.
McMasters' History of U. S.
Metternich, Memoirs de.
Moniteur.
Monroe, James, Correspondence.
Montholon & Gourgaud, Memoirs de.
Moore's, Sir John, Journal and Dispatches.
Morse's Geography.
Napier, Gen., Peninsular War.
Napoleon, State Papers.
" Memoirs de St. Helena.
Narrative and Critical Hist. of U. S. — Windsor.
Naval Glory of England. — Russell & Jacques.
Navarette.
Nelson's Correspondence.
" Life of, by Southey.
Niles' Register.
North American Review.
Parliament, Acts of.
" Reports of.
Pitt, William, State Papers.
" Life of.
Quincy, Josiah, Speeches.

Rambaud's History of Russia.
Randall's Life of Jefferson.
Randolph, John, Speeches.
Recamier, Madame, Memoirs of.
Remusat   "   "   "
Romilly, Sir Samuel, Diary.
Rotteck's History of Europe.
Schlosser's [F. C.], Geschichte des 18 Jahrh.
Scott, Sir Walter, Life of Napoleon Buonaparte.
Segur, Memoirs d' Count.
Seward's Life of J. Q. Adams.
Slater, Samuel, Memoirs of.
Spanish Acts and Decrees.
Sparks' American Biography.
Spalding's Italy.
State Papers of Various Nations.
Sweden, History of.
Tactics, Systems of.
Talleyrand's Correspondence.
Teft's Webster.
Thackeray's Four Georges.
Thiers, Adolphe, Consulate et l' Empire.
Treaties of Several Nations.
Tucker's Jefferson.
Ukases of Russia.
War Bulletins.
War Office Papers.
Watt, James, Life of.
Webster, Daniel, Speeches of.
Wellington (Duke of , Dispatches.
Wilson, Henry, Rise and Fall of the Slave Power. And numerous others.

INTRODUCTION.

History for American or British readers must recognize the fact that all persons are naturally entitled to common rights, fairness and humanity; that rulers have no just right to deprive any people or any innocent person of comfort, by making needless war, or by useless or pernicious acts; that a ruler may not seek merely his own will or pleasure, but is bound to act only for the best good of his people; that every person is accountable to the same moral principles of action, and an act or a motive that would be crime in a pauper is also a crime in a prince, and that any admiration we may indulge for an eminent man must yield to any adverse verdict that may be given by our own conscience.

The times to which this history relates, although recent, were very different from ours of today. We are not accountable for the errors of our ancestors in that hating, warring period, unless we approve of those errors. Our century began in a wicked, a cruel period; the European race was then war-mad; it was an era of distrust, of enmity, of active malignity; benign religion was not active; generous sentiments were suppressed; grand humanities, such as asylums and hospitals were almost nonexistent; newspapers, now public educators, were few, and under strict censorship everywhere except in America and Great Britain; outside of New England and Scotland few public free schools existed; neither the British, French nor German law systems had yet been reformed by such men as the great Romilly, Tronchet and Savigny; international courtesy was almost unknown.

We have German, Swiss, Dutch, Italian, Portuguese and Turkish history mainly from writers unfriendly to those peoples; Swedish, Danish and Spanish from their rivals; British, from their bitter enemies or their ardent apologists. Instead of these let us have honest, actual history—the real facts. Too many writers conceal or palliate errors. The despotism of the murderer of Palm, the bookseller, and censorship suppressed so many facts, that history has not usually done justice to the grand German people, who have stood in the dense shadow of incapable Frederick William III.

If the person is greatest who most influences and benefits mankind, then James Watt is greater than all the Cæsars; educators are greater than politicians; a free and well-directed press is a nobler instrument than cannon; editors are greater than generals.

The history of our country or of any country, to be understood, must be read and studied in close connection with that of those with which it has considerable intercourse. To judge of our own progress, we must also study our neighbor nations. To admit the idea that all errors are foreign and all wisdom exclusively our own would destroy the lessons of history. It is not well to be dazzled by any brilliant man or splendid career. Let us estimate every person, a powerful emperor, an American president, or the most lowly laborer, by the same just principles of honor, conscience, fairness and humanity; if his deeds be right let us honor him; if his acts be wrong let him be unto us as a wrong-doer; only such study of history can be profitable.

To prepare this history I have examined a great number and amount of evidences, with care and labor. I have investigated with honest candor. I now report the facts as the evidences show them, which are, in numerous instances, different from what I expected and desired.

AUGUSTA, ME.   H. B.

ALPENMARCHEN; DREAM OF SWISS LIBERTY.

PAINTED BY K. DIELITZ.

HISTORY OF THE UNITED STATES AND EUROPE.

I

THIS Century began in exciting times. On its first day, January 1, 1801, Great Britain and Ireland united as one nation. King George III was apprehensive that Bonaparte would possess himself of Denmark's navy, so Admirals Nelson and Parker demanded its surrender to England; and on refusal they bombarded Copenhagen and destroyed most of Denmark's fleet. The bad Russian Czar, Paul, was strangled by some of his officers, because he was cruel. These two events broke up a great coalition of north Europe and Russia, and Austria made the peace of Luneville of February 9, 1801, with Bonaparte, who ruled France. Only Britain and France remained at war.

William Pitt, head of the British ministry, wished to give common political rights to Irish Catholics. George III refused and Pitt resigned. George formed a new tory ministry.

The French in Egypt, beaten in battle by the British, March 21, surrendered on condition of being carried home to France.

Bonaparte compelled Holland to receive a French constitution. Of 416,419 Dutch voters, 52,219 voted against it, the rest, dissatisfied, refused to vote, but Bonaparte insisted that all who had not voted against it had tacitly consented to it, and he put it in force. But he soon set it aside to give power to a few persons whom he could control, and Holland remained in his power till 1814.

The foolish king of Spain, Charles IV, gave to Bonaparte five Spanish war ships, a large sum of money, all Louisiana, and promised to force Portugal to close its trade with England, for all of which Bonaparte gave the king's boy son-in-law, Ferdinand, duke of Parma, the title of king of Etruria (Tuscany), then a republic; but Bonaparte held his own power over this new king and his domains, and seized Parma, too, as soon as this boy died, in 1803.

In January, 1802, Bonaparte assembled 452 Italians at Lyons, and, when many of them were absent, obtained from the remaining fraction a vote that he be president of the Italian Republic. This was all the election that took place; on this he took the great office. His constitution ordained that no law could be made unless offered by him; only 700 Italians were allowed to be voters, and a French army was kept there at Italy's expense. Then Genoa came into his power.

In France Bonaparte suppressed liberty, organized a spy police, made summary courts to punish with promptness, and held a court like a king. He built roads, canals and public buildings and infused energy. Churches were already re-opened all over France. He made a Concordat with the Pope, July 15, 1801, which regulated the church and allowed him to select the bishops, and he hoped to compel the church to promote his own ambition, and for the same object he allowed banished monarchists to return.

Britain and France agreed, October 1, 1801, to make peace, and it was made March 27, 1802. After all the immense damage done by the long war it left all as it was when the war began, in 1793, except that Britain kept Spanish Trinidad, and Surinam, and Dutch Ceylon.

Able lawyers formed a law code which was gradually adopted in France. But Bonaparte's power was nearly absolute. Against opposition he originated the Legion of Honor, but it soon became popular.

In May, 1802, the Senate voted him consul for ten years longer. This did not satisfy him, so the proposal that he be consul for life was voted on by the people. It was dangerous to vote "no." The Senate announced the vote as 3,577,379 yeas and 8,494 noes. Bonaparte had appointed the senators and the councilors, and they were servile to him; they changed the constitution for him, reduced the council from 500 to 258, and the tribunate from 150 to 80, and gave him power to add 40 senators. His servile Senate was to control all laws and courts and appoint the Legislative Body and Tribunate, but all the Senate's acts were first to emanate from him.

Rulers were held to be owners of their peoples, and Bonaparte, with concurrence of Alexander, Czar of Russia, partitioned, traded, and gave away several of the provinces, cities and peoples of Germany. Of 45 free towns only six, Frankfort, Augsburg, Lubec, Bremen, Hamburg, and Nuremberg, were left free. It was a dividing of prey among princes.

The colored race of St. Domingo had revolted, freed themselves from slavery and liberated their country.

In 1802, Bonaparte's government made a law to reestablish slavery, and to restore the frightful slave-trade, and to put St. Domingo for ten years under his own exclusive control.[1] He sent about 40,000

[1] Act relative to colonies, 1802.

French troops, under Gen. Leclerc, to re-conquer and re-enslave the San Domingans. The natives made gallant resistence; the war was terribly fierce, bloody, destructive; that lovely island was devastated; many French fell victims to war and climate. The colored chief, Toussaint L'Ouverture, capitulated May 8, 1802. Then the French ill-treated the conquered men. By order of Bonaparte, they, by treachery, seized Toussaint and sent him to France, where Bonaparte placed him in the cold mountain prison of Joux, where he soon died. This treachery so enraged the colored men that they rose again in arms, and terrible scenes followed. In a few weeks many thousands of both parties were destroyed by war and fevers. Gen. Leclerc died. Reinforcements came from France, but this only increased the already frightful losses. In 1803 the remnant surrendered to Toussaint's successor, Dessalines, and British ships carried them away. A massacre of whites followed. In 1804 Dessalines proclaimed himself emperor, but he was killed in 1805 and Christophe and Petion's wars made of the island two states, the kingdom of St. Domingo, and the republic, Hayti, and bloody wars raged between them.

In September, 1802, Bonaparte annexed Piedmont to France; he compelled Naples and Sardinia to give him Elba; he ruled Holland and compelled it to support a French army; he invaded and occupied Switzerland. Not one of these acts was just. The English press severely condemned them. Bonaparte's official *Moniteur* bitterly replied. He could not tolerate a free press, even in England; he entered on a newspaper war with it. He became very much enraged and wanted the British government to suppress his newspaper opponents. It was said that he sent military men accredited as commercial agents, but really spies, to report plans of best ways to enter British ports. England dismissed them, and Bonaparte was still more furious. The French anti-Bonapartist refugees in England taunted him. The contest of words aroused Britain for war again. Its ministry replied to Bonaparte that it did not control the British Press, yet the *Moniteur*, which abused England, was Bonaparte's official organ; suit for libel could be had in British courts. But Bonaparte demanded that England stop the press from injuring his character and measures; and cease to give asylum to his enemies. England always offers asylum to refugees. But a libel suit was brought against one Peltier. He was convicted, but his lawyer, James Mackintosh, made for a free press, and against Bonaparte's abuse of the rights of mankind, a speech that rang throughout Europe. Then Bonaparte seized some British vessels driven to France by a storm; he also demanded that the English leave Egypt and Malta, as agreed in the terms of peace. England complained of Bonaparte's annexation of Piedmont and Genoa and aggressions in Holland and Switzerland, and demanded that Europe be as when the peace was signed March 27, 1802, she said this increase of France had impaired the treaty; France might occupy Egypt to injure the British in India.

Then the *Moniteur* published a report of Col. Sebastiani, who had been sent to examine eastern places; he said that 6000 French could take Egypt. Then a vain account of French power was officially published February 23, 1803. It summed up that "England, single-handed, is unable to cope with France."

George and his Addington ministry took this as a defiance, and wanted satisfaction for this "singular aggression."

George announced French "considerable military preparations" and "differences" and new British measures of precaution. On news of this message Bonaparte violently upbraided the British ambassador in presence of the European ambassadors. He had done this once before, February 18, and said, " sooner or later Egypt will belong to France." In this remark George fancied a threat. England gave its ultimatum, — England to retain Malta for ten years, then it to be independent; Naples to cede Lampedusa to England; the French to quit Holland and Switzerland; the king of Sardinia to be indemnified; England to recognize the Italian Republic and Kingdom of Etruria.

France replied with offer of transfer of Malta to Russia, Prussia, or Austria, and to treat on all new points. George refused; he wanted to keep Malta, which he was pledged to surrender to France. On May 20, 1803, his licensed privateers seized two French vessels without declaration of war, and the war was thus begun which was to last for eleven long, bloody years, to the distress of all mankind. Bonaparte retaliated by seizing, as prisoners, all English travelers in France, and he kept them for eleven years.

The king of England was also elector of Hanover. Bonaparte sent a French army and seized Hanover and the free cities of Hamburg and Bremen. He compelled them and Holland to give him large sums of money, — a plain robbery. England blockaded the Elbe and the Weser. Prussia, Russia, Austria, and

Denmark, were displeased. Bonaparte offered Hanover to Prussia in exchange for an alliance offensive and defensive. Prussia refused it.

Thomas Jefferson became president March 4, 1801. Louisiana was all the country west of the Mississippi to the Rocky Mountains, and a broad strip of coast from New Orleans east to the Perdido River, where it joined Spain's Florida. So the United States had not a foot of the coast of the Gulf of Mexico. It could reach it only through foreign ground. In 1803 the officials at New Orleans denied to Americans a treaty right to deposit goods for shipment at New Orleans. Kentucky was indignant; it called for war. Congress authorized President Jefferson to prepare 80,000 volunteers, and appropriated $2,000,000. Then came news that Spain had sold Louisiana to Bonaparte. Jefferson did not propose to buy Louisiana, but he instructed our envoys, Robert R. Livingston, and James Monroe, and Van Murray, to buy New Orleans and the mere strip east along the Gulf. This was all; it would give us an outlet. But Bonaparte refused. This ended the commission from Jefferson.

But Bonaparte offered to sell the whole of Louisiana. Our envoys had neither instructions, authority or money to buy it; they lacked time to hear from America; but they were equal to the great occasion; they bought it all. Bonaparte signed the treaty just on the eve of opening his war with England, April 13, 1803. The price was $15,440,000, of which $11,-580,000 was to be paid to Bonaparte, the rest to Americans, whose ships and cargoes France had confiscated. Our envoys found a market for American 6% bonds in Holland, and thus obtained the money to pay France. Jefferson believed our constitution did not authorize this purchase. But he accepted the great act of statesmanship of Livingston, Monroe and Van Murray, and intended to have an amendment to legalize it, but it was never done. Congress passed an act to issue the bonds. The Federalist party opposed the purchase. Louisiana was made an organized territory. Spain disputed its boundaries.

The other notable events of Jefferson's first three years were the admission of Ohio as a state, in 1802; payment of $1,250,000 to Georgia for its claim to Indian lands; the killing, in 1804, of Alexander Hamilton, the Federalist leader, by Aaron Burr in a duel; Lewis and Clarke's explorations in Oregon; a threatened war with Spain, about Florida; and Gov. W. H. Harrison's purchase from Indians for trifling sums, of vast northwest lands.

Spain objected to aiding Bonaparte in his British war. But Bonaparte assembled an army on her border. Spain ordered a levy for 100,000 soldiers; war seemed imminent. Bonaparte threatened and Charles IV yielded; he agreed to pay Bonaparte nearly $14,000,000 a year, and to compel peaceful Portugal to give him 1,000,000 francs a month. Thus by robbery of Holland, Hamburg, Hanover, Spain, and Portugal, and also Italy and Naples, and sale of Louisiana, Bonaparte obtained money for his British war. In June, 1803, Bonaparte proposed that Russians garrison Malta; that Lampedusa be given to England; that the French troops quit Holland and Switzerland;

GOVERNOR W. H. HARRISON TREATING WITH INDIANS.

that French acquisitions in Italy be acknowledged by England. Britain offered to refer it to arbitration of Alexander, the French to first leave Hanover and north Germany. But Russia was a party to the quarrel, so Bonaparte refused. England made great conquests in India, but the results of her war against France were meager.

MODERN SLAVERY.

THE slave trade is older than history. Bancroft[1] says it would have ceased before America was discovered, but for the bigoted hostility between Christians and Moslems who enslaved each other. Rome, Madrid, Bristol Hamburg, and Lyons had their markets for white Moslem slaves.

Negroes enslaved negroes. From A.D. 990 this trade is known. Spaniards and Portuguese traded in negroes in 1443, a half-century before Cabot found our continent.[2] Bigots and brigands agreed in stealing unbelieving Africans and heathen Indians to be slaves in Spain. Columbus[3] made slaves of five hundred Indians to be sold in Seville in 1494. Ferdinand and Isabella claimed one-fourth of the Indian slaves.[4] But Indian slaves died rapidly. Spanish and Portuguese brought negro slaves into the West Indies a full century before the first British settlements at Pemaquid and Jamestown of 1605 and 1607. In 1501 a royal edict permitted, and in 1511 ordered, Guinea slave trade.[5] Las Casas, a bishop in Mexico,

[1] Bancroft, i, 163-64. [2] Galvano, Hakluyt iv, 413.
[3] Irving's Columbus, viii, chap. v. [4] Navarette ii, 245.
[5] Herrera.

wanted to spare the Indians from slavery, so he urged the use of negroes [1503]. Charles V consented; the year that began Luther's reformation Charles sanctioned the import of four thousand negroes a year into the West Indies, a monopoly sold to Genoese, who bought negroes of Portuguese to whom the pope had given monopoly of commerce with West Africa.[1]

Sir John Hawkins first led the English into the odious trade. He made so profitable a voyage [1562] that the avarice of Queen Elizabeth was aroused; she took share in and protected the stealing of slaves and smuggling them into the American islands, against the laws of Spain. Hawkins said he set fire to a town of eight thousand inhabitants and seized two hundred and fifty for slaves.[1] The slave trade was thrown wide open in 1620, and then, in August, Virginia received its first negro slaves in a Dutch vessel. It already had a trade in white servants from England, who soon became free.

In 1645 Massachusetts forbade buying and selling of any but captives and convicts, and in 1646 Boston denounced man-stealing and sent back to their own country a cargo of negroes just arrived.[1] In 1650 Connecticut made kidnapping a capital crime. Providence enacted in 1662 that all bondmen be free after ten years' service or when twenty-five years old.[2] This is the earliest emancipation law that I have found, but it was not obeyed. Swedes in Delaware had still earlier forbade slavery. But in 1650 in Boston a debtor might be sold to service to pay his debt, and Indians might be sold or shipped out and

Bancroft, i. [2] Moor's Notes on Slavery.

exchanged for negroes, if they did not give satisfaction for injuries.

In 1702 Queen Anne ordered some of the colonial governors to aid the disgusting trade of her "Royal African Company." Massachusetts opposed it with a tax on the import of slaves. Virginia had laid such duties in 1699, but royalty cancelled them.

Bancroft estimates those imported into our country before 1776 at above three hundred thousand, and, including the West Indies, at three millions, and that two hundred and fifty thousand more died on the sea passage and were thrown into the ocean ; and reckons the trade profits at four hundred million dollars![1] But Raynal estimates the numbers taken by Europeans from Africa before 1776 at nine millions !

Petitions against slavery appeared in Boston in 1701, and in Pennsylvania in 1712. Many persons thought it wicked to hold converted slaves ; heathens might be deprived of every human right, but a baptized slave ought to be freed ; but Gibson, bishop of London, combatted the idea ; so did the Assemblies of three Southern colonies.

In 1727 South Carolina complained of the vast imports of slaves. Most of its rice and Virginia's tobacco were raised by slaves ; negroes were bought on credit, but their produce fell in price; debts became heavy, white laborers were preferred, so colonies tried to lessen the imports of blacks. But Queen Anne and the four Georges were always in favor of slavery ; Anne insisted on pushing the trade with vigor ; she delighted in its profit to herself. From 1680 to 1700, under the Stuarts and William

[1] Bancroft III, 407-411.

and Mary, the English took about three hundred thousand slaves from Africa.[1]

No general European opinion spoke out against it;[2] no general feeling of humanity rebuked the stealing of millions of human beings; no general national sentiment was indignant at the horrible sufferings by which numbers so enormous perished in the frightful sea passage; men cared for creeds, made war for them, fought desperately against belief different from their own, but to be as great Jesus preached on the mount, "meek," "pure in heart," "merciful," "peacemakers," was not the forte of those whose avarice sought profit in the inhuman slave trade.

One great man rose who was somewhat of the sermon on the mount pattern, the merciful hero, soldier, scholar, statesman, James Oglethorpe.

The English code hanged men for petty offenses; kept men in prison for life for debt if the creditor insisted. Oglethorpe planned a colony for an asylum for poverty and devotion. June, 1732, George II granted to trustees a charter to all the land between the Savannah and Altamaha and west to the Pacific,— regardless of the fact that much of this country did not belong to England,—" in trust for the poor" for twenty-one years.

Charities furnished money, and in 1733 Oglethorpe arrived and began to build Savannah. A few Indians made treaties with him. Moravians, given free passage, food for the season, land, freedom of worship, came singing through Germany, and holding wide-awake worship on the vessels on the ocean, and settled *Ebenezer*.

[1] Raynal, quoted by Bancroft, iii, 411.   [2] Bancroft iii, 412.

From this "Georgia" slavery and ardent spirits were forever to be excluded. No Maine law could be more stringent. "Slavery is against the gospel," said this gallant Christian, this man whose career is a remarkable romance, an epic poem, a hero's tale. He called slavery a "horrid crime." Then came Scots and settled New Inverness.

But in about two years some of his Savannah jail colonists, disliking to work, began to petition for slavery. They might buy negroes on credit. Oglethorpe refused.

More religionists, anti-slavery men, devout Moravians came. And, too, came John and Charles Wesley, "not yet settled in heart," but enthusiastic "to live wholly to the glory of God;" as Bancroft says, "to enjoy the exquisite delights of religious sensibility." John preached at Savannah, but he and his charge disagreed and he went home.

More settlers came and prospered, but the Savannah lot still asked for rum and slavery; the honest settlements seem to have supported Oglethorpe in refusing these evils. But when in ten years, in 1743, Oglethorpe left Georgia the idlers gained their points, rum was smuggled and they hired slaves from South Carolina, at first for short time, then longer, and then for a hundred years, and soon slaves were brought direct from Africa to Savannah.

Whitefield[1] believed that God would make slavery a help to the Africans; he pleaded before the trustees for it as needed in Georgia. The Moravians regretted, then hesitated, then became reluctant converts to slavery "in a Christian spirit," "with intent

[1] Bancroft iii.

to bring them to Christ" [1751]. In 1749 slavery was established on condition that masters must teach slaves the Christian religion. A slave must be worked but fifteen hours a day in summer and fourteen in winter.

Judge Holt of the King's Bench declared in 1697 that "as soon as a negro comes into England he is free,"[1] but public sentiment did not sustain Holt's doctrine, and in 1735 Judge York reversed it.

Till our independence in 1776, England allowed no manufacturing in America. English manufacturers wanted our whole market; to enlarge the sales of their goods they insisted on slavery and the slave trade. Anne and George II gave land to settlers in the British West Indies on condition that they keep four slaves to every one hundred acres.

Virginia, dismayed at the increase of negroes, tried in 1761 to check their import by tax, but the king disallowed the act. Whites might wish to make goods, tools, cloth; slaves would never do so; slaves would raise crops,—indigo, rice, tobacco, corn,—crops different from those of England, so there could be no competition with English farmers; slavery added wealth to English trade, made markets for English goods; both slave-trade and slavery increased English profits. English ministries did not allow the Americans to make a hoe or a web, all goods must come from England, so George III insisted with all the stubbornness of his ill nature to give force and vigor to the horrible cruelty.

Treaties of commerce first appear just before 1700. That of Utrecht, in 1713, gave England monopoly of

[1] Smith vs. Brown and Cooper.

the African slave trade. England engaged to furnish the Spaniards with one hundred and forty-four thousand negroes within thirty-three years. A great slave-trading company was formed in England; Queen Anne took one-fourth of the stock, the King of Spain another fourth. Thus these two sovereigns became the greatest slave traders. They extended slavery in America. Anne gave all her influence for slavery, and Georges I, II and III followed her bad example.

In the peace of Westphalia, in 1748, England secured monopoly of slave trade for four years more. In 1750 Spain gave £100,00 to be allowed to share in it.[1]

Negroes bought in Africa with rum, sham goods, and old muskets were, with extreme cruelty, brought across seas in small, crowded vessels, packed below decks too close to turn over, stifled with heat and lack of air, ironed, whipped if they made trouble,—a system more revolting than the barbarities of savage Africa. Of some cargoes one-half died, one-third was not unusual loss.[2]

England, Spain, Portugal, and France claimed all America, all but France used vigorous exertion to fill it with slaves. The negroes were from the youth of Africa between fourteen and thirty years old, and were born slaves in Africa or were captives, kidnapped or convicts.[2]

In most of the colonies were Indian slaves. They were poorly protected. In North Carolina in 1750 a person found guilty of manslaughter of a slave was "to incur no forfeiture or punishment."[3]

In some countries they fared better. In Boston in

[1] Koch ii, 82.   [2] Bancroft.   [3] Hildreth ii, 424.

1773 a slave won a suit against his master for wages. In 1772 Sumerset, a negro brought from Virginia to England, was freed by decision of full court of King's Bench on the ground that a slave could not be held in England under American laws.[1]

In July, 1774, the Virginia Assembly, on Jefferson's suggestion, resolved that:—

"After November 1, next, we will neither ourselves import nor purchase any slave imported."

October 20, 1774, the Continental Congress, except three South Carolina members, signed articles of association containing:—

"We will neither import nor purchase any slave imported after the first day of December next, after which we will wholly discontinue the slave trade."

April 6, 1776, Congress resolved that "No slave be imported." Jefferson wrote in July, 1774, "The abolition of domestic slavery is the great object of desire in these colonies." This was not then true of the Carolinas and Georgia, and slavery had many supporters in both North and South.

The clause of the Declaration of Independence of July 4, 1776, that all men are born free and equal with natural rights, led many persons in Delaware and Virginia to expect early abolition of slavery.

But in forming the Articles of Confederation in 1777, a vote in Congress to exempt property in slaves from tax was carried against northern opposition, and Congress received no power to stop the slave-trade; each state was to decide what it would import. No doubt a majority desired that the trade should cease, but slavery was a vested property, it held its ground;

[1] Mansfield was chief-justice.

three hundred thousand blacks remained slaves. Virginia's efforts were not against slavery but against *import* of slaves, a very different matter.

Free negroes were in the Revolutionary army. Rutledge of South Carolina moved their discharge, but his motion was voted down. In October, 1776, a conference at Washington's camp proposed to reject them from the service. Washington reversed the decision. Congress allowed those who had been in the battle of Bunker Hill to re-enlist. In 1774 the Royal governor, Dunmore, tried to raise black troops against Virginia, but he had little success.

The suppressed article of the Declaration of Independence written by Jefferson, calls the slave-trade "war against human nature," "piratical," "this assemblage of horrors," and charges George III with "this execrable commerce" and veto of attempts of the colonies to restrain it. "To please some southern gentleman," says Jefferson, this clause was "yielded" though all the thirteen colonies then respected the prohibition of Congress of April 6, 1776.

South Carolina returned the Articles of Confederation for the right of inter-citizenship to be confined to whites, but Congress, eight states against South Carolina and Georgia, refused it, although in every state were slaves. Free blacks were citizens. Bancroft says they were in every regiment of Gates' army against Burgoyne in 1777. In 1778 Rhode Island, by sanction of Washington, gave freedom to every slave who enlisted.

In 1777 a prize brought into Massachusetts several slaves. They were to be sold, but the state liberated them.

Hildreth estimates the number of slaves carried off from Virginia during the war at above thirty thousand.[1] The British treated them as property and plunder. I find that James Madison (afterward president) wrote[2] in 1780 advice "to liberate and make soldiers at once of the slaves."

Pennsylvania in 1780 and Connecticut and Rhode Island in 1784 forbade import of slaves, and gradually freed those already held. Virginia, in 1788, prohibited their importation.

In 1789 Parker of Virginia, supported by James Madison, moved for a tax of ten dollars each on import of slaves. A lively debate resulted in nothing.[3] Georgia and South Carolina were the champions for the odious trade.

Before 1743 the Friends began to actively oppose slavery. In 1780 the Pennsylvania Abolition Society became active to relieve free negroes illegally held as slaves. The great Franklin was then its president. It labored against slavery for about fifty years.

In England an anti-slavery society was formed in 1787 in London. William Wilberforce was the anti-slavery parliamentary leader. In 1791 parliament voted down his bill to end this trade, which was a horror as frightful as the French "Reign of Terror" of the next year. A law was made intended to lessen its enormities but with meager results.

All territory west of the thirteen colonies was conjointly won and belonged to all the states. But southern states made claim to all of it. Virginia, in March, 1784, released its bad claim to all north of the Ohio river, and it was expected that the other

[1] Hildreth iii, 354.   [2] Madison to J. Jones, November 28, 1780.
[3] Hildreth iii, 392.

southern states would relinquish their bad claims to all west of the Alleghanies. A committee of Jefferson of Virginia, Chase of Maryland, and Howell of Rhode Island reported a plan in Congress to forbid slavery after 1800 in all this immense territory from which seventeen states were expected to be made.

New England, New York, and Pennsylvania voted for the plan; Maryland, Virginia, and South Carolina against it; North Carolina was divided; Delaware and Georgia not present; New Jersey gave one vote for it, but its other vote was absent; sixteen members for it, only seven against it. But to carry it required nine states; so it was lost and slavery won Kentucky, Tennessee, Alabama, and Mississippi and its power of further extension to still newer territory later, which, finally, spread it over Missouri, Arkansas, and Texas after 1803.

In March, 1785, Rufus King of Maine moved to forbid slavery extension. His motion failed. In 1787, Nathan Dane of Maine reported an ordinance to forbid slavery in all country northwest of the Ohio. It was passed by the vote of all the thirteen states, Yates of New York alone voted against it.

In the Constitutional Convention of 1788 South Carolina and Georgia demanded that there be no export duties, and no tax on import of slaves; and that to pass any navigation law should require a two-thirds vote. This would let a state control its imports and exports unless two-thirds decided otherwise. The North, too, owned the vessels; this would let the South control navigation, and the South hated the commercial interests. After an exciting debate, in which South Carolina used threats, its standard argument, the matter was referred to a committee of one from each state for compromise. The committee reported to have no export duties; Congress to have power to tax imports of slaves; and navigation laws to require only a majority like other bills; and slaves might be imported until 1800. Maryland, Delaware, and Virginia had slaves enough and did not favor import of more. C. C. Pinckney of South Carolina moved to extend the time for slave imports from 1800 to 1808. This was done by the votes of New Hampshire; Massachusetts and Connecticut joining with South Carolina and Georgia against the votes of New Jersey, Pennsylvania, Delaware and Virginia. Thus New England gave eight years' extension to that wicked trade. South Carolina insisted on and obtained the clause for the return of fugitive slaves, which caused immense damage for many years to the friendly feeling between states, and, finally, in 1857 set the North into a blaze of furious indignation by the Dred Scot decision which remanded to slavery a man and his family after they had once been taken by the owner to a free state and had resided there.

February 11, 1790, Friends, ever on the side of mercy, petitioned Congress against slavery as they had done in 1783. South Carolina and Georgia members violently assailed the petition and the petitioners. Madison and Parker of Virginia, Elbridge Gerry of Massachusetts and Hartley of Pennsylvania, insisted on receiving the petition, but it was laid with contempt on the table. The next day came in a memorial from the Pennsylvania Society, written by Franklin, the greatest American of his times except Washington. It is almost the last of the many wise counsels of that illustrious sage ; he died soon afterward. Tucker of South Carolina bitterly attacked it; he said the southern clergy did not condemn slavery or the slave-trade, a case too true. Scott of Pennsylvania, from humanity, opposed the slave-trade; Jackson of Georgia replied that religion is not against slave-trade, that Scott "will see from Genesis to Revelation the current setting strong the other way." After a sharp debate, bitter on the pro-slavery side, the petition was referred to a select committee who, later, reported that Congress has no power to stop the slave-trade until 1808 ; that it could not free slaves in states, but could tax each slave imported ten dollars ; that it could interdict the trade to foreign ports, and might regulate the trade at home, or prohibit the fitting out of vessels by foreigners in our ports. South Carolina and Georgia members discussed it with hard words, threats, coarse invective; they demanded an end to freedom of discussion of the subject ; they declaimed, as they had done in the Convention, of disunion, the same cries which those states kept up for seventy years longer, till 1861. Varnum of Delaware replying to their rancerous tirades spoke for human rights. This great debate closed March 23, 1790, with the adoption of a substitute declaring that Congress could not prohibit import of slaves until 1808, nor interfere with slavery in states, but could restrain Americans from supplying foreigners with slaves, and regulate their treatment in the sea passage. It was observed that members from Virginia, Pennsylvania and Delaware, spoke in grave, dignified and courteous manner. Anti-slavery societies in Virginia, Pennsylvania and other states, petitioned Congress to exercise these declared powers, but nothing came of it. In November, 1792, Mr. Ames of Massachusetts, presented a petition from a Delaware Friend against slavery. Again Smith of South Carolina rang the familiar cry of "disunion," "rant," "fanaticism," and the alarmed House voted to return the petition to the good Friend.

In February, 1793, Congress passed the act to give masters power to seize and return to slavery their escaped slaves; the House gave seven votes against it, the Senate none. Under it many free negroes were kidnapped and carried off into slavery. So far did this evil go that in 1795 the Delaware Legislature asked of Congress protection against this man-stealing. Smith, South Carolina's champion, opposed this relief; he demanded that the matter be dropped, and it was dropped.

But the Friends and other humane persons frequently protected negroes. In this humanity Isaac T. Hopper of Philadelphia was distinguished. "Colonel" Ridgly's own mulatto son escaped from south Virginia to Philadelphia. After several years he sent an offer to buy himself from his white father. Ridgly asked two hundred dollars. But he came to Philadelphia, seized the man and refused the money. Friend Hopper reproached him for trading his own flesh. The slave-master replied:—

"What if he is my son? I have as good a right to sell my own flesh and blood as that of any other person. It is none of your business."

By aid of Friend Hopper the son escaped.

In January, 1794, a convention of delegates from societies in ten states was held in Philadelphia. It asked Congress to stop the slave-traffic by Americans to supply foreign nations with slaves, and to bar foreigners from outfitting slavers in our ports. The Friends at yearly meeting also petitioned. Congress then prohibited the trade between foreign ports. This act was made more effective in 1800. But Brown of Rhode Island wanted free trade in slaves. Newport was engaged in the trade. He spoke of its large revenue. Bayard of Delaware replied that "a more dishonorable item of revenue could not be imagined."

In January, 1797, some free negroes who had been sold into slavery under a law of North Carolina, petitioned Congress for rescue. Some of them appear to have attempted to escape. Swanbach of Pennsylvania denounced as atrocious the offer of ten dollars reward for one of them if taken alive, or fifty dollars if found dead, "and no questions asked." Madison wanted to table the petition. The House refused to receive it thirty-three to fifty votes. Since the invention of Crompton's spinning jenny [1775], Watt's steam engine [1783], cylinder printing of cottons [1785], slave produce had raised in price, and the invention of Whitney's cotton gin [1793] made the cotton crop very valuable, so the value of slaves and popularity of slavery had greatly increased.

On a new petition the North Carolina affair was again bitterly discussed in November, 1797, and it was voted to be a judicial question to be let alone by Congress.

In December, 1799, colored men in Philadelphia petitioned for revision of the Fugitive and Slave Trade Acts, and for steps towards liberty. South Carolina members opposed receiving the memorial; so did H. G. Otis of Massachusetts and Henry Lee of Virginia (father of Gen. Robert E. Lee) ; John Brown of Rhode Island said he thought "slaves as much property as a farm;" John Randolph wanted action so decisive as to stop such petitioning; Christie of Maryland hoped the petition would go "under the table;" Jones of Georgia echoed Christie's remark; and Goode of Virginia proposed to "give it the pointed disapprobation of the House." Thacher of Massachusetts alone defended the petition. Rutledge of South Carolina, as usual, made threats. Then a vote of eighty-five against brave George Thacher alone, denounced the petition.

In 1798 Georgia prohibited the foreign slave-trade.

The arrival of negroes who had fought for liberty in St. Domingo and been expelled excited South Carolina imaginations with fears of a servile revolt. It called on Congress for protection. In 1803 South Carolina was really alarmed. Slaves were being imported from the incendiary French West Indies. They might spread free ideas. Excited South Carolina called sharply for help. Something must be done to quiet her fears. So Congress passed an act laying one thousand dollars fine and forfeiture of vessel for importing a slave contrary to state laws. Since 1798 each state had laws against imports of slaves.

But in 1804 South Carolina, lately so afraid of imported negroes, passed an act reviving the slave-trade. This act caused a struggle with Congress where it was resented. But an act to tax each import of a slave ten dollars failed to pass, and this fearful trade went on with vigor.

New Jersey gradually freed its slaves by act of February 15, 1804.

The ordinance of 1787 barred out slavery north of the Ohio river. But in 1803 settlers in Indiana petitioned Congress for suspension of that ordinance; they wanted slaves. It was referred to a committee of which John Randolph of Virginia was chairman. He reported against the petition, but in 1804 a Jefferson democrat committee reported in favor of allowing slavery in Indiana for ten years. This would have made Indiana a slave state in the end. It does not appear that Jefferson (then president) opposed this attempt to extend slavery over free territory. Jefferson himself owned about two hundred slaves.[1] It is error to suppose that the South did not value slavery in those times. It was then popular in all the South but not popular in the North except in Indiana. Vermont prohibited slavery in 1777, Massachusetts in 1780, New York, finally, in 1827.

Fiery debates on prohibition of the slave-trade occurred in Congress early in 1807. A majority wanted the traffic ended. But how? By what penalties? What should be done with negroes imported in defiance of the proposed act?

The death penalty for violation of the act was struck out of the bill by vote of sixty-three to fifty-two. To forfeit such negroes, to give them to the state where imported, were discussed with acrimony; to not sell them was lost by majority of one; the proposal to make apprentices of them outside of the slave states caused angry debate for a whole day; it was settled that the importer should hold no legal title to them; the Senate accepted the House bill, all but the clause allowing domestic slave-trade; the House insisted on

[1] Tucker's Life of Jefferson, p. 298.

the clause; a committee amended it to forbid "transportation of slaves coastwise in vessels under forty tons with a view to sale." John Randolph extravagantly denounced the bill. Williams of South Carolina — violent as usual — expressed crazy visions of massacres, but the Bill was passed, March 2, 1807. South Carolina was hurrying the imports in order to get as many as possible before the prohibition could take effect, January 1, 1808. It got nearly forty thousand in those last four years of legal import; about half of them brought in by British, the rest by Rhode Island vessels.[1] But the slave-trade, both foreign and domestic, went on after it became illegal.

In Canada, after several attempts in the Assembly at Quebec to abolish slavery and the slave-trade, it was summarily done by decision of Chief-justice Osgood at Montreal in 1802, on the grand principle that such barbarism is repugnant to the genius of Canadian liberty; a decision broad and sound and highly honorable, both to its author and to Canada. Yet in 1801 England had nearly eight hundred thousand slaves in its other colonies. This fact makes Judge Osgood's act still more conspicuously creditable.[2] In our thirteen colonies slavery had rested rather on custom than on law. In 1801 Spain and Portugal had six hundred thousand slaves, and Brazil had two million.[3]

In 1802 France had two hundred and fifty thousand slaves in its colonies, and in May of that year Bonaparte restored slavery and the slave-trade in the possessions he had recovered by the peace of Amiens of

[1] Hildreth.
[2] Lalor's Cyclopædia of Political Science "Slavery."   [3] Lalor, ibid.

March 20, 1802. The American slaveholders held Bonaparte in high admiration.

The colored people of St. Domingo had won their freedom. Bonaparte sent there forty thousand French troops to destroy their new free government and reduce them to slavery. They resisted, and a frightful war devastated the country; the suffering was extreme, but these former slaves maintained their liberty. This is a dark chapter of history.[1]

For twenty years the British parliament had refused to pass the bill which William Wilberforce introduced at every session. In 1805 an " Order in Council" forbade the slave-trade in conquered colonies.

January 2, 1807, the Whig minister, Grenville, brought in the Bill. George III's sons opposed it. Says Miss Martineau (English), "A miserable exhibition it was . . . . the best men perceived the least to hope from the royal family." But many of the British people were for the measure, and it was passed against the opposition of many British ship owners. It was enacted March 25, 1807, twenty days after the American act and six months after the death of Charles J. Fox, who had labored for years for such a law. Both acts took effect the same day, January 1, 1808. The Whig ministry went out on the very day of its enactment. One day later the Tories were in power and the Bill might have failed.

British subjects continued the trade under the Spanish and Portuguese flags. The slave ships were terribly crowded, and to avoid capture blacks were thrown overboard on pursuit by war vessels. For many years longer the sickening horrors of this trade shocked the world; it died hard.

[1] For its history see "The World's Greatest Conflict."

In 1811 Brougham's act made it a high felony. In 1824 the trade was still active, and England made it piracy, a capital crime. But now, as this century is closing, it is not piracy by international law, though made piracy by several nations.

By treaty of February 9, 1820, England obtained the pledge of Portugal to co-operate against the trade, the first treaty stipulation of the kind.

The slaves were from negro-land, only a part of Africa, mainly from the country back of the Gulf of Guinea, a district of two hundred languages.[1]

Russia had no negro slaves but had a vast number of white serfs attached to the soil and saleable with it. They might hold land, transact business and acquire property.

When this century began, slavery existed in some form in almost every land. It was in all North and South America, except Canada, Vermont, Massachusetts, Maine, and Ohio. New York then had 20,613, New Jersey 12,422, Pennsylvania 1,706, Rhode Island 380. Southern states and West Indies had great numbers. In the United States more than one-sixth of the people, or 869,749 were colored slaves.[2] India, Burmah, Siam, Arabia, Barbary, Egypt, and all Africa, had either black or white slaves. In Germany was limited serfdom. English law bound English colliers and salters to perpetual service and transfer with sale of the mine till ten years after the French Revolution began.

[1] Koch ii, 235.   [2] United States census.

WHEN THIS CENTURY BEGAN,

Laborers in some parts of England got forty cents a day, in Ireland but half that pay, and in Poland still less, and from this they must live and support their families,[1] but an Irishman paid in potatoes had nutriment for more persons than an Englishman paid in wheat, and both could buy clothing cheaper than could an American on his sixty-five dollars a year and board. Those were hard times for the poor. From 1735 to 1755 an English day's labor would buy a peck of wheat, but not so much from 1790 to 1815. In Norway laborers fared better than in England. They had no white bread, but had more fish, meat and milk.

In the best parts of America wages though better than in Europe were very low and furnished little more than bare subsistence ; common houses were rudely made and poorly furnished ; with huge chimneys and big fires it was difficult to make them comfortable in winter ; in summer, mosquitoes and other insects entered through the many cracks. Rooms were few, walls were not papered, floors were not carpeted, the furniture was rude and strong, musical instruments for homes hardly existed, except here and there, a fiddle. Clothes were made at home, and the village shoemaker went around staying long enough in each family to make up the shoes for the season. Clothing was in most part made of the home product of flax and coarse wool ;

[1] Matthias.

the first merino sheep sent to America from Spain at large expense were used for mutton by a man who did not know their value.

Invention was not brisk; the patent office had but one clerk; goods must be foreign; the buyer asked eagerly, "Are you sure it is not American?" before purchasing, for nobody wanted American make of any goods except rum and whisky. Rum, cocoa, and hides made up one-half the cargoes brought from the West Indies; in exchange we sent out lumber and fish. Under the embargo of 1807 business was ruined, but, but when our lumber could not be sold for decent goods it could always be exchanged for portly barrels of rum,[1] — then regarded like molasses as a necessity of life, — even when it added to the hunger and utter poverty of the people in whose windows old hats and bundles of rags served in place of glass.

Postage was from six to twenty-five cents, according to distance, for each sheet; envelopes were not in use. Jefferson complained in 1792 that the post-riders carry the mail but fifty miles a day; it was carried on horseback.[2]

Sunday-schools in England and America taught reading, writing, and ciphering; the teachers were sometimes hired. These schools were still strongly opposed as Sabbath breaking, but Methodists, Universalists, Dunkers, and others aided them. Song books were few; libraries came in later.

As late as 1811 Jefferson placed "spindles" and rude looms on his farms, and exulted in them as wonderful innovations.[2] In 1809 Madison became pres-

[1] Kendall's Travels, 1807.   [2] Jefferson's Works.

ident in a complete suit of American make, a fact that attracted great attention.

All inventions and the growth of civilization are largely indebted to paper. It was not until about 1776 that writing paper was made at all in America. The first German paper mill was at Nuremberg in 1490, but English paper manuscripts are found that date in 1340. The first recorded English paper mill is in 1496, the next in 1588; one in Philadelphia in 1732 made only coarse paper for tailors' press-boards. Not paper, but cloth was used by the luxurious to drape walls in palaces.

Down to one hundred years ago, Europe received its small cotton supply mainly from the East and West Indies and the Levant. India has raised and used cotton from ancient times. The first known shipments from English America were a few pounds in 1754 and two thousand pounds in 1770. It was not known as a valuable article of export till after our Revolution, hence slaves were of low value. In 1791 but 189,316 pounds of our whole crop of two million were exported. England's first import of East India cotton was not till 1783, and its average till 1792 was but 65,550 pounds.

Cotton.

Clothing was made of wool, linen and silk. The present system of using cotton to wear has grown up in Europe and America,since 1760. The inventions that brought cotton into use are Hargreave's spinning jenny [1767–70], Arkwright's spinning by rollers [1769], the American card-making machine later, Crompton's mule jenny, first in full use about 1780; color printing [1785] — improved by Perkins' steel stamps; Cartwright's power loom [1785], and especially Whitney's cotton gin of 1793, and Watt's steam engine, and the use of water power, and the dressing machine of 1802.

Spinning and weaving were domestic industries; the spinning was done with the distaff and the then more recently invented spinning wheel of one thread.

The first mule jenny had but thirty spindles and was worked by hand; now mules may have two thousand spindles. From 1793 Whitney's gin added enormous value to the cotton crop. Before 1791 it could hardly be called an article of export, its amount was so small. In 1801 the average price in Liverpool was fifty cents a pound. In 1786 a pound of cotton yarn (one hundred hanks) was worth thirty-eight shillings,— more than nine dollars. In 1807 it was ninety-one cents. Calico, as good as now retails at eight cents a yard, brought one dollar and forty-six cents in 1789. France used 3,330 tons of Levant cotton in 1750, twice the amount the British used. The Swiss first used a spinning machine in the year of Eylau [1807].

Arkwright's first mill with water-power, which gave the name "water-frames," was in 1771. Samuel Slater built his spinning mill at Pawtucket in 1790. He used all the patents of his teacher, Arkwright. Cotton was so little raised in America that his supply came from Barbadoes.

In 1812 Lowell and Jackson, barred by the war from getting a power loom from England, or even a pattern from which to make one, invented their loom and built their mill at Waltham. It was, probably, the first in the world completely prepared to convert raw cotton into cloth, Slater's and others were spinning mills only. English weavers bought their yarn of spinners.

James Watt so much improved the steam engine that he may almost be said to have invented it. He led all its improvers.

In 1443 Blasco de Garey [Spanish] showed his paddle-wheel boat at Barcelona. In 1736 J. Hull took English patent for paddle-wheel tow-boat. Auxiron in 1774, and Perier in 1775, experimented on the Seine, and in 1782 de Jeffroy built a steamboat that went on the Saone, but it was deficient in power. *Steam Travel.*

The double boat with paddle-wheel in the interspace, made by Taylor, William Symington and Patrick N. Miller in Scotland, tried in 1788, was a success. In 1789 Miller's steam vessel moved seven miles an hour on the Clyde canal.

In 1784 James Rumsey propelled a boat by machinery on the Potomac. In 1786 his steam pump, driving a stream of water from the stern, propelled his boat. Later he exhibited it in England, Holland and France.

In 1786 John Fitch's steamboat appeared on the Delaware. In 1787 he made the first American condensing engine. Watt patented his in England in 1786. In 1788 Fitch's steamer moved four miles an hour, but its boiler burst, which disgraced it in the public estimation. Some of the first steamers were worked by paddles as an Indian uses them. In 1790 Fitch built a boat with paddles at the stern, to carry passengers on the Delaware, but his company failed. In 1793 he tried to introduce it in France, but he failed and came home discouraged.

In 1802 Symington built the steam tow-boat, "Charlotte Dundas." It did the work, but as its wash injured the Clyde canal banks, it was discarded.

Richard Trevithick, a Cornwall engineer, improved steam engines, invented the extremely valuable high-pressure engine,— Watt's engines were too heavy for roads,— and in 1804 his engine, which I have lately seen preserved at South Kensington, drew ten tons at the rate of five miles an hour. But it exploded and no practical use was made of it. The idea was generally prevalent that for an engine ever to draw carriages the track rail and wheels must be cogged. Trevithick was a great inventor ; one of those rare men whose works help all mankind.

In 1804 John C. Stevens, a great American engineer, drove his steam screw propeller on the Hudson; and another great man, Oliver Evans, drove his steam dredge a mile and a half on land, and then on the Delaware and the Schuylkill, by his high-pressure engine. He had made the first high-pressure engine in America.

Robert Fulton, the illustrious American, built a steamboat and tried it on the Seine, in Paris, in 1803. He tried to interest Bonaparte, but the Consul thought him a visionary. Fulton saw the "Charlotte Dundas," took drawings, and in 1806, with Robert R. Livingstone of New York, built the "Clermont" with side wheels, with Watt and Boulton's engine. In 1807, jeered by a crowd, he started on his famous trip from New York to Albany, against wind and tide, and astonishing the people on the shores of the Hudson, and at night frightening those who saw the belching fire and smoke, he went to Albany, one hundred and ten miles, in between twenty-four and thirty hours. From September 2, 1807, the "Clermont" was a regular passenger boat, pioneer of the floating palaces of today. His patent for exclusive steam navigation of New York waters required twenty tons burden and four miles an hour speed. The "Clermont" was one hundred and sixty tons.

By 1812 Fulton and Livingstone had six steamers on the Hudson. When their "Richmond" went nine miles an hour Fulton called it "the perfection of steamboating."

Soon after the "Clermont's" success, John C. Stevens' "Phœnix" went from New York to the Delaware, the first steamer ever on the ocean.

In 1811 Henry Bell started his steamer the "Comet," on the Clyde. It was James Watt's invention of his engine that made a steamboat possible.

James Watt, born in 1736, died 1819, was the great inventor, the great man of that generation. His was a broad, capacious intellect, and he was a manly man. He was the great improver of the steam engine to make it of general use. He possessed greater mental capacity, a more magnificent executive ability, more good-conferring qualities, and was far more the arbiter of human destinies than any English statesman of his time. Pitt, Fox, Burke, Grattan, or Sheridan were far inferior to him in grasp of mind, sound judgment, widely acquired attainments, practical knowledge, and in good character. It is too much the custom to regard him as only an engineer. Nature placed him on earth as one of her best specimens of a noble, grand man. His learning was extensive, varied; he knew several languages, was a great mathematician, and had a remarkable store of well-considered information, and was a kind, gentle, good, Christian gentleman of refined culture and pure, gentle sentiments, humane and honorable.

Watt found the steam engine crude, clumsy, and of but limited uses. He took up the great battle of man against natural obstacles,— far more honorable than war of man against man,— and, greater than Napoleon, he is still winning it and will continue to win it for unnumbered ages to come. He made steam capable of the heaviest work and of the most minutely delicate adorning; it dashes ships across the ocean in six days, and it weaves gossamer laces; it enriches all branches of private enjoyment, adds immensely to the sum of public comfort; it is in business what good government is in politics, what pure religion is in theology, what love is in human nature, the central, warm, healthy heart of its life; its blessings are to be universal; it is the greatest, best gift to man since he received the love of God and of woman.

Except only Washington, Watt was the greatest man of modern ages, perhaps of any age. In varied and exact learning he was almost peerless,— his mind was quick, his memory prodigious, his method complete. He knew, where other men merely surmised; his information on many subjects was almost exhaustive; even in ancient medicine, German philosophy, poetry, architecture, music, law, modern language, recent literature, he was a marvel. He was a cyclopedia of all that is rich and desirable in intellectual companionship, was social, unassuming, quietly humorous, gently bantering; this kind, loving man of genial eye and face of "finer expression of reposing strength," and of mild, friendly pleasantry; who, though of deep, strong voice, commonly spoke in low and welcome tones. Heaven loved the good, great man and blessed him with length of days, and when old he invented machinery to copy fine sculpture and used it and called himself "a young artist just entering his eighty-third year."

Of all men who ever lived he did most to make the world more inhabitable, he was the most creator-like, Godlike. Compared with the conquests of nature made by aid of this glorious man, all the marvelous conquests of Napoleon dwindle to brilliant inutility. Man is creation's noblest work; Watt is one of its masterpieces. He was nature's and culture's kingly man, and his iron rule is mild as was his own great, tender, womanlike heart; his glory did not, like that of Napoleon, red blaze in continuous gleam of scintillating war bulletins and then relapse into immortal uselessness, but steady, and warm, and calm as the great sun, it daily shines on and on and will still shine and bless mankind until nature's great subterranean, central boilers shall explode in liquid flame and hurl all earth, seas, land, mountains, in fiery fragmentary missiles into dread abyss.

It was the invention of Watt that made other machinery far more effective and productive of wealth. In the long wars from 1793 to 1815 it was his steam engine that enabled Britain to stand the tremendous expenses, the heavy outlays, and the taxes; that made it possible to carry on so great a struggle; this it was that added to Britain's resources to finally overthrow the less great man, Napoleon.

II

FRANCE.

FEBRUARY 4, 1804, the French Consul's government discovered a plot. It made a wild excitement in Paris, and rang through all France. It was said that Pichegru, the exiled French general, and Georges Cadoudal, had come back from England; had suddenly appeared and were to destroy Bonaparte the First Consul, and the Bourbon Prince D'Artois was to rally the royalists and proclaim Louis XVIII.

Plot against Bonaparte.

What if Pichegru had been for months in Paris; had been seen on the streets a hundred times; had met several opportunities to shoot Bonaparte, if he so intended? France itself did not know these facts. France heard the flying report that it was England — hated, long abhorred English — who had sent these men to destroy the French military leader, the great general of Marengo and Arcola. The public spirit of France was aroused. Men spoke to each other in tones of indignation, doubt, half-dismay. What if the First Consul had fallen? The odious Bourbons, a new revolution, a fresh reign of terror? Should England, who harbored the banished class of French; England, their hereditary enemy, force a Bourbon king on Frenchmen? And that, too, by foul conspiracy and murder? Such was popular French talk.

Troops blockaded Paris; police searched everywhere for the strangely escaped conspirators. Amid the uproar, the suspension of business, the everywhere buzz of gossip, the tramp of armed men through the streets, the police visits, it was twenty noisy days till Cadoudal was seen in a carriage. The officers made sure it really was the right man; they made a rush for him; he shot dead the leading officer but he was arrested. Pichegru had been caught in ten days.

Bonaparte's soldiers made a raid into the grand duchy of Baden; there kidnapped the Bourbon Duc d'Enghien, and hurried him to Vincennes castle, near Paris. Bonaparte ordered his trial by a court martial of French colonels. Bonaparte selected these colonels. They knew that he expected, intended that they should condemn the helpless prisoner. They were there not to fairly try but to pronounce judgment on him; but some of them were under a delusion that Bonaparte wanted him condemned only that he might make an exhibition of lenity by pardoning him, that he might make a gift of life to a Bourbon. Savary, who was there, knew better; he was to execute, to practically murder the captive in the darkness of that very night. He did it, and the civilized world was shocked by this assassination. But France did not know the real facts. Bonaparte controlled the muzzled French press.

The life of d'Enghien was not specially precious because of his being a royal duke. He had justly incurred Bonaparte's hostility; he had watched for a chance to aid to transform old Stanislaus Xavier into Louis XVIII on a French throne. But this kidnapping by French, in a neutral country, was an outrage on the laws and customs of mankind; a crime against all nations, a blunder against reason. The Russian court, indignant, went into mourning, and the Czar urged the grand duke of Baden to demand redress. Baden was too small for that.

Next to Bonaparte the most eminent general of France was Moreau, hero of Hohenlinden. Paris was startled, France was astonished, when Bonaparte caused his arrest. The alarm was almost panic when Pichegru was found dead in his prison cell. Parisians shook their heads; they congregated in knots; they asked, excitedly, "Who killed him?" Officials said he committed suicide. Paris shrugged its shoulders and doubted; many persons still doubt.

Bonaparte sent Moreau, the great republican, to trial, if inquisition can be called trial; he was not proven guilty; it appeared entirely probable that he was innocent; he almost proved a negative of guilt; it availed him nothing, he was too great a man to be allowed so near to power; the arbitrary inquisition, overawed by the First Consul, condemned him. But Bonaparte could hardly dare to execute Moreau; he banished him.

Bonaparte saw his opportunity. He made adroit use of this affair. In this excited state of France, in the tumult of passion against England and assassins, which he associated in the official mind dependent on him, he obtained numerous addresses from all sorts of officials. France was in just the right temper to readily catch his ideas that his government must be made hereditary so that his assassination could not disrupt it. He controlled the servile senate, and the tribunate; they were ready to serve his ambition and their own; neither body was representative. So all was in his power.

The Senate voted to declare him Hereditary Emperor. He gave a gracious answer. The Tribunate approved and added the delusive words that "Equality, liberty and the rights of the people be preserved in their integrity." Liberty had already ceased. The Senate formulated its "Consultum." Bonaparte arbitrarily altered it and accepted it. France was bound anew.

All that France was allowed to vote on was whether or not his crown be hereditary. He became Emperor without France's votes.

Bonaparte, Sieyes, and a few others directly made a "Constitution," often afterward violated by him; the Senate decreed it the next day, with no authority from the people. France itself was entirely silent in the matter of this May 4, 1804 constitution.

He made as heirs to the throne: 1. Any son or adopted son of his own. 2. His brother Joseph, and then Louis, or their sons. 3. He excluded his brothers Lucien, who had saved him when he lost his wits at his first seizing power in December, 1799, and Jerome, because they had married women without rank.

The Tribunate was reduced from one hundred members to fifty. It lost influence, got increased salary, and was a shadowy state council till 1807 when he abolished it.

The Corps Legislative was silenced, was allowed to debate only in secret committee.

To render the servile Senate still more abject, Napoleon took to himself the appointment of senators. He made his brothers princes and senators. He named to dark age titles, Joseph, Grand Elector;

Louis, Grand Constable; ex-Consul Cambacèrès, Arch Chancellor; ex-Consul Lebrun, Arch Treasurer; Duroc, Grand Marshal of the Palace; and Berthier, Grand Master of the Hounds!

A senate committee was to guard the liberty of person and of the press; but it only made Napoleon's suppression of all liberty of person and press the more thorough. France was silenced. It had liberty only to applaud and support Napoleon. During his reign prisons received many persons who were never allowed trial.

May 4, 1804, the Senate declared Napoleon Bonaparte Emperor. He was to have twenty-five million francs a year and use of all crown lands and castles, and each of his brothers and sisters received a million francs yearly with which, at the expense of France, they set bad examples of luxury and extravagance. The great bribe which senators received were rich estates and splendid residences in the departments. Those who had made him Emperor received pay for delivering France into his power more completely.

In place of former republican simplicity Napoleon restored old dark age court etiquette; the stale absurdities, the old nonsense, all the old trammels to good society. Men in ridiculous dresses mingled all styles of manners, and women in finical robes and tinsel trickeries aped old court ceremonies and absurd styles at this court of the most unmannerly and uncouth monarch in Europe.[1]

At great expense to France, court clergy appeared with Napoleon's uncle, Cardinal Fesch, as grand almoner. More than this, the Jesuits, expelled by

[1] Remusat; Talleyrand; d'Abrantes.

good Catholics from many Catholic countries, obtained special favor from some of the ladies of his new court, when France was barely Catholic and certainly not Jesuitical. Metternich, the best of authority as a witness, says it would be difficult to give any idea of the prodigious expense of the court and the ministers. The only country of Europe that still preserved any freedom was Great Britain, and there it was very limited.

The vote of France on the question whether or not the empire be hereditary was nearly all in favor. The omnipotence of thinkers; the glory of the divine sentiments of equity; the sacred liberty of person to abstain from bloodshed, were not yet for France.

A popular craze once hurled a good part of Europe into Asian crusades; a popular craze crucified Jesus; a craze for equal justice once rushed France into the bloodiest injustice of the "Reign of Terror;" now a craze for security hurled her into imminent insecurity, resulting in war with all Europe; France wanting peace, confirmed its destinies to him who was a very Mars of war.

Prussia secretly joined with Russia in a treaty, May 24, 1804, to declare war on France, at its first further encroachment on north Europe.[1]

The French conspiracy trials lasted from May 28 to June 10, 1804. Twenty prisoners were condemned to die. Cadoudal and eleven others were executed; others were imprisoned. Yet three nobles, Reviere and the two Polignacs, who were condemned to death, were pardoned at request of *noblesse* friends who had become Bonapartist courtiers; a marked favor to the

[1] State papers.

old nobility, whose aid Napoleon was seeking ; but these men were afterward sent to prison.[1]

February 15, 1804, the French Admiral, Linois, with a ship of the line and three frigates, attacked a British trade fleet from China with rich cargo. The British were armed. In a severe fight in the Indian ocean they defeated the French war vessels. This caused great joy in England. It was highly creditable to British seamen.

WILLIAM PITT AGAIN PREMIER.

In spring of 1804, to the excitement and hope with which the war began in 1803 had followed disappointment and discontent. England had gained little, for little was in its reach. So the Fox party had foretold. Britain's power was on sea, not on the continent. England blamed its Addington ministry.

May 4, 1804.

George III was to blame for this useless war. Now he became again insane. England was almost despondent. It ought to have retired George from the throne as incompetent to reign, as Sweden, later, retired Gustavus IV ; as Spain barred out Prince Philip. But even the corrupt tories dared not trust his son George, the bad prince royal, to act as regent. The plan to put kingly powers into a commission of able men, separate from the two incapable Georges,

[1] Schlosser vii, 346.

was favored by some statesmen, but was too wise a course for Pitt and Addington and the tory majority. So dull George III, now a maniac, remained the head of a very great nation.

A crisis in public opinion came; something must be done, some change must be made. Pitt, the ministry's adviser, wanted to be again premier. He attacked his own protegé, the Addington ministry, March 15, 1804. Fox and Sheridan again protested against the war and its ruinous mismanagement.

After several weeks of insanity, George mustered what little wits he ever had and required the ministry to resign. With strange infatuation the tory majority imagined that Pitt, the misadviser of the late ministry and of George, could remedy the bad condition of affairs; this opinion seemed to accuse Pitt of not having given honest advice.

Never did country more need an able ministry. It needed to unite all parties in its support. It was a triumph of all enemies of powerful Britain that foolish George III, with his usual stubbornness, utterly refused to receive into the new ministry the great Whig, Charles J. Fox.

Mr. Fox opposed useless war, advocated humane non-interventions, such as find more favor today, and he was a champion opposer of African slave-trade.

George ruined the best prospect; he prevented forming an able ministry, and Britain, "A power which has dotted the surface of the globe with her possessions and military posts, whose morning drumbeat, following the sun in his course, and keeping pace with the hours, circles the earth with one continuous and unbroken strain of the martial airs of

England,"[1] was committed to Pitt, a proud, cold orator,[2] little but a debater. He was a very bad war manager; he was a hero of brave words and wine; of foreign briberies and blunders; of able speeches and bad campaigns; of winning words and unwinning wars; the very genius of inefficiency; hero in speech, vanquished in wars. His speeches elated Tories as much as Napoleon's victories cheered the French.

Macaulay, a British Whig, wrote:—

"For assuredly one-tenth part of his errors and disasters would have been fatal to the power and influence of any minister, who had not possessed in the highest degree the talents of a parliamentary leader. While his schemes were confounded, while his predictions were falsified, while the coalitions he had labored to form were falling to pieces, while the expeditions he had sent forth at enormous cost were ending in rout and disgrace, while the enemy against whom he was feebly contending was subjugating Flanders and Brabant, the electorate of Mainz, and the electorate of Treves, Holland, Piedmont, Liguria, Lombardy, his authority over the House of Commons was becoming more and more absolute. There was his empire. There were his victories, his Lodi, his Arcola, his Rivoli, his Marengo.

"If some great misfortune, a pitched battle lost by the allies, the annexation of a new department to the French republic, a sanguinary insurrection in Ireland, a mutiny in the fleet, a panic in the city, a run on the bank had spread dismay through the ranks of his majority, that dismay lasted only till he rose from the Treasury Bench, drew up his haughty head, stretched his arm with commanding gesture, and poured forth, in deep and sonorous tones, the lofty language of inextinguishable hope and inflexible resolution. Thus through a long and calamitous period, every disaster that happened without the walls of parliament was regularly followed by a triumph within them."

This eloquent marplot, this persuasive deviser of disaster, who had so discredited the honorable English name, was now again made the head of George III's ministry, where he had once been so prolific of

[1] Daniel Webster.   [2] Alison, ii, 294.

damage to Britian, so fertile of bloody reverses to British arms, so fruitful of calamity to British policy, where he was again to run a career of expensive defeat. He became again Prime Minister on the very day,— May 18, 1804,— when Napoleon, who had so greatly baffled and beaten him, became Emperor of the French : these men were head contestants in the gigantic struggle; the one a great orator, an active schemer, an incompetent war minister, a bad financier, a bad strategist, and handicapped by a meddling, stupid king : the other, without conscience, faith, or honesty, with not a moral scruple ; but avaricious, grasping, eager, and ambitious ; and yet the ablest soldier of all the ages.

King George III would not receive the able Whig, Charles J. Fox, into the ministry. Charles Knight, the English historian, says : —[1]

"'The King would risk something far higher than his crown . . . the lives of his people, the independence of his country . . . . for a miserable personal pique, which he was compelled to lay aside two years afterwards.''

And English Thackeray said : —[2]

"His mother's bigotry and hatred he inherited with the obstinacy of his own race. Like other dull men, the king was, all his life, suspicious of superior people."

The other able Whigs would not enter this madman's ministry without their great leader, Mr. Fox. So the ministry was made up of men whose heavy weight is still felt in all Brician in the heavy taxes required by the great debt.

George III required of Pitt assurance that he would never agitate for or support removal of the legal

[1] History of England.   [2] Four Georges.

restrictions upon British Catholics. Pitt dishonored himself by stifling his own convictions, and accepted the terms. Yet he had left the ministry in 1801 on that very issue. Now he backed down. He liked office well enough to subdue his own conscience.

George and Pitt went on wasting British blood and treasure for a very un-British cause,— that of the old continental monarchs. The British had not a single interest in common with the pretended "king of Sardinia," who was really not a king, yet the British government stuck to his shadowy fortunes through the whole bloody struggles from 1803 to 1815, and then made him a tyrant over unwilling Piedmont, which he ruled badly on un-British principles, by measures hostile to British doctrines.

French arms had won Italy from Austrian tyranny. But Pitt used British money to bribe Austria to war to win back Italy to be again her victim. A bargain was made. Pitt drew up the terms of Europe's subjugation; tyrant's terms; a great wrong to the people of Europe. The terms suited despotism so well that they were put in force in Europe when Napoleon was overthrown. They set back the world's progress. Pitt and George III meant that the war should continue till arbitrary monarchs and nobles, instead of Frenchmen, should rule against the rights of men and of labor.

Russia. In 1754 the Russian subjects were about twenty million, and in 1804 thirty-six million. The revenue in 1754 was fifteen million dollars, and in 1804 sixty-six million dollars; raised mostly by poll tax of five roubles for each freeman and two for each serf. The

CHARLES J. FOX.

WILLIAM PITT.
OB. 1806.

spirit tax added about fifteen million dollars in paper in 1804. Russia was gaining in property.

The Czar, Alexander I, was young, romantic, dreamy. He aspired to ascendency over Turkey and Persia and influence in Europe. He was subject to great changes of opinion. The sagacious Metternich who knew him intimately, says:—

"This prince, vehement and full of energy, impulsive, always in danger of acting rashly and viewing things from the standpoint of his own ideas, had, on coming to the throne, surrounded himself with a council formed of persons of his own age, whom he honored with the name of friends."

The Russian army,— all conscripts,— nominally three hundred thousand men, had so vast territory to protect that it could concentrate in 1805-7, against Napoleon, less than one-fourth that number at any spot. Its army on paper and the force it can use in battle or campaign, is always quite different. Its supply and its hospitals were wretched. The pay of an infantry man was less than three dollars a year; that of a Cossack still less. Government fed and clothed them. They were hardy, could bivouac in snow and subsist on scanty fare. They believed that Russia was to conquer the world.

The Czar was alarmed lest Napoleon should disturb his relations who held Oldenburg and Mechlinburg. But the British blockade disturbed his commerce.

Markoff, Russian ambassador at Paris, intrigued against Napoleon. The French seized his secretary, Christin, in Switzerland, on charge of aiding banished French royalists. The Czar gave money to the Bourbon Princes. The French arrested Vernegas, a member of the Russian embassy at Rome, and carried him to France, an insult to the Czar. In an audience, September 21, 1804, Napoleon went up to Markoff and said before the assembled envoys, that it is very strange that a Russian ambassador has a dependent, a Swiss, whose business seems to be simply to aid all sorts of conspiracies. "In future I shall cause arrest of all persons who shall act against the interests of France." The Czar recalled Markoff, but assured him of his esteem.

England, Russia, and Sweden, tried to draw Austria and Prussia into coalition with them against France. The Czar and Gustavus IV king of Sweden urged the German Diet at Ratisbon to demand satisfaction for the French seizure of the Duc d'Enghien on German soil of Baden. But Baden expressed its satisfaction and the German emperor, Francis of Austria, feared Napoleon too much to protest. Napoleon recalled his ambassador from Russia. The prospect was warlike.

The Czar sent his final terms by D'Oubril, whom Napoleon hated, — That Russia have part in arranging Italian affairs; that the promised "compensation" be given to the "king of Sardinia;" that the French troops leave Naples and north Germany; that small states may be neutral. Of these four items only the last could be of much importance to Russia. France hardly noticed these absurd terms, but Talleyrand replied that Russians correspond with enemies of France; that Markoff in Paris gave asylum to hired agents of England; that the Russian court wore mourning for d'Enghien; that Russia had broken its agreement that Ionia should be left free of foreign troops, but had changed Ionia's government: four points that were true. He proposed that Russia avoid partiality for England and unite with France to consolidate general peace, equilibrium, and liberty of the seas.[1] This correspondence was based mainly on the treaty of Luneville. Diplomatic relations ceased; Russia and France stood at point of war.

Prussia aspired to be protector of northern Germany. Frenchmen arrested Rumbold, British minister, at Hamburg, October 5, 1804, and sent him to Paris. This made great sensation at Berlin. The anti-French party declaimed that Prussia's honor was wounded; redress must be had or influence lost in north Germany; that Napoleon's ambition was unbounded. The king wrote to Napoleon, his envoy protested, and Napoleon released the prisoner. But the insult rankled in Prussia.

On condition of no increase of the French army in Hanover, and no burden of war on north Germany, King Frederic William agreed to be neutral and not permit Russians or others to march across Prussia, and Napoleon said he would augment Prussia. Then the ministry changed. Count Haugwitz, friendly to France, was retired; Baron Hardenburg, an enemy to French influence, friendly to Russia and England, took power.

To gain the alliance of Prussia in order to awe the continent, was Napoleon's aim. This gained, he could restrain Russia and Austria. The king wanted to be bribed to this alliance; Napoleon meant that George III's Hanover should be the bribe; but Frederic William, fearing Russia and England, hesitated to accept Hanover.

[1] State Papers.

Foolish Gustavus IV broke relations between Sweden and France in a letter addressed to "Monsieur Napoleon Bonaparte." He forbade French journals in Sweden [Sept. 7, 1804]. This was not the wish of the Swedes. He might have kept Sweden in peace, but December 3, 1804, he engaged with England to form a depot in Swedish Pomerania for Hanover troops to enter British pay, and for a station for sale of British goods, thus antagonizing Sweden to Napoleon's vast power. His bribe was eighty thousand pounds from Pitt.

<small>Sweden.</small>

The Legion of Honor was opposed by many French. But Napoleon forced its adoption. July 14, 1804, this new order was grandly inaugurated at the splendid church of the Invalides, Paris, and its crosses given out by generals in all French camps. The people soon approved, it became permanent and an object of aspiration. By thus celebrating the date of the taking of the Bastile, Napoleon adroitly blended in the public mind the republican triumph and his imperial splendor. But the next day he struck a new blow at liberty by restoring Fouché's spy police.

At Boulogne, August 15, called his birthday, around his high throne were grouped the high dignitaries, the marshals, the ministers; and before him, radiating from his throne like the spokes of an immense living wheel, was displayed a mighty army,— eighty thousand men,[1] — destined to fight and perish in every part of Europe from Moscow to Cadiz, from Denmark to Dalmatia. The great spectacle was very magnificent. The thrilling martial music, the gay uniforms,

[1] Bourrienne, ii, 202.

the inspiring spirit of military glory, the memory of many victories, the hopes of coming distinction, the presence of so many great military leaders, all animated the grand occasion. With splendid ceremony the Emperor gave the crosses of the Legion of Honor.

Cavalry and artillery formed the brilliant border of this gorgeous array, while beyond, a countless multitude covered the slope to its summit. On each side of Napoleon the bands came and excited the vast concourse with stirring music.

The Emperor ascended the throne amid the thunder of cannon and flourish of trumpets. Around were seen many standards; some new, many stained by the blood and blackened by the smoke of many battles.

The Emperor took the oath. Raising his voice he said:—

"And you, soldiers, swear to defend, at the hazard of your life, the honor of the French name, your country, and your Emperor."

Many voices responded.

The Polytechnic school at Paris held a republican spirit, so Napoleon changed it into a military academy.[1]

Napoleon had the German princes in his power. Filled with hopes and fears they hastened to meet him at Mainz. He formed a Confederation of the Rhine of the German princes, under his "protection," which put south and central Germany for years helpless in his power and forced it to furnish troops and money for his wars, a vast damage to Germany.

Genoa gave itself to Napoleon, October 20, 1804.

[1] Bourrienne, ii, 206.

He got six thousand seamen, its arsenals, and its grand harbor, worth more than Malta, and made it a great naval station, a mutual advantage to Genoa and France. He was to let Genoa's goods into Piedmont and Parma, and compel the Barbary states to respect its flag. He would build there ten ships of the line. This made business lively at Genoa.

Lord Nelson tried, October 2, 1804, to burn the French flotilla at Boulogne. He sent at night floating torpedoes into the harbor. The failure made much ridicule in England and France.

Napoleon tried to connect his glory with Charlemagne. Ten centuries before, in A.D. 800, Pope Leo III crowned that great monarch, who went submissively to Rome. Napoleon, more powerful than Charlemagne, required Pope Pius VII to render homage by coming to Paris to crown him. No more of empire bowing to the pope; the pope must bow to empire.

Pius VII objected. Five cardinal advisers objected. Fifteen demanded conditions. They all prayed for light. But necessity decided. The question might divide the church. It was dividing it. Pius hoped for great gifts from Napoleon. Napoleon's uncle, Cardinal Fesch, at Rome gave presents and made threats.[1] Pius objected, hesitated, hoped Napoleon would give him the two Legations regardless of the will of the Legation people, then he yielded.[2]

Most Frenchmen then disliked the Church of Rome. Napoleon's Concordat of 1801 gave his rule a ruder shock[3] than his abrogation of the liberties won by the Revolution. The army hated it. Many

---

[1] Guizot vii, 101.   [2] Remusat.   [3] Bourrienne ii, 213.

civilians hated it. Many Royalists hated it. It did not please the Republicans. But it conciliated some of the Catholics of which there were still many. He wanted the prestige which church and religion could add. Some persons regarded his anointing and crowning by the pope as essential to sacred authority.[1] He always grasped every means of power. No scruple deterred him. He knew that the Roman church, like the Greek, had ever been a bulwark of strength to monarchs good or bad.

France had above 27,000,000 people. Napoleon controlled the election officers. No means exists to verify their returns of votes. December 1, 1804, the Senate, whose members he had appointed, reported the popular vote as 3,572,329 in favor and 2,569 against making the empire hereditary in his family.[2] This was claimed as a sacred ratification.[3] It was no more sacred than the votes which ratified several preceding governments. These had been recalled; the people had always a right to recall this or any form of rule. A people have a natural right to change their government at their pleasure provided it is done without oppressing opposers. No act is final by which a people lose their liberties. Plots had stimulated the French to vote heredity lest death of Napoleon should leave it to anarchy or to return of the Bourbons. With gay fêtes the French rejoiced at this death of liberty. The cost of the gayeties were said to be 85,000,000 francs.[4] The pope came and was received with pomp.[5] Metter-

[1] Bourrienne ii, 213.
[2] Bourrienne: Remuset.   [3] Lanfrey.
[4] Schlosser viii, 356.   [5] Bourrienne ii.

nich says that only the evening before the day fixed for the coronation : —

"The holy father perceived with surprise that it was intended to crown the empress at the same time with Napoleon. The pope was undecided as to the part he ought to take. . . . . He had no proofs of the validity of the Emperor's marriage"

which was made when marriage was only a civil contract as it is in Protestant countries. He : —

"Declared that he would not appear at the august ceremony . . . if he did not receive direct proofs of the validity of their marriage. . . . . The bishops reassured him and gave him details of the marriage of Napoleon and Josephine and the sacramental bond . . . . The Holy Father crowned them the next day, and it was not till several days after the ceremony that he learned that his credulity had been abused . . . . and that he had, so to speak, sanctioned a concubinage, ... a wrong for which the pope has never forgiven him."[1]

Madame Remuset says Josephine states that : —

"Two days before the coronation Cardinal Fesch married them in presence of two of his aides-de-camp, and gave her a written certificate of the wedding."

And Remuset adds : —

"It is since said that religious marriage not witnessed by the curé of the parish where it is celebrated, is a nullity, and by that expedient the means of breaking the marriage in the future was purposely reserved."[2]

Napoleon had already contemplated divorce, but it did not come until December 16, 1809.[3]

At Notre Dame, December 2, 1804, amid great pomp, the pope anointed Napoleon's head with oil, and Napoleon placed a crown on his own head and crowned Josephine. He solemnly declared he was satisfied with his grandeur and would make no more additions to his empire, a pledge quickly broken.

[1] Metternich Mem. ii, 184–85. [2] Remuset ii, chap. x.
[3] Ibid ii, chap. ix.

This remarkable man, incapable of friendship, with few personal friends, admired by many, loved by no man, had raised himself to be a power dreaded by all Europe.

Next day at a great martial display in Champ de Mars, Napoleon gave to the colonels the eagles to be the army standards. On a throne he addressed the troops.

The Bourbon Stanislaus Xavier, who called himself Louis XVIII, was brother of Louis XVI, issued a bombastic protest. It was so silly that Napoleon had it printed in the "Moniteur."

Pius VII had given the church's approval of Napoleon. Now he wanted his price. But with lack of sharpness he waited until Napoleon had no further present need of him. Then he coolly asked Napoleon to give him Avignon, Bologna, and part of Italy, once papal; he ought to have known better; Napoleon was not that sort of a man; he never let go anything that he could hold; this time his language was dignified. He replied: —

"France has dearly purchased the power which she enjoys. We cannot sever anything from the empire which has been the fruit of ten years of bloody combat. Still less can we diminish the territory of a foreign state which by confiding to us the powers of its government has imposed on us the duty of its protection, and never conferred on us the power of alienating any part of its territory."

This refusal cooled Pius VII toward Napoleon. Still worse, Pius VII had, by this demand, asserted the wicked principle that states and peoples may be traded, given away, squandered from one power to another without asking the people's consent. The pope soon had ample cause to repent the sanction of so monstrous a doctrine. Many good Catholics disapproved this affair as well as several of his other acts.

The United States and the European governments, except England, Russia, Sweden, and Turkey, soon recognized Napoleon as Emperor.

Forming the Confederation of the Rhine had destroyed the old German empire; its power had gone to its "Protector," Napoleon; he ruled it. So its Emperor, Francis II, was crowned by the archbishop of Vienna in the year 1804, as Francis I, Emperor of Austria, and dropped the title "Emperor of Germany," which his family had borne for nearly five hundred years. He united his states in one empire. The present title, "Emperor of Germany," is a new creation, made in 1871.

By treaties of 1796, 1801 and 1803, Spain and France were bound to mutual offensive and defensive aid. This fact excited British jealousy because it helped Napoleon to cash from Spain to use to injure Britain in the war. It was well known that Napoleon compelled unwilling Spain to give him this money. The amount was concealed. The British ministry intimated that it would not regard a small forced sum as cause for war on Spain. But rumors that the sum was large got abroad. Mr. Frere, British ambassador to Spain, remonstrated against the payment and against the passage of French troops through Spain to Portugal. In February, 1804, Mr. Frere protested against sale of French prizes in Spain, and called for "cessation of every naval armament within" Spain. In September, 1804, the British learned that fifteen hundred French troops had gone in small parties to Ferrol, in Spain, where were four large French war ships, and that Spain had ordered the arming without loss of time of three ships of the line and other vessels at that port; that three line ships should go from Cadiz to Ferrol, and that packets should arm as in war. This was startling news. It received the alarming addition that within a month eleven Spanish ships of the line would be ready for sea at Ferrol, and though said to be bound for America, victualled for but three months. Then came reports that French soldiers were daily arriving at Ferrol. Then followed tidings that they only awaited arrival of the Spanish treasure ships from America, to throw off the mask and be hostile to England.

Mr. Frere warmly remonstrated. Manuel Godoy, Prince of Peace, governing Spain for the incapable, worthless Charles IV, replied : —

"The king of Spain has never thought of being wanting to the agreement entered into with the British government. The cessation of all naval armaments against Great Britain shall be observed as heretofore, and whatever information to the contrary may have been received, is wholly unfounded."[1]

Here was a chance for Pitt and George III to again blunder. They did blunder, as usual. They decided to seize the Spanish treasure at sea, and so managed it that only four British frigates met these four Spanish frigates [October 5, 1804]. Captain Moore informed the Spanish Admiral that he had orders to detain the Spanish ships; that he hoped to do it without bloodshed. The Spaniard, of course, declined to submit to an equal force. A battle took place; one of the Spanish frigates blew up; the British took the others with above $10,000,000 on board. The

[1] Parliament Debates, ii. 93—98.

Spanish lost about one hundred killed and wounded, besides two hundred and forty on the exploded ship. Had it been right to seize these ships, then common sense should have dictated to George and Pitt to send a force so large as to compel the Spanish commander to surrender without battle, and to justify him to do so without loss of his honor. England had a vast navy; it could send a strong force. This senseless catastrophe made a great shock in England; it angered the British sense of justice and honor. The Whig leaders, Fox and Grenville, urged:—

"That there appeared nothing but inattention, negligence and mystery on the part of the British government on this occasion."

Some Tories, blinded by partizianship, did not denounce the deed. But the extreme Tory historian, Alison, wrote:—

"A large and conscientious body of the ministry's usual supporters beheld with pain what they deemed an unwarrantable invasion of the rights of nations, and loudly condemned an act derogatory to the British name . . . . no defense can be maintained for the conduct of England." [1]

The eminent Englishman, Charles Knight, says:—

"It was a complicated question, and one in which the British government was, upon the face of it, open to very serious blame." [2]

Dr. Coote (British), remarks:—

"It cannot be justified by any arguments drawn from reason or equity." [3]

Crowe (British), says:—

"It was a flagrant act of injustice, in the very style of Bonaparte's own conduct, and proceeded from the same imbecility which threw upon us the blame of the renewal of the war; an irresolute, wavering system, which was but weakness, and which looked like treachery." [4]

---

[1] History Europe ii, 305.   [2] History England vii, 199.
[3] Modern Europe vi, 71.   [4] Crowe's France iii, 189.

As the king of Spain was a fool, and Godoy held power only by the king's will,— an uncertain tenure, — and the real manhood of Spain was out of power, so that appeal to the manly conscience of the brave Spanish nation was impossible, I can hardly join with the great British authors whom I have quoted, in so strongly condemning the arrest of that great treasure on board those frigates from going into the hands of the enemy of Britain, Napoleon; but the manner of arresting used by George and Pitt, merits the severest condemnation as opposed to every sense of honor and decency; it was great folly not to send force sufficient to overawe the Spanish admiral and so prevent the battle.

Debate in Parliament on this outrage was vigorous, but the Tories sustained the ministry by a large majority.

Hoping for peaceful adjustment, Spain delayed to declare war until sixty-eight days later, December 12, 1804.

In January, 1805, Napoleon compelled unwilling Spain to make a new treaty of alliance with him, offensive and defensive, by which Charles IV must furnish him thirty-two ships of the line and five thousand soldiers. Spain had practically nothing in return.

Napoleon calculated that he had 193,000 men on the coast, ready to invade England. He had sixty-nine ships of the line and many smaller vessels. France was then a great naval power; at sea it rivalled the British.

Napoleon wrote to George III proposing peace. British kings do not negotiate: the minister,

Hawkesbury, replied for him, refusing full answer "to the overture" till he had "time to communicate with the powers on the continent with whom he is engaged in most confidential connections and relations and particularly with the emperor of Russia."

<small>Napoleon proposes Peace, Jan., 1805.</small>

Few rulers ever sent such stupidity. Had George and Pitt tried to end the war, success was then possible. Some day they must negotiate. It is treaties that end wars. Common sense, honor, and religion command to "agree with thine adversary quickly." George and Pitt wantonly repulsed overture. They did more; they stupidly betrayed their own country and plans. Their words, "most confidential connections," revealed just what was of extreme importance to conceal; just what Napoleon most wanted to know; a new coalition; that he must fight Europe; that he must attack and cripple Austria before Russia could aid her. Thus stupid George and Pitt helped France to victory at Ulm and Austerlitz, and, in consequence, to later Aerstadt and Friedland. "It was but weakness which looked like treachery."

These two letters did still more damage; they made Napoleon appear nobly forbearing, humane, and England disreputably quarrelsome. The French press, controlled by Napoleon, blazoned this aspect to all Europe; the French and many others thereon, credited him with love of peace.

The emperors of Russia and Austria hoped to drive Napoleon from Germany, Netherlands, and Italy and place there a tyranny even greater than his. It was war between oppressors. Neither would allow liberty or rights to Germans or Italians. Either would trample common rights, that nobles might have plunder and oppressive power. The people had not even choice of masters; they must fight for the one who then held them. Napoleon was false, unjust, selfish, grasping; so were Alexander and Francis. Under him common men might rise to high station; not so under them. There all was heredity, and it had given to Russia the mystic dreamer, Alexander I; to Austria the dull, despotic Francis I; to England the dark-minded George III; to Sweden the crack-brained Gustavus IV; to Portugal the insane Maria; to Spain the moral idiot, Charles IV; to Naples Charles' worthless brother, Ferdinand; to Denmark the dissipation-crazed Christian VII; to Prussia the inefficient marplot, Frederic William III: hardly one with morals that would have been decent in a peasant.

January 19, 1805, Pitt showed to the Russian ambassabor a basis of principles which he desired should actuate the coalition. Reduced to plain language it was in substance: —

1. To rescue from France its conquests made since 1789.
2. To divide this plunder among sovereigns, and to make these countries barriers against France.
3. To protect each other in holding fast our robberies.

Such was Pitt's monstrous basis. It was used in 1814–15 to give Italy, Germany, and the Rhine provinces to grasping despotism, to bar the people from their natural rights and liberties. George III wanted this bad plan "established in its fullest extent."

Said Pitt:

"If the arms of the allies should be crowned with such success as to despoil France of all its conquests made since the revolution, it would certainly be their first object to re-establish the United Provinces (Holland) and Switzerland, and the territories of the kings of Sardinia and Naples, as well as the dukes of Modena and Tuscany . . . . As to the Italian provinces that have been mentioned, experience has demonstrated that they have neither disposition nor resources to resist the aggressions of France. The last measures of Genoa and some of the other Italian states, give them no title to appeal either to the justice or the generosity of the allies . . . . It is certainly a matter of highest importance, if not of absolute necessity, to procure the efficacious and vigorous co-operation of Austria and Prussia, but there is little reason to hope that either of these powers will embark in the common cause unless they have a prospect of advantage to indemnify them for their exertions."

This proposed restoration of Switzerland and Holland is right. But the rest of this basis is evil. Thus after admitting that Italy had no "disposition to resist" France, he practically admits that only prospective plunder of the liberties and substance of Germany and Italy and the Rhine can bribe Prussia and Austria to re-enter the war on France. Such was Pitt's real meaning. Pitt described what large spoils Prussia and Austria should have.

Russia, Prussia, and Austria still held back from the awful crime, that of the Devil on the mountain, of trading countries not owned by the seller. But George and Pitt actually bribed them to re-enter on the wicked career of crime against the rights of mankind. So depraved was Pitt's plan that these hardened plunderers of Poland, these veteran gamblers in German and Italian countries so much hesitated that only Pitt's British cash set their armies in motion.

Pitt wanted to join with the despotic monarchs to guarantee security of each other's plunder, to sup-

KREMLIN AT MOSCOW.

ROYAL PALACE, MADRID.

press any attempt of downcast manhood to right itself.

In stating these facts of Pitt and the monarchs I do not arraign their countries; many British, Prussians, Austrians, Russians deplored the great transgression. All but Britain were absolute monarchies; their people had no rule. England had limited monarchy, with a hard, stupid king: the whole British people did not then, as they do now, elect the members of the House of Commons. The English had little control of the king and ministry. England was not under the enlightened policy that governs it today.

Within a few years each of these great powers had much increased its domain. To the advantage of civilization the British had conquered large empire in India. It was trying to conquer more in India. It was wisely extending its dominion in many parts of the world. Russia, Prussia, and Austria had divided Poland. Russia had conquered parts of Turkey, Sweden, and Persia. Austria had got Venice. Much of Russia, Prussia, and Austria was made up of conquests. Their policy was aggressive. Such were the governments that Pitt hired to try to take from France its conquests.

To preserve the "equilibrium of power" was a pretense. Pitt would preserve the "equilibrium" by reducing France alone below the new equilibrium made by increase of the others' powers, an odd way to make powers balance!

It is true, though it seems incredible, that to bring Russians of that day to attempt conquest of enlightened Germany, and to divide it as other bandits divide spoil, Pitt gave great bribes of borrowed cash, for which Englishmen are still taxed to pay the interest.

Lord Melville was in the ministry. He was detected in making his own private use of public money instead of giving it away as Pitt did to Bourbon intriguers and absolute monarchs. This shocked Pitt, the great misapplyer. Public opinion, for once too strong for Pitt and George, drove Melville from the ministry.

By great wrong in former times, royal and other adventurers took a large part of the land of Ireland from the people (who owned it collectively as tribes before Irish landlords existed), and gave it to nobles and favorites. Most Irish laborers were Catholics, and these laborers created the value of Irish land. In 1805, in some parts, Presbyterians, Methodists and other disfranchised were a majority. Prosperity required that all outside the established English church should have their natural rights and privileges, subject only to wholesome laws that should bear on all alike.

<small>Ireland and Religion.</small>

Yet to this great Catholic majority was denied common rights. They might not sit on juries; they might not be tried by juries of their own kind; they might not hold commissions in the army outside of Ireland; they had no part in making the laws which they were to live under; they could not choose one of themselves as their legal representative in making laws; they had no part in executing Irish laws. In their own land, the land of their forefathers, they were practically outlawed. They were compelled to pay the taxes for the salaries and expenses of the English church in which not one of them communed. Habeus corpus writ was suspended; an Irishman could be arbitrarily imprisoned indefinitely without trial.

For years had been efforts to remove religious disabilities. Grattan and the British whigs, Fox and Grenville ably advocated this relief. Lords Hawksbury, Sidmouth, Eldon, and others opposed this justice and argued: —

"Can there be any doubt of the complete dependence in which the pope is placed to Bonaparte? Would it not be the height of madness in us, knowing of his [Bonaparte's] inveterate hostility to this country, to weaken our means of resistance by the admission to political power of those who are necessarily subject to a power over which he has such control? The priesthood interfere in a great part of the civil and domestic concerns of life. It is submission to a foreign power that renders them dangerous."

George III aided French Chouan and Vendean Catholics to revolt and war against their French government; he used his utmost efforts to destroy in Italy the new governments that allowed freedom of religious opinion; he tried hard to force on Italy the "king of Sardinia," the pope, the bad king of Naples, the dukes of Tuscany and Modena, and rule of Austria in Italy; all of these were Catholics; all of these would refuse freedom of Protestant worship of George III's own church in Italy. Yet stubborn old George said his conscience and his official oath restrained him from consenting to allowing civil rights to Catholics in Ireland. Pitt wanted to give their rights to Catholics; he had promised it to them in 1801. But Pitt, hard, unmerciful toward the happiness of many millions of Germans and Italians, was so in fear of hurting the feelings of hard George, that he debased his manhood by yielding his own conscience, his sense of right and wrong in the religious question; he deserted his principles and no longer supported Catholic emancipation, and the Commons voted it down, three hundred and thirty-six to one hundred and twenty-four. It was not adopted till 1829. Irish Catholics, Methodists and other dissenters were compelled to pay taxes to support the English church in Ireland until relieved by Mr. Gladstone's Irish church disfranchisement act in 1869.

North Italy followed all the changes in France, — Directory, Consulate, Monarchy. Napoleon convened the "estates of the Italian Republic" in Paris. There it proclaimed him king of Italy, March 18, 1805. These "estates" of Italy had no authority from the Italian people; nobody in Italy elected them; the whole thing was assumption of authority. It was added that his sons, natural or adopted, should succeed him on that throne, but the crowns of France and Italy should never be united after him.

Napoleon said to Bourrienne: —

"The union of Italy with France can only be temporary, but it is necessary in order to accustom the nations of Italy to live under common laws. The Genoese, the Piedmontese, the Venetians, the Milanese, the Tuscans, the Romans, and the Neapolitans hate each other . . . . When manners shall be assimilated and enmities quenched, there will be an Italy, and I will give her independence. But for that I must have twenty years."

The iron crown of Charlemagne had reposed for a thousand years in the cathedral of Monza. It was brought forth, and with it, in the presence of the bishop of Milan, the pope having refused, Napoleon crowned himself king of Italy.

The occasion was one of great splendor. He appointed as viceroy, Eugene Beauharnais, son of Josephine. As in France, Napoleon revived the regal customs of the old Byzantine court. He appointed grand dignitaries; he compelled a concordat with the pope; he enacted the same civil code as in France, except trial by jury; he made a new order,—that of the iron crown.

Napoleon had made Eugene a French prince. He did not expect him to govern; he selected Mejean, a Frenchman, to conduct business; he did not perceive that an Italian might know better what was best for Italy; this offended Italians; Mejean was surrounded by Frenchmen. Napoleon bestowed honors on a few Italians; he put a large French military force in Italian pay, and thus saved their subsistence to France. But he kept them at his own disposal. He ordered many improvements which now adorn Milan. His rule was good and popular for Milan.

At Marengo he held a splendid pageant to imitate the victory there in 1800, though he had there been badly defeated by Melas, before Dessaux came up to turn it into decisive victory.

As secretly arranged by intrigue, a deputation from Genoa asked him to unite Genoa with his empire. They said:—"We are the naval power of Piedmont, we must be united with Piedmont." Piedmont was already annexed to France. Although he had solemnly declared five months before that he would not extend his empire, he annexed Genoa in June, 1805.

Thus sank the old republic that for fourteen hundred years had kept a separate existence. He wanted Genoa for its naval resources. Said he:—" I had but one object in view, viz.: 15,000 seamen." He wrote to Lebrun, his governor of Genoa:—"Govern but to collect seamen." Union with France seemed to give Genoa great added importance and business, and to France a great harbor, many vessels and trade advantages. But in Genoa these were already had. Genoa had placed its arsenals and harbor at his disposal, had engaged to furnish him with six thousand seamen and ten line ships, at Genoa's expense. The annexation was needless; it was almost a wanton act; he well knew it would offend Russia and Austria; it was a blunder; it was more, it was defiance to Europe.

Russia and Sweden made a friendly treaty January 12, 1805. England, Russia, and Sweden made alliance April 5, 1805; England and Russia drew still closer by treaty April 11, 1805. They counted on 300,000 Austrians to make up 500,000 men against France. Britain and Russia were to form a great league to exclude the French from north Germany, make Holland and Switzerland independent, destroy the new kingdom of Italy, re-establish the old kingdom of Piedmont, and aid the bad king of Naples. They were to intimidate Prussia into joining the league.

War Coming.

England refused to leave Malta to the Czar. Then Alexander would first try to make peace, he would mediate. He started an envoy, Novasilzoff, with French passports for Paris obtained by Frederic William, who wanted peace.

Napoleon wrote to Frederic William:—

"I expect nothing from this mediation. Alexander is too fickle and too feeble. Russia is too far, too foreign to colonial and maritime interests . . . . I owe Russia no more as to Italian affairs than she owes me with reference to Turkish and Persian affairs. All peace with

England, to be solid, ought to contain a clause stipulating that she cease to give asylum to Bourbons and emigrants, and that she restrict her miserable writers."

To the glory of England she did not refuse asylum to exiles.

The Russian peace envoy reached Berlin. Russia had been offended by the d'Enghien affair; by the seizure of Rumbold in Hamburg; by the occupation of Hanover, whose offense was its great misfortune that George III of England was its Elector; by the erection of the kingdom of Italy, with Napoleon as its head; by the giving of Lucca by Napoleon to his sister Eliza, and by the aggressive and rude temper of Napoleon; but Alexander wanted peace. Then came this useless annexation of Genoa, and Napoleon's threat that he would not leave the bad queen of Naples land enough in her kingdom for her tomb. Alexander recalled his peace envoy.

War was resolved on; Austria was arming rapidly and with attempted secrecy; Alexander ratified his treaty of British alliance. Thus Napoleon had driven these two powers, Russia and Austria, to take part against him in the great coming war.

By treaty of Luneville, February 9, 1801, Napoleon had agreed to allow Switzerland, Genoa, and Lombardy republics to choose their own constitutions. He had violated his faith in each case.

The fatal coalition proceeded. Pitt and George engaged to give a bribe of £1,250,000 ($6,082,500) for every 100,000 regular troops brought into the field.[1] Parliament voted £3,500,000 ($17,031,000). It might be used at discretion by Pitt to bribe governments or officers.[2]

[1] Treaty of April 11, 1805.   [2] Parliament Reports.

War was to begin as soon as 400,000 troops could be ready. Of these Austria was to furnish 250,000, Russia 115,000, Hanover, Sardinia, and Naples 35,000. Russia engaged to march 60,000 men forthwith to the Austrian frontier and 80,000 to the Prussian border, to keep a reserve on the frontier, and to bring 180,000 men into the field if needed.

But Austria held back. It desired the war, but its finances were crippled. It required a Pitt bribe of £3,000,000 ($14,598,000), one-half down, the rest by monthly installments; so Pitt and George bought Austria's aid with that sum.

George and Pitt had much wronged Sweden's seamen and ships. Sweden's commerce needed that freedom of the seas which George and Pitt denied and abused. France had shown some favor to neutral commerce, which was of great importance to Swedes, and Sweden had received no injury from France. But vain Gustavus, a grief to the allies and a derision to the French, a marplot that heredity had thrust upon the brave and honorable Sweden, hastened to sell the lives of his subjects. He wanted a better bargain with Pitt than Russia and Austria had made. Pitt knew that Sweden's interest was against the foolish king's policy, that the Swedes disapproved it, so he accepted the king's terms. He promised $8.75 per man, each month: later, in October, the Swedish army to be used in Pomerania was fixed at 12,000 and Pitt was to pay the same as to Austria, $60.81 per annum for each man, beside five months in advance, and 50,000 pounds sterling to fortify Stralsund.

Gustavus IV.

Green, the English historian, says : —

"Pitt's offer of subsidies removed the last obstacle in the way of a league, and Russia, Austria, and Sweden joined in an alliance to wrest Italy and the low countries from the grasp of the French emperor."

But the people of Italy and the low countries showed no desire for rescue. Alison, whose opinions seldom favor progress or freedom, admits that the Italians liked the rule of the kingdom of Italy, that they were gratified by its honors, that they "look back with fond regret to the Regno d'Italia as the brightest period of their modern existence," that "Lombardy felt the foreign yoke only in the quickened circulation of wealth, the increased vent for industry," and that "hardly a magistrate or civil functionary was of foreign birth. Everywhere great and useful undertakings were set on foot, splendid edifices ornamented the towns, useful canals irrigated the fields."

Such were the situation and feelings of Italians when Pitt hired Europe to plunder them of their admired government. And Pitt was trying to force them back under a very bad form of absolute tyranny.

Mr. Fox, a real statesman, who disliked the war, warned Pitt of the dangers of a league without Prussia; that it might result in Napoleon's triumph and increased power. But Pitt ridiculed this wise caution and went on in his perverse errors.

Sir Walter Scott wrote : —

"Great Britain and Russia were the animating sources of this new coalition against France; but it was impossible, considering the insular situation of the first of these powers, and the great distance of the second from the scene of action, that they alone, without the concurrence of the emperor of Austria and the king of Prussia, should be able to assail France with any prospect of making a successful impression. Every effort therefore was used to awaken those states to a sense of the daily increasing encroachments of Bonaparte, and the extreme danger to which they were respectively exposed by the rapidly increasing extent of his empire."

All Spanish fleets were controlled by Napoleon. April 4, 1805, the British admiral, Lord Horatio Nelson, learned the French admiral, Villeneuve, with a French fleet, had put to sea and been joined by the Spanish fleet off Cadiz with 4,500 soldiers on board, the whole amounting to eighteen line ships and ten frigates, which was a very powerful fleet. With but ten line ships and three frigates Nelson had the audacious courage to pursue Villeneuve.

Napoleon's grand plan was to get Nelson away at a distance from Europe while his own great fleet should circle the West Indies, put Nelson on the wrong track, return quickly and surprise the British on his coast and overpower them before Nelson could return.

But the French fleet at Brest was so well blockaded by the British that it could not get out. So in May Napoleon sent orders to Villeneuve at Martinique to return with his fleet, raise the British blockade of Ferrol and Rochfort, unite all the fleets, appear before Brest and break its blockade, and then suddenly appear, with the immense combined fleets of France and Spain in the English channel before Boulogne, overmatching the British fleet, ready to assist Napoleon's great army to cross the channel and invade England.

Nelson was deceived. He lost time in searching the West Indian seas for Villeneuve. "London was in the greatest alarm for the West Indies."

So far luck had favored Napoleon; Nelson was decoyed away; Villeneuve was returning; the enormous combined fleet was expected.

Napoleon was at Boulogne, August 3, ready to invade England. His great fleet had not arrived. Irritated at the delay, impatient, he drilled his troops every day in maneuvers of embarkation. Eagerly he scanned the western horizon for a sight of the great squadrons.

Days sped by; more and more impatient grew the French emperor. In the depths of his soul he saw himself baffled, defeated in his darling design by this delay. He hurried off ship after ship to sail with speed with the most urgent orders to Villeneuve to hasten to appear. His anger was violent. Still the west showed a clear horizon; where was the tremendous fleet?

Napoleon held a great review of 80,000 men. The line occupied from right to left, nine miles. He inspected his great flotilla; it was an immense fleet of 1,800 small craft.

A mighty army — 120,000 men — with 10,000 horses, were ready to embark. Enormous as was this powerful army, another was ready on the Texel, and still another at Brest; in all, 155,000 disciplined men.[1]

All was ready; every man knew his exact place; so complete was the drill that in seventy-five minutes each 26,000 men could embark.

All was ready but the grand fleet. Where was it? It should have arrived; it should be before Boulogne, covering the waters with its naval grandeur. It had

[1] Napoleon to Tréville, July 2, 1805.

been prepared at enormous expense; it should have come, a force so great as to defeat any fleet that England could possibly assemble in the channel; it should be occupying and holding open the channel for the passage of the grand army, led by the man who proposed to suppress free British speech and the British free press; for him who hoped to conquer the world at London; for him who would suppress independence on sea and land. So thought Napoleon, who hoped to rule the world despotically for the benefit of Bonapartes and Bonapartists.

Two years and a half of vast preparation had culminated. All along the coast signals were arranged and waiting to announce the coming of the eagerly expected navy. It was estimated that in two hours after orders given the great army could be out of the harbor.

Napoleon wrote to Decres:—

"If we are masters twelve hours of the passage, England has lived."[1]

He wrote exhortations to Villeneuve:—

"Set out. Lose not a moment. Unite with my squadrons: come into the channel. England is ours. We are ready. All is embarked. Appear within twenty-four hours and all is finished."

Still the army waited for the navy.

Napoleon had great genius for war and for governing, but he had no genius for naval affairs. On sea Nelson was much his superior.

French and Spanish ships were less well built, and more poorly fitted, were harder to manage than the British ships. Their crews were less trained for sea service. Too many of them were raw hands. Ships,

[1] "Si nous sommes maîtres dous heures de la traversée, l'Angleterre a vécu."

masts, rigging, all were defective. French and Spanish seamen did all that was possible; no men could do more.

When Nelson found that Villeneuve had left the West Indies he sent a fast sailer to warn England, and sailed for Gibraltar. This news arrived in England July 9. Instantly Sir Robert Calder was sent with fifteen line ships to intercept Villeneuve. He met Villeneuve's fleet of twenty line ships and eight frigates July 22, 1805. A battle ensued. It was British victory. Calder captured two Spanish line ships, but the British court-martialed and reprimanded him for not inflicting harder defeat. Villeneuve knowing that it was more important to raise the blockades than to fight Calder, sailed away. He reached Ferrol August 2, one day before Napoleon arrived at Boulogne, to expect him there ready to aid the invasion of England. Villeneuve believed that Nelson had joined Calder, so he lingered at Corunna lest the British united fleet should destroy him.

Had Napoleon landed in England with his 155,000 men, victory was far from certain, was doubtful, even improbable. With the available British force, if such a soldier as Moore or Wellington could have been in command and free of the ministry and war office incompetents, and considering the stubborn defensive qualities of British soldiers and the aid of the militia, it is hardly to be believed that even with 200,000 men Napoleon could ever have arrived at London.

In his wars against Austria, in Italy and Bavaria the people were not against him; the soldiers had little personal interest in fighting him; those were not the people's wars. But invasion of England would have aroused all the British people; he would have found himself in such a war as he never saw until 1813 when aroused German people so gallantly aided to hurl him and his veteran hosts across the Rhine in terrible defeat. England's great danger lay in the unfitness, incapacity of king, ministers, and high officials, not in its soldiers or its people.

Once in England, the return of a French army must have been well-nigh impossible. All Britain's enormous navy would be called around it. It was strong enough to defeat and disperse Napoleon's combined navy. Then while Napoleon's veterans would be blockaded in England, the armies of united Russia, Austria, Sweden, Naples, and perhaps Prussia, already preparing, might have marched on his empire and anticipated 1814.

Napoleon's victories had been over troops compelled to fight for rulers, not for themselves. With British, defending their own England, protecting their rights, their liberties, their homes, it seems improbable that Napoleon could have conquered even had he safely landed.

The original claim of the house of Austria (Loraine-Hapsburg) to the Netherlands was founded, not on right, but on a shadow, the mere accident of a royal marriage, a terrible accident for the people. Misgovernment, cruelty and suffering marked periods of the Spanish rule. Oppression drove the Belgians to resistance. They defeated the Austrians, took possession of Brussels, and, in 1790, declared their independence. But Austria forcibly re-occupied Belgium. The French, under Pichegru, obtained it in 1794 by driving out the Austrians; later it was annexed to France. Through Napoleon's reign Belgium was French; even at Waterloo the Belgians did not wish to fight against Napoleon.

By treaty of Campo Formio, October 17, 1797, Austria ceded to France all its claim to the Netherlands, Milan, and Mantua, and received in full compensation, Istria, Dalmatia, Venice and its ground east of the Adige, previously independent, but made the spoil of France and Austria; this contract was renewed at Luneville in 1801. These gains proved more valuable than the Netherlands to Austria. Thus Austria had already first lost by conquest the Netherlands and Milan, and then had sold them to their conqueror, Napoleon, in 1797, and again in 1801, and had been more than paid in full for them in spoil, and now she sold herself to George and Pitt, to try by bloody combat and waste of human life to wrest them back. This hardly looks like fairness and honor; in common life such a deed would be disgrace; but Francis I was only an emperor, and George was only a king, and both were bad monarchs.

In 1801 Austria's income was about $50,000,000 net, equal to a much larger sum now. Like most of Europe it was forced to use paper money not convertible into gold, but a forced legal tender. There was little silver and gold. **Austria.** Brass coin was issued at double its intrinsic value. The state debt was large. The interest was paid in paper or by forced loans. The population was 27,600,000, almost exactly that of France. The army was 300,000 men, including 50,000 cavalry.

The emperor, Francis I, dispensed all army and civil appointments. He could crush freedom anywhere in Austria.

Archduke Charles was war minister. He was an able soldier. But the powers of the ministry were mainly held by Count Cobenzl, the vice-chancellor, and Count Colloredo, the emperor's intimate.

The political robbery of Germany in 1802 had given to Bavaria the "Equestrian Order," knights who held various possessions, long subject only to the emperor. After 1802, till 1806, the German empire had hardly more than nominal existence. The Elector of Bavaria held that these useless knights had become his subjects. He summoned them to meet him at Bamberg. They refused. They appealed to Francis I. He supported their claims. Thus he violated the German settlement of 1802. The Elector appealed in 1804 to Napoleon. Bonaparte then wished to please Francis, so the Elector had to submit. This left the knights under Francis. Francis pretended great amity toward Napoleon, but quietly he was preparing for war against him. Austria complained of the annexation of Genoa, but expressed a wish for the amicable settlement of all the disputes. Austria was playing a double game.

Talleyrand replied with a complaint of the coalition of Russia with England, and, later, of Austria's distrust, and he urged a reduction of its army.

Francis again insisted on the faith of the Luneville treaty; he referred to French preparations in Italy; he said he must arm to maintain that treaty and his own security, that he was ready to treat in concert with Russia, that he wanted peace, that

France had instigated the princes of the frontier circle [German] to take arms against him.

The Archduke Charles said Austria lacked means and generals for a war. It was true.

Before Russia was ready, against the able advice of Charles, who for his common-sense views of military affairs was driven by Pitt's friends from the head of the Austrian war department, Pitt hurried Austria to the great blunder. Little use for the counsel of the able Russian veterans, Kutusoff and Bagration, the marplot Pitt was ahead of even Mack himself to ruin the great campaign in advance of battles. Cobenzl, long head of the peace party, resigned; Count Ballet-Latour and Prince Schwarzenberg came into power. The change was decisive, the war party had triumphed, Pitt's advice was taken.

Austria tried to compel Bavaria to join the coalition. The menaced Elector replied:— "On my knees I implore you for permission to remain neutral."

Austria refused this prayer. It dictated that his troops must be taken into the Austrian army, not even to be a separate army in the coalition. The Elector sought escape from these odious terms which denied the nationality of the Bavarians. Between dangers on both sides the Elector agreed, August 24, to the substance of alliance with France, but fearing the results he delayed to sign it. Austria demanded of him to join his forces with hers September 6; but he hastened to Wurtzburg and sent his army into Franconia, nearer France where it could join Napoleon easily.

<small>Bavaria.</small>

III

WAR. THE ULM CAMPAIGN.

THIS war of 1805 was never declared at all. Without waiting for the Russians to arrive, Francis ordered his army to invade Bavaria. Mack, with 80,000 Austrians, crossed the Inn into Bavaria September 8; 30,000 more under Archduke John were already in the Tyrol; 55,000 more, to be greatly increased, were under Archduke Charles to attack Massena's 35,000 French in upper Italy. So 165,000 Austrians were already in the field, and 116,000 Russians were advancing by forced marches to join the Austrians in Bavaria! Where were the French? But the Russians were still distant; they might not join Austrian Mack in a month.

What if the French were to confront Mack before the Russians could arrive? But a week ago the French were in Boulogne, ready to cross the British Channel into England.

Mack marched right on to Munich; he arrived two days too late; the Bavarian army was gone; it could not be seized and mixed into the Austrian army; another blunder of Pitt's in treating Bavaria so haughtily.

Pitt chose Mack to this command. Mack had not been efficient at Naples. Pitt blundered, as usual, for Mack lacked quick perception, ready decision and firm will. Should the great Russian soldier, Kutusoff, arrive in time he could now act but as a second to Mack. But Mack's soul was at the feet of hereditary nothingness which Pitt loved, and for whose benefit

Pitt had made this war. A young archduke nothing, Ferdinand, was placed as figure-head above Mack, but Mack was the responsible chief. The emperor Francis joined his army, but quickly retired when he saw how great was the lack of ardor and discipline. Austrian soldiers had nothing at stake; as honest men they did not wish to fight for no good purpose.

A great statesman would have taken into account the marvelous skill, celerity and secrecy of Napoleon. Pitt omitted all this. Accustomed to the champion dullness of his own king, Pitt could not credit the wonderful military abilities and resources of the French emperor.

At Boulogne Napoleon had organized his army into corps, divisions and brigades. It was in admirable discipline. This army, the army in Holland, that in Hanover, Bavaria's 24,000, and others from Germany, gave Napoleon about 225,000 available men[1] to open the campaign. Yet Pitt, head of the coalition, allowed his chosen Mack to advance with 80,000 Austrians, clear across Bavaria, unsupported, to Ulm, to meet the ablest soldier of all times!

Napoleon ordered his armies of Boulogne, of Holland, and of Germany, to concentrate in Bavaria. September 23, 1805, he violated[2] his new constitution by requiring the subservient Senate to illegally decree levy[3] at once of 80,000 conscripts not legally due till 1806. He reorganized the militia (National Guard).

The four corps from Boulogne crossed the Rhine at and below Strasburg, September 25. Bernadotte with the French armies in Holland and Hanover, and

[1] Lanfrey iii, 30-33.   [2] Schlosser vii, 418.   [3] Lanfrey iii, 37.

troops of Darmstadt and Baden, was ordered to push on through Prussia's Ansbach by Eichstadt to Ingoldstadt and Munich, to cut off Mack from Austria. Had he gone by Nuremberg he would have been delayed only from twenty-four to thirty-six hours, and would not have thus insulted the neutrality of Prussia.[1]

A strong point of Napoleon's tactics was to always have superior numbers and force at the assailed part so as to overwhelm the foe at that vital spot. To be strongest at the point of attack, he drew troops freely from other parts, where was less danger of disaster. His was the genius of concentrating force; where most needed there were his ready regiments, his concentrated strength, his best combinations. Whether inferior or superior in numbers to his enemy, he did not expect to defeat them mainly by the attack "all along the line." He did it by finding the vital point and throwing just there sufficient force to win the battle at that point; just there he made his supreme effort; just there his superior celerity brought numbers and bravery so great as to confuse and overwhelm his most powerful adversary; such was his system. Neglect of it at Waterloo, and its use there by Wellington, aided to the defeat of that terrible day.

He now formed a strong reserve; every able-bodied man from twenty to sixty years was called; only those between Geneva and Calais were put into active service; four corps,— 20,000 men,— under Marshal Brune, remained at Boulogne.

France was uneasy, dissatisfied. Financial panic was coming on. Paris murmured aloud. Dangers

---

[1] Schlosser vii, 417.

were everywhere. France itself dreaded Napoleon. The army admired him; there was his strength. But the army was hastening to a foreign war.

September 26 Napoleon arrived at Strasburg. Mack at Ulm looked direct toward Strasburg for the French. With little more of ability than Pitt, Mack expected the great soldier to march direct on Ulm through the intricacies of the German Black Forest. Murat in the Black Forest confirmed Mack in his opinion. He would fight and defeat the French at the edge of the Forest. Many of the Austrian lower officers knew better than to expect such good fortune. Charles was right when he said that Austria lacked generals. It did not lack good subalterns or good soldiers.

From the fourth to sixth of October 180,000 French crossed the Danube. The troops of Baden and Wurtemberg and Bavaria's 24,000 joined the French. Better that Pitt had granted Bavaria's prayer to be allowed to be neutral. Better that Austria had permitted it. Says Sir Walter Scott: —

"And thus Austria had arranged against her those very German princes whom a moderate conduct toward Bavaria might perhaps have rendered neutral . . . . France at the outset of the contest scarce having the power to compel them to join her standard."

From this time [1805] Napoleon made war nourish war. His soldiers foraged, robbed, and plundered. Friends did not escape their ravages.[1]

Napoleon intended to overwhelm Mack's army before the Russians could arrive, but he did not expect that Pitt's general would advance away from support, clear across Bavaria. Still Mack was at Ulm. Did he not see his grand error? Why did he

---

[1] Napoleon to Eugene, Sept. 22, 1805; Napoleon to Bernadotte, Oct. 2, 1805.

not retire to Bohemia or to the Inn, to unite with Russian Kutusoff? Or to John in the Tyrol which is easy to defend? Either course now had its dangers. But either was better than to remain at Ulm. The prime object of his advance had ceased with the escape of the Bavarian army. He should hasten to retire to keep connection with Austria, to receive the Russians.

Bernadotte was marching on Ingoldstadt. He took it. He marched on Munich. He occupied it. Mack was thus cut off from Austria and the Russians; the investment of Ulm was begun. Poor Mack and Pitt were really astonished at this vigorous strategy. The situation was already very alarming. The Archduke Charles weakened his Austrian army in Italy to send in haste thirty battalions to Mack. This took from Charles the overbalance by which he was to crush the French Marshal Massena in Italy. Why did not Mack then march in haste to meet John and these battalions in the Tyrol? Then with above 115,000 men in those mountains, on the flank of the French route down the Danube to Austria, he could have paralyzed Napoleon's march on Vienna. Thus could Napoleon have been detained until Mack, John, and Kutusoff had united above Vienna.

The corps of Marshals Ney, Soult, Lannes, and Murat's cavalry crossed the Danube at Dillingen and Donaworth and penned Mack closer. Still the way to the Tyrol was open. But Mack began to retire into Ulm where food for so great an army was deficient.

Soult marched on Augsburg. Murat and Lannes advanced to Wertingen where in an action an Austrian corps lost its cannon and four thousand men. Ney advanced from Stuttgart, attacked the Danube bridges at Gunzberg still nearer to Ulm. Here in a battle Prince Ferdinand lost three thousand Austrians and many guns. Almost the entire French army were now between Ulm and Austria. Bavaria and Suabia, so lately seized by Mack, were now held by the French and Bavarians.

Fugitives bore to Mack the news that Napoleon was at Donaworth, that overwhelming numbers menaced the Austrians. Gunzburg defeat induced him to draw close around Ulm. The German Schlosser says : —

"The issue of these battles was such as to entirely destroy the confidence of the brave Austrian soldiers, driven into Ulm, and their officers of middle rank, in the aristocratic generals by whom they were commanded."[1]

Incapable, high-place men had done it.

Napoleon's army was officered by men who had won their commands by their own skill and bravery; it was led by men whose merit had elevated them from the ranks, so it was invincible to an army whose officers gain commands by mere aristocratic birth.

Ferdinand attacked Dupont's French division north of the Danube at Haslach, not far from Ulm. The Austrians were above 20,000. The battle was fiercely contested. Dupont saw his retreat impossible; he knew that he was fighting superior numbers; his defeat was imminent. He must act decisively. He intrepidly attacked; and held on till at last aid arrived. The fierce battle continued. The bloody conflict was incessant. Six times the village of Jun-

[1] Geschichte, des 18 Jahrh. vii, 420.

gingen was taken; six times it was retaken. Finally the Austrians held the bloody ground. They took cannon and baggage, but the defeated French carried off fifteen hundred prisoners.

Soult advanced from Augsburg, cut to pieces an Austrian regiment, and invested Memingen. This important garrison about five thousand Austrians, ill-fed, not interested in royalty's war, surrendered. Next day Soult hastened with three divisions to Biberich to bar the open road to upper Suabia. His fourth division took post before Ulm to the southeast with Lannes' and Marmont's corps.

With the Imperial Guard Napoleon advanced from Augsburg to Burgau, while Ney on the north completed the circle. The Austrians fighting for their masters, were surrounded by the French fighting for the new tyranny. Neither Austrians nor French could expect good from it. The Bavarians fought for their own invaded country.

The autumn weather was severe; snow was falling in large flakes. The French soldiers, loaded with their arms and several days' provisions, toiled over rough, muddy roads. Napoleon formed a mass of private soldiers around him and described to them the situation and prospects of the campaign. He thanked them for their endurance; he described Mack's situation, cut off from Austria, surrounded, obliged to fight for a chance of escape; he promised them victory if they continued to act with resolution and constancy. This speech, then characteristic of French armies, was loudly applauded by the soldiers.

In Ulm opinion was divided. The best plan was to try in force to break through the French and join

NAPOLEON AND HIS SON: 1814.

"HIS SOLDIERS FORAGED, ROBBED AND PLUNDERED."

the Russians in Bohemia, or John in the Tyrol. Again patriotism was sacrificed to a noble. Archduke Ferninand was of little value as a soldier. Better for Austria could it have retired his whole class and filled their places with men from lower social position. The silly idea that he must be saved prevailed. The army was divided. Ferdinand with three divisions, followed by Warneck with two divisions, marched away, passed the French blockade and Warneck got a start of the French. This fact shows that Mack, with his whole army, could still have broken away.

Early on October 14, Napoleon on a height was watching the advancing line of outpost fire. Suddenly a violent cannonade thundered away on his right. It was Ney with 16,000 men attacking Elchingen; 15,000 Austrians under Lander were in that elevated, strong position. The village of stone houses rises like an ampitheater from the Danube to a vast convent that crowns the summit.

At every point cannon flashed and thundered down upon the French. The windows blazed with Austria musketry.

Ney attacked with tremendous energy and intrepidity. The French hurled the Austrian outposts on the north bank pell-mell across the bridge; hotly pursued them up the steep streets where the plunging fire from the top of battlements, and a blaze of enfilading fire from an abbey tore through the French ranks and threatened to sweep down every man. Fresh assailants arrived; a desperate conflict went on in front of a wood held with terrible firmness by the Austrians; fragments of regiments held their ground desperately after three out of every four had fallen. French cavalry crossed the bridge; they were making their way around the Austrian rear to isolate them; more French infantry were arriving and plunging into the terrible fight. At last the terriffic combat ended; the Austrians retired; the French had won the bloody hill. The losses of both were heavy. From this frightful action came Ney's title, "Duke of Elchingen."

One division of Austrians made a feint of advancing toward Biberach, while Werneck with another moved on Albeck and Herdenheim and fell with superior force on Dupont's division, already so severely weakened at Haslach. Murat arrived in force with cavalry, and the Austrians were driven toward Herdenheim. Next day Murat assailed them again and took eighteen hundred prisoners. Ferdinand returned from his feint toward Biberach; he joined Werneck and tried to force his way through the French. But this archduke, whose only chance was in celerity, incumbered his light troops with five hundred heavily laden wagons; a corporal could have advised him better; these wagons, with their escort, were quickly captured by French cavalry; then this stupid heredity abandoned his infantry and ran away with the light horsemen in the night. With good soldiers, led by such generals, Pitt and George III expected to crush the best troops in Europe led by the greatest soldier of history! Yet men existed who called Pitt a statesman!

The French pursued with vigor and celerity over very bad roads in bad weather, and surmounted every obstacle. The archduke saved his worthless person at the expense of loss of his troops. It was only with a few hundred[1] out of his great divisions that he escaped; 10,000 of his soldiers,[2] fatigued, hungry and deserted by this hereditary unworthy, surrendered October 18.

Ulm lies in a valley, overhung by the heights of Michelsberg and La Tuileries, which, on the other side of the Danube, command every part of it. Ney took Michelsberg. Suchet took La Tuileries. The French guns began October 19, 1805, to throw shells from these heights, carrying terror to every part of Ulm.

Napoleon summoned Mack to surrender. Mack refused and expressed great indignation at the summons. He insisted that the Russians were within five days' march. Finally he proposed to capitulate if in eight days he was not relieved. Napoleon accepted with the condition that the eight days commence from October 17. This would reduce the time to six days. "Eight days or death," replied Mack. But on further information Mack agreed to surrender on October 25, if not sooner relieved.

Every day to Napoleon was precious. He felt the burden of maintaining his army without magazines and at a single point. He sent for Mack. He completely bewildered Mack by a recital of his great disasters, the impossibility of escape to the Tyrol, or the arrival of the Russian army; he urged that it would be cruel and useless to expose the Austrians and the citizens of Ulm to the want and the sufferings of war for the eight days. Mack's higher officers seemed to expect a surrender; a large park of artillery and baggage at Bopfingen was taken; Mack was confused;

[1] Alison ii, 315. [2] Bourrienne ii, 297.

he consented to cut short this time already agreed on; and October 20, 33,000 Austrians and eighteen generals marched out past Napoleon, laid down their arms and forty stands of colors, and delivered up sixty cannon.

Napoleon, surrounded by a numerous and brilliant staff, stood before a bivouac fire on a rocky eminence north of the city, and for five hours this immense array defiled before him.

Napoleon addressed their leaders : —

"War has its chances. Often victorious, you must expect sometimes to be vanquished. Your master wages against me an unjust war. I say it candidly, I know not for what I am fighting: I know not what he desires of me. He has wished to remind me that I was once a soldier; I trust he will find that I have not forgotten my original avocation. I will, however, give one piece of advice to my brother, the Emperor of Germany, that he hasten to make peace: it is the moment to remember that all empires have their limit. The idea that the end of the house of Lorraine may arrive should alarm him.

"I want nothing on the continent; it is ships, colonies, commerce that I desire, and they to you would be advantageous as well as to us."

Thus spoke Napoleon, October 20, 1805. The very next day the empire of the seas was decided by the tremendous battle of Trafalgar. On that day, eight years later, Napoleon was himself flying from the great disaster to his arms inflicted at Leipsic.

Napoleon released the Austrian officers on parole. The private soldiers were marched to France and distributed among farms to replace conscripts withdrawn from labor.[1] This experiment was successful.

Mack's surrender freed Napoleon's army so that it could advance against Austria.

[1] Scott's Bonaparte, 74.

UNITED STATES AND EUROPE.

RELATIVE NUMBER OF SOLDIERS FOR THE ULM CAMPAIGN, are shown by the length of the lines given here.

Intended against Napoleon by the Coalition of England, Russia, Austria, with Naples, Hanover and Bavaria, . . . 425,000

Proportion that did fight in Ulm Campaign, Only Mack's Austrians, . . 80,000

Proportion of Napoleon's troops engaged, . . 225,000

An Austria court-martial afterward sentenced Mack to lose all honors, dignities, and positions. He was not pardoned till 1815.

IV

THE GREATEST OF NAVAL BATTLES.

I HAVE carefully examined among the treasured manuscripts preserved by the British government the original rude drawing that Nelson made of his mode of attack at the battle of the Nile, by which he explained to his commanders how to attack at Trafalgar. It was to sail in two columns into Villeneuve's line so as to cut off both from his right and left six or seven ships, and thus give use for every British cannon in both broadsides at once, while the twelve or fourteen ships cut off could bring but one broadside to bear.

Trafalgar.

Russell finds, according to James, the vessels at Trafalgar rated in cannon, British, 2,336; French, 1,636; Spanish, 1,270; the enormous aggregate of 5,242! But they carried, British, 2,542; French, 1,736; Spanish, 1,306, a total of 5,584! Nearly twelve times the 466 which Napoleon, Wellington and Blücher used in all at Waterloo!

Since Chaos the world has seen but one Trafalgar; most massive of all great battles; but one grand aggregate of gigantic battling ships so vastly colossal; of forests of great masts and spars, and rigging so immense; of clouds of broad sweeping sails so extensive.

Trafalgar thundered more stupendous, more frightful crashes of heavy cannon fire than earth had ever heard; larger volumes of blazing sulphur smoke infernal than had ever rolled over battle.

It had a spectacular sublimity, a luxuriant magnificence of horror, a splendor satanic, far exceeding anything man may expect again to behold.

Vice-admiral Villeneuve commanded the two enormous, terrible fleets of France and Spain, thirty-three monster ships of the line, beside several frigates. The Spanish "Santa Trinidad," four decker, alone carried a hundred and thirty heavy cannon, and alone threw a heavier weight of shot at every discharge than all of Wellington's one hundred and eighty field cannon at famous Waterloo.

Admiral Horatio Nelson, greatest of sea warriors, nothing but a seaman and sea fighter, commanded the truly Titanic British fleet, twenty-seven ships of the line and four frigates.

A single one of these mighty ships of the line under peaceful sail was alone a grand spectacle. They carried each from seventy-four to one hundred and twenty of the largest cannon of the time, much larger than army field cannon. They were wonderful ocean fortresses, now forever gone, that in stately majesty far exceeded all other ships the world had seen. Two hostile war fleets each so prodigious had never met and fought. Sixty-four sailing mountains; above five thousand more cannon than at Waterloo. No wonder its collision shook the world. It was one of the greatest wonders of that wonderful, warring age, a spectacle indescribably majestic. It was terrible.

Waterloo's cannonade was tremendous, terrific, but far inferior to Trafalgar's massive explosions. Thirty rounds for every one of Napoleon's and Wellington's four hundred and twenty-six cannon and the forty used by Blücher at Waterloo would hardly load Trafalgar's cannon once.

Nelson, but a fragment of a man, with but one arm, a Cyclops with but one eye, so small that the blue, four-starred coat in which he was killed — which I have examined at Greenwich — looks too small for a large boy, was a more powerful, a more effective warrior than all the mighty Achilles and great Hectors of old Homer.

At daybreak, October 21, 1805, Nelson saw Napoleon's whole allied fleet about twelve miles off, in a vast semicircle, ready for the great conflict for ocean supremacy of the world. Villeneuve's order of battle was strong. Plainly he was a great commander. But Napoleon, never great in naval affairs, had, against the advice of his minister of marine, Decres, and remonstrances of his admirals, and against Villeneuve's better judgment, by threat of removal and disgrace goaded him into this great battle.

Villeneuve's enormous first line was twenty-one ships, alone a stronger force than man had ever yet attacked at sea. Twelve more ships were the second line to fire double and triple broadsides through openings in the front line. In all he had 3,042 cannon.

Napoleon's highest tactical skill was displayed at Ulm and at Austerlitz. Studying those famous plans, I fail to see how in either he exceeded the skill with which Villeneuve planned Trafalgar.

BATTLE OF TRAFALGAR.

Abler sea warriors than Nelson and Villeneuve never crossed cannon shot. Now came the grand contest of the greatest masters of naval war for supermastery.

Intrepid Nelson ordered the most superb assault, the onset at once of his entire fleet in two grand columns. It is the grandest charge of all history. Compared with it the great charge of the Old Guard at Wagram loses in importance and in spectacle, Valmy becomes a skirmish, and Lodi almost a trifle. It was extreme intrepidity; but only audacious daring could hope for victory over an enemy more formidable than man had ever fought on the ocean.

Nelson's plan was to break Villeneuve's line in two places at once and quickly bring every British ship and every one of his 2,542 cannon [1] into close action.

Collingwood on the right in the "Royal Sovereign" led the first column, fourteen ships against Villeneuve's left.

Nelson in the "Victory" led all the rest against the allied right. At his masthead Nelson showed the famous signal:—

"England expects that every man will do his duty."

The silence of expectation which precedes the first crash of battle is thrilling; I have seen the bravest men then turn pale who never paled in the midst of fierce conflict itself. The uncertainty, the deep sense of death's coming havoc, the wide opening of eternity's doors to receive your comrades and friends, these stern realities press dread upon the soul. All was this awful stillness as the two great columns came forward, so superb, so terrible.

[1] Russell & Jacques' Nelson.

Collingwood's ship was a fast sailer. Far ahead of his own grand column that daring man, with only his own ship sailed into the tremendous conflict with all sails set. It was a gallant sight. "See how that brave fellow takes his ship into action," exclaimed Nelson.

Instantly the enemy broke the awful silence with the explosion of a thousand cannon, and the unearthly shrieks and screams and crash of many tons of flying missiles. Yet the intrepid hero sailed his ship grandly alone right into the hostile embrace of the enemy's cannon-blazing line.

He attacked thirty-three times his own number! Where, even in fable of Trojan classic story, is the equal of this intrepidity of real life?

Probably this superb daring was dictated by his cool judgment, for this brave man "never permitted his ardent courage to outrun his cool judgment;" he was "at once firm and mild in command."[1] He knew that ocean's great empire was at stake; he meant to win.

Eagerly Nelson crowded all sail. At long range single shots were fired at his ship, the enemy were getting the range. As he came nearer a single shot went through his sail; they had got the range.

Then a moment of awful suspense; the foe were taking aim. Then flashed from their right wing, tremendous volumes of fire and battle smoke; two thousand cannon thundered; frightful tornadoes of deadly missiles howled and shrieked in the air like wild screams of frantic demons.

Both British columns sailed into closest action.

[1] Chamber's Cyclopedia.

War in its wildest, grandest act was played by Cyclopean ships on Titanic stage.

Then the terrific battle was superbly appalling, magnificently awful. Five thousand cannon were at once blazing with red death fire. The tremendous crash of two thousand heavy guns on one side was instantly answered by the roar and flame of more than two thousand on the other, while still a thousand more swelled that stupendous concussion as if worlds had come into crashing collision of universal destruction. Then flamed the heaviest masses of continuous cannon fire, from double the whole number of guns carried by the famous Spanish Armada of 1588, from more than forty times those of Lake Erie of 1813.

Any one of these sixty-four ships could have defeated all the fleets of both Greeks and Persians at Salamis the famous, whose fighting glory has rung down to us through almost twenty-four centuries. The bombardment of Port Royal in 1861, witnessed by the writer, was of grandeur indescribable, yet at Trafalgar blazed and thundered fifteen times the number of Port Royal's heavy guns.

At Trafalgar, incomparable in the infernal, great broadsides, forty to sixty cannon almost touched muzzles as each sent its smashing cyclone of shot full into the other's bosom. One broadside from Collingwood's ship struck down four hundred Spaniards on the "Santa Anna."

Many men were destroyed, blown to atoms; masts were shivered; ships were shattered; volcanoes of projectiles crashed through vessels; more than Plutonian volumes of battle smoke filled all space and nearly suffocated Nelson's men on his own ship. I have witnessed in battle a frigate before it had fired two minutes, completely hide herself from sight by her own dense battle smoke, through which I could still see the streaming of her long flashes of cannon fire; imagine then the somber effect of a hundred times her number of constantly flaming cannon.

On the French ship "Redoutable" six hundred men were shot. Every instant ships were torn and retorn.

In this jubilee of devastation the great Spanish ship, "Achilles," took fire and was quickly wrapped in flames; her men were burning alive. Then she blew up with tremendous crash and concussion, flinging her very guns, her masts and timbers at her foes. The waves quickly closed over the fatal spot where the now vanished ship a moment before existed.

Ship after ship of Napoleon's great fleet struck her flag. The battle was dying away with his fleet which was terribly shattered.

The spectacle was frightful. Nineteen of the largest ships in the world, carrying over fifteen hundred cannon, lay helpless, ragged, and crippled wrecks in mingled confusion with their British conquerors.

Ruin was everywhere. Everything was battered, smashed, splintered, blackened. Everywhere lay or crawled mutilated, crippled, powder-stained creatures, lately strong men, now bleeding, suffering, wishing themselves dead. Everywhere lay torn bodies, fragments of men.

Nelson was dying; Magon, French vice-admiral, was dead; Spanish Admiral Alava was mortally wounded.

Villeneuve was a prisoner and longed for death. He afterward killed himself for chagrin at Napoleon's injustice to him. He died for Napoleon's fault.

Spanish Vice-admiral Gravina, with nine Spanish ships, sailed off for Cadiz. French Vice-admiral Dumanoir, with but four French ships, crowded sail, pouring in broadsides as he past. In the confusion of friend and foe he fired into Spanish surrendered ships as well as into British; this was remembered with bitterness by Spain.

The next day nature, too, was furious. A wild storm raged. The damaged British could not keep in tow their battered prizes nor repair them to stand the fearful gale. Many sank or were driven on the coast or were scuttled by the victors. Only four were brought into port at Gibraltar. One retaken by prisoners reached Cadiz. French frigates retook two others.

Tall ships, shivered, staggering from the avenging thunders of man's cannon to the vengeance of God, went to their doom in the wild tornado, sank to quiet rest forever in the deep sea.

The British ship "Indomptable" made terrible wreck in which a thousand British and their prisoners perished.

The British ship "Swiftsure," captured by the French, was sunk by British cannonade.

Fourteen colossal ships had gone under the waves.

This, the greatest of naval victories, gave the British 20,000 prisoners, including soldiers on the ships. Less in number, they were of far greater value in the war than the 33,000 Austrians that Napoleon took but one day earlier at Ulm, for Napoleon could not easily replace his lost seamen, his trained sailors.

Dumanoir hoped to escape into Rochfort or Brest. But he met Strachan's fresh British fleet which chased him two days and forced him to fight in his crippled condition. His four battered ships made four hours of battle against eight fresh British ships, lost 750 men killed and wounded, and then were taken.

In both battles Napoleon lost twenty first-class ships, nearly two thousand cannon, and vast stores. Several of his thirteen ships that escaped were disabled from service. His number of killed and wounded is large.

Spanish and French admirals said their ships were badly equipped and some of their men untrained at sea, that they were not prepared to fight. It is Napoleon himself who is responsible for his great disaster.

Because England refused to yield him Malta as agreed in 1803 was Napoleon's main pretext for the war. Now that Trafalgar gave England control of the route to Malta, its recovery by France was hopeless, and the war might well have ended. Napoleon could conquer stupid hereditary leaders but not Nelson, the village clergyman's son, nor Collingwood, a sailor from his tenth year of age.

Trafalgar was a blow from which Napoleon's navy never recovered; Great Britain ruled the seas; his invasion of England was made impossible. England passed from great alarm to confidence. America was made safe from Napoleon.

Trafalgar seems to be the great decisive battle of

modern times. On what battle since Hastings in 1066, or Tours in 732, have hung interests so wide and momentous? Not on Waterloo, for had Napoleon won Waterloo, the great Russian, Austrian, and German on-coming armies must have overthrown him a few weeks later. Not alone Britain, France, and Spain, but all the world had something of our destiny at stake in dread Trafalgar. Its victor was to rule the seas for a generation.

Had Trafalgar's great decision been completely reversed, the French and Spanish fleet intact, and the British navy as crippled as was that of France and Spain, then Napoleon would have controlled the naval resources of France, Spain, Portugal, Holland, Denmark, Prussia, all Germany, Italy, Naples, and Genoa, and, probably, those of Russia, Sweden, and his ally, Turkey,—every war vessel of the entire continent. And that man who, during the brief, only time the Atlantic was ever open to him, sent in 1802 40,000 French veterans to not only suppress liberty, but to actually restore slavery itself in St. Domingo, could, with far greater incentive, send a vastly larger force to attempt the conquest of the United States.

Let him who doubts that, hoping to be emperor of two hemispheres, Napoleon would have attempted it, point out a single instance where he ever missed a chance to conquer and possess, right or wrong?

Napoleon had just said at Ulm, only one day before Trafalgar, "It is ships, colonies, commerce that I want." Conquest of America could give him these. But Trafalgar denied them to him, barred him from world-wide power.

Forty-two days after Trafalgar Napoleon humbled

Austria and Russia at Austerlitz; less than a year later he overran Prussia. The Peace of Tilsit, July 7, 1807, saw him ruling or allied with every country of the continent except Sweden, Austria, and Portugal, and with these he was at peace or semi-alliance. Only Great Britain, the sea power, withstood him. Had he conquered the British navy, then many Spanish and Portuguese colonies of both Americas and the West Indies must have fallen with Spain and Portugal to Napoleon in 1808, and the British Peninsula war could never have been.

Napoleon did not like republics; he destroyed several; he never omitted to oppress liberty. France asked "tribute" of America in 1798, Napoleon freely robbed our commerce, seized our vessels. He said to our minister in 1810 that small pretext would "make me seize all the American marine if I could." In 1810 he ordered his brother Louis, king of Holland, to rob American ships and cargoes, and quarrelled with him because Louis did not do the robbery more effectually, and then did the foul deed himself in Holland. Napoleon expressly uses the word "American" in that wicked correspondence. His minister, Fouché, then only second to Napoleon in French power, had, in 1810, an elaborate plan for the conquest of the United States to be attempted on making peace with England. But England was unwilling. How far Napoleon instigated that plan is, of course, unknown, the blunders of both himself and Fouché exposed the plan. His sending Fouché to Dalmatia does not prove that it was not Napoleon's own plan, that his anger was for anything but its miscarriage by England's ill-reception of it

WRECK OF THE INDOMPTABLE ON SPANISH COAST.

HORATIO, VISCOUNT NELSON.

and its exposure to the world; he never published his plans in advance of their action, but he executed them before the victim country could learn of their existence and prepare against them.

Friendship could not restrain Napoleon, he hardly knew the sentiment; he had no capacity to be a friend for friendship's sake. Charles IV of Spain was his devoted, slavish friend, yet in 1808 he dethroned Charles and seized Spain; the Czar, Alexander, was his fervent friend, but Napoleon wasted 400,000 human lives to invade Russia in 1812. Turkey was his friend and ally, yet at Tilsit in 1807 he sold to Russia the privilege of conquering Turkey's Roumania.

It was with troops drawn from sixteen countries that he invaded Russia in 1812. With Trafalgar reversed he could after Austerlitz of 1805, or Tilsit of 1807, have invaded America with vast armies from many lands. He could have landed in America many times the effective veteran troops that England ever sent against us in any war.

While Napoleon was emperor America had little money, few manufactures; our own embargo and the war in Europe had caused our ocean carrying trade to be mainly between foreign lands; our vessels staid abroad for years; we had mere vestige of an army; a very small navy; not a single first-class war ship. Had America resisted with the greatest desperation, as did Spain, yet such a war would have been ruinous.

England insulted our commerce, but she employed it profitably to our ship owners; she barbarously impressed our seamen, but she barred Napoleon from access to our country.

Great Britain was then far from being the British semi-republic of today; but her semi-free speech and half-free press, even under Pitt's gag laws, her guarantee to citizens of rights which British laws and British juries would maintain enraged Napoleon; he hated England for her liberties, which the French might wish to imitate again; he wished to destroy this menace to his absolutism.

How much less then would he have tolerated our larger American liberty and our elective republic, if access to it had been open?

Conquest offered also the American-European trade which in 1801 and since 1815 has been and is the richest trade in the world.

Southey says: —

"The death of Nelson was felt in England as something more than a public calamity; men started at the intelligence, and turned pale, as if they had heard of the loss of a dear friend. An object of our admiration and affection, of our pride and our hopes, was suddenly taken from us, and it seemed as if we had never till then known how deeply we loved and reverenced him."[1]

V

Prussia.

PRUSSIA then small, began to rise in power under Frederic William of Brandenburg, the great Elector. He found it in 1640, in social and financial misery. He freed it from dependence on Poland, regulated the finances, raised an army of 25,000 men, and, despite of disastrous war, more than tripled its area. He received 20,000 Protestant French exiles,

[1] Life of Nelson.

aided industrial arts, and constructed canals. He left a full treasury, a fine army of 38,000 men, a population of about 1,500,000, and an area of 42,000 square miles.

His successor, Frederic III, was greedy for aggrandizement, admired Louis XIV of France whose pomp he imitated to the distress of his then poor country. He lent 6,000 soldiers, under the famous Schomberg, to William of Orange for his expedition to England in 1668. He traded the services of his troops to the emperor of Germany for the title of king, as Frederic I of Prussia [January 18, 1707]. Next Frederic William reigned from 1713 to 1740. That eccentric, brutal, and partly insane king liked tall soldiers; he used flagrant outrages to kidnap tall men and force them into his service. He was despotic, fond of military drilling, averse to mental cultivation, and he liked illiterate and low society. He held the utmost ideas of his own arbitrary power and divine authority and made his people suffer. He left a well-drilled army, a treasury of 9,000,000 thalers, a people more than 2,240,000, and an area of 45,000 square miles. Frederic II (the Great) ruled from 1740 to 1786, raised Prussia to rank as a great power, and favored agriculture, trade, and commerce, but his wars scourged all central Europe. The "Seven Years' War," begun in 1756, crippled all the powers engaged in it, and caused widespread suffering. He left a powerful, strongly organized kingdom, one-half larger in area than he found it, an army of 200,000 men, and a full treasury. Religion was free; so was the press: order and property were secure. His reliance was his army and his money.

His nephew and successor, Frederic William II, in his reign of eleven years, from 1786 to 1797, exhausted the surplus of 70,000,000 thalers left by Frederic II, and left the state 22,000,000 thalers in debt. His fondness for improper favorites, his strict censorship of the press, and his stringent church laws offended his people. By the second partition of Poland in 1793, and by other means, Prussia was increased by more than 46,000 square miles and 2,500,000 people.

Frederic William III came to the throne in 1797 at the age of twenty-seven years. I call attention to him here as he reigned till 1840. He dismissed his father's bad favorites. He lacked ability and fairness, was greedy, unscrupulous, and unworthy of that brave and honorable nation. He usually had able ministers, but his meddling with the public business caused great disaster. Had he let politics alone, like Queen Victoria, it would have been far better for Prussia.

Since the war against France in 1792, Prussia had wisely preserved a wary neutrality and had prospered by it. It was then good statesmanship. All Europe took offense at Prussia's efforts to avoid giving offense. It has been the fashion to decry it. Against this verdict I protest that injustice has been done to the Prussians. The king deserves all censure, but his people, the real Prussians, until 1804, set a better example than their enemies were ready to follow. After 1804, Prussia's policy was bad because its king made it bad. The Haugwitz ministry, which the great Von Stein, the leader in the later awakening of Germany, entered in 1804, was the ablest in Europe outside of France. Had its counsels been acted on the great coalition war of 1805 would not have occurred. Prussia's mistake during that war was very great, but less than Pitt's and Russia's and Austria's mistake of beginning that war without Prussia. She became simply the victim of Pitt's great blunder. Had Europe taken Haugwitz advice then the tremendous disasters of Ulm and Austerlitz would never have been. Haugwitz used prudence — a high quality not less valuable than bravery, far better than Pitt's temerity — and for this wisdom in avoiding war, Prussia has been censured by many writers. Austria had repeatedly fought the French and had lost Italy; Prussia had kept the peace and had gained in extent and in prosperity. Prussia saw this situation with secret pleasure, for Austria was her old rival. Till 1805 peace was wisdom, it served Prussia and served her well, but in the war of the autumn of 1805 the situation had changed, peace had become fatal, and the king had not the wisdom and resolution to change his policy to suit the new conditions.

The people had good motive in desiring peace, the king's motives were less good. He wanted more dominion. He was ready to allow Napoleon to seize German states or German dominions in the south, provided Napoleon would permit him to snatch domains from north German states. He desired to be the co-despoiler of weaker states. To gain Napoleon's aid in such plundering, he had flattered and aided him; he had persuaded William of Orange, the Dutch Stadtholder, to recognize the Batavian republic (Holland), which allowed it to remain under Napoleon's control; he recognized the Italian republics and the kingdom of Etruria (Tuscany); he omitted to protest against union of Piedmont with France. In 1802 Napoleon rewarded his subserviency by allowing him to seize Hildesheim, Paderborn, Munster, and other territory, nearly four thousand square miles and half a million people, and to imagine himself protector of neutral north Germany.

While the ministry kept peace with France and the king stole his neighbor's territory, the good Prussians were prospering and increasing in numbers; the ruinous war expenses of other nations increased the sale and profits of Prussian products; German trade came to them; their neutral navigation was profitable; the people were on the high road to wealth; the population of 7,000,000 in 1786 had become 9,500,000 in 1804; order, economy, and wisdom pervaded the state; in few countries were the expenses of State so moderate. The Prussians had much yet to do to improve their condition, and they were doing it with manly energy.

The Prussian army was nearly 200,000 men, a good army made up of good men, but as there was no promotion from the ranks for military merit, the leaders were hereditary incapables, a great weakness should it ever meet the French, to whom the Republic had given the chance for good soldiers to rise from the lowest to the highest places.

Strict suppression of freedom of the press left little chance for a pronounced type of the people's opinion on public affairs.

Apprehensive of a coalition against him in 1802-4, Bonaparte tried to draw closer the ties between France and Prussia. But as co-operation with that willful man would be simply to surrender Prussia to his dictation, the ministry could not consent. It did not wish to provoke war with him, so it temporized. What else could it do? Alliance with France would be but peaceful conquest by France as had occurred with Holland, Switzerland, Naples, Piedmont, Genoa, and Tuscany; to oppose France would bring war with Napoleon who could brook no opposition, as it brought war to Russia and Austria. No power of Europe could be simply Napoleon's peaceful friend, he would compel all to take part in his wars either for or against him.

Several attempts of Napoleon to overreach Prussia in German affairs, the division of so much German territory in 1802–3, his aggrandizement there of the rulers of Bavaria, Baden, and Wurtemberg, the giving a German duchy to Murat with the addition of territory claimed by Prussia, and many other annoyances by Napoleon [1] had shaken Prussian friendship and strengthened the anti-French Hardenberg party against the Haugwitz French sympathizers. A sentimental interview in 1802 between the king and Czar Alexander had resulted in their swearing a mutual personal friendship.

When in 1805 Napoleon foresaw the third coalition war he tried to secure the alliance or at least the neutrality of Prussia.

He wanted to make of Prussia a barrier against the march of Russian troops against the French in north Germany, the very region where he had most wounded the pride and the hopes of the king. After much negotiation the king promised for himself and for Russia that no such Russian march should occur.

[1] Napoleon ruled the "Confederation of the Rhine."

But Russia's consent had not been obtained, the Czar was preparing to advance against Napoleon.

At the Prussian court party feeling ran very high between the Haugwitz and the Hardenberg parties. All was excitement. The dull king, dazed, undecided, knew not what to do next. The Hardenberg party was gaining; the king favored both sides and neither side. Napoleon threw in a bait by declaring his intention to augment Prussia. This would suit the king. But for a time the court's patriotism triumphed over the king's greed for acquisition. What would it avail for Prussia to be augmented if all Prussia were to be dominated by Napoleon? The other party drove Haugwitz from the ministry and from Berlin; Hardenberg came into power.

Hardenberg was a man of pleasure, a voluptuary,[1] a disbeliever in the rights of the people, was on the side of old abuses, saw no visions of a regenerated Prussia, no improving of the army, no training of Prussia's forces into an irresistible power: all those great ideas that have made Germany and Prussia the great Germany and Prussia of today, except the concentration of power, he left to the far greater men, Von Stein, Scharnhorst, and the gay, lively, enthusiastic patriot,[2] Blücher, whom the king hated. Hardenberg favored alliance with England and Russia.

When, in 1805, the French had taken Hanover because George III of England was its Elector, Prussia offered to occupy it with Prussian soldiers and in due time to return it to George if he would remove the British blockade of the Weser and the Elbe which seriously injured Prussia and all north Ger-

[1] Schlosser vii, 405.   [2] Bourrienne ii, 352.

many, including George III's patrimony, Hanover. By it Pitt was punishing England's friends. This British blockade was at great distance from France, did Napoleon little harm, but was at the commercial gateway of Prussia and Hanover. George's ministry refused this justice, lost this great opportunity of conciliating Prussia, and then wondered why Prussia did not attack Napoleon! Of course this foolish Pitt policy produced its natural results, Haugwitz, unfriendly to England, friendly to France, soon returned to Berlin from his enforced absence. Pitt and George had scored another point against England!

The weak Prussian king consulted both Haugwitz and Hardenberg, the leaders of opposing policies; he mixed their advice. Extremely jealous of his own royal power, he knew neither how to use it, nor was willing to delegate it to able men. He became alternately angry with Napoleon and then pacified. Had either Haugwitz or Hardenberg been unhampered by him, then Prussia might have been saved. But the king obstructed the policy of both, he received the derision of Europe, but angered Europe had not comprehended that it was the king and not his worthy people that was to blame.

Pitt and Alexander and Austria still tried to bring Prussia into the coalition of 1805 against France. Haugwitz still made energetic efforts to avert that terrible collision. In the summer and early autumn of 1805, before the Ulm campaign, Haugwitz was the great minister; he used more of wisdom than any other minister in Europe; he advised such a peace as would have so united the strength of central and eastern Europe as would, by well-placed and well-provided armies, have made the Elbe, the Bohmerwald, and the Inn a line forever impassible by Napoleon, and, still more, would have kept Prussia, Russia, Austria, Denmark, Sweden, and Norway free from his trade restrictions, but open to ocean trade, and thus have added to their own wealth to strengthen in war and bless in peace. Yet admirers of Pitt and apologists for Napoleon have censured Haugwitz.

Prussia wanted trade. Pitt blockaded it. She wanted to move only so fast as she could move safely. Pitt tried to precipitate her. The Prussian king coveted Hanover, so Napoleon removed 12,000 French troops from Hanover. Napoleon cheated, wheedled, but he persuaded; Pitt's cruisers threatened, harassed Prussian vessels, and impaired Prussian thrift. The Prussians did not want war; they wanted peace. They desired prosperity. They wanted to exercise their manly industry. They wished to compete with the French and the British only in the products of skill and labor. In that summer of 1805, whose autumn and winter were made so frightful by war, Prussia, the much maligned, was the nation of Europe most in the right, but its king was the least reliable.

The fickle king at last intimated a willingness to make alliance with France, offensive and defensive. Napoleon sent to Berlin his able, silent Duroc, almost the only man in Europe that really loved Napoleon. But the intimation proved only a slight to France. Duroc came, but the king was not ready to sign, the treaty remained unsigned. The unsafe king wished to keep himself out of all the risks of the contest, but wanted to share in all the spoils of war. But neither Napoleon nor his antagonists were willing to let the king alone; whoever should win would be likely to turn upon the king.

September 21, 1805, a month before Ulm and Trafalgar, the Russian envoy presented to the king the Czar's request, very like a threat, for an interview at their frontier and for permission to march Russians through Prussia en route to Bavaria against Napoleon. The king accepted the interview, but he refused the passage, and he assembled an army in Prussian Poland to prevent the passage of Russian troops over Prussian soil.[1]

Says Metternich:—

"The Prussian king was full of hesitation. The Czar Alexander, wearied by the evasions of Prussia, made dangerous move by attempting to coerce him to decide, by marching a Russian army to the east Prussian frontier. This act only increased opposition. The vacillating king was resolute against Russia, but more irresolute toward France. The Austrians were on the eve of their catastrophe at Ulm. Alexander threatened to march through Prussia. But the king said he offered neutrality, if either party violates this by entering Prussian territory it makes war. . . . The violent measures of Napoleon and Alexander, similar in character and coincident in time, left the king only the choice of which of two insults he should resent."

Great was the surprise and anger at Berlin when news came that Napoleon had violated Prussian soil by marching Bernadotte's corps through Anspach to get in rear of Mack at Ulm. Prussia demanded satisfaction for the great insult. Indignant, the king gave permission for Alexander to march through Prussia. Three powerful Prussian armies of observation were directly ordered, one of 60,000 men into Franconia toward Napoleon's position and on the flank of the route from Ulm to Vienna, another of

[1] Metternich's Mem. i, 30-32.

50,000 in lower Saxony, and one of 20,000 in Westphalia toward France. Had Bernadotte not saved twenty-four to thirty-six hours by insulting Prussia he could still have arrived at his objective point in time. So Napoleon's insult to Prussia was almost wanton audacity.

On the news of Mack's surrender the king opened negotiations with both belligerents. Among the many givers of advice he could not decide what to do. He could find plenty of good soldiers, but generals cannot always be furnished to order. Suddenly and wholly unexpected the Czar arrived at Berlin. This still further embarassed the king. He received Alexander pleasantly. Together they went to Potsdam. There occurred the sentimental night scene at the tomb of the great soldier, Frederic II, by torchlight; the Czar and the king threw themselves down before it; the Czar kissed the tomb; he gave his hand to the king over it; they pledged themselves to eternal friendship; the Czar, the king, and the beautiful young queen then tenderly embraced each other.[1]

While at Potsdam the news of Mack's capitulation reached them. Then the king joined with Russia and Austria in a treaty of prospective alliance, November 5. It was a half-way measure. The Prussian army advanced toward the distant French. Haugwitz was to present to Napoleon the king's ultimatum: if Napoleon did not halt in his career before December 15, the king would feel bound to join the coalition.[1]

Prussian public feeling was aroused; Prussia was

[1] Metternich's Mem. i, 34-35.

angry, indignant. A Berlin crowd broke Haugwitz' windows because he favored peace and they believed him the friend of France; they gave a noisy popular congratulation to Hardenberg because he disliked the French and favored war.[1]

The Potsdam agreement was to remain at present a secret, but it was published by the Austrians, probably to intimidate Napoleon. He was deeply offended at this agreement of the king whom he had goaded to it by his own arrogance.

October 26, six days after Ulm, Prussian troops entered Hanover. They did not disturb the French still there. Russians and Swedes also came, with them Gustavus IV, the half-lunatic, — in those days royalty seems almost synonymous with incapacity. He increased the Elbe tolls and purloined them. The Hanoverians were oppressed with civil and military exactions — such was the "protection" of the allies — the people were at once the victims of Russians, Swedes, Prussians, British, and French, all consequent on their greater misfortune that George III of England was their Elector.

In November and December the allies in Hanover were reinforced to an army thought sufficient to conquer Hanover and coerce Prussia into joining the alliance and then moving on the almost undefended Holland and Flanders. This augmented force amounted to 15,000 Russians, 8,000 Swedes, and 12,000 British, in all 35,000 men[2] to do the work that needed 150,000! This was Pitt's statesmanship!

In December misery prevailed in ravaged Ger-

[1] Schlosser vii, 433.   [2] Bourrienne ii, 303.

many; hatred of the French enabled the British to recruit rapidly in Hanover.¹

Advantageous as Napoleon's rule had been to Italians and Belgians, it was disastrous to Holland; had ruined its rich commerce, lost its valuable colonies, depressed its prosperity, taken away its liberty, compelled Great Britain to prey on its foreign possessions, and placed Holland and Great Britain unwillingly at war. Holland needed liberation.

The autumn of 1805 was England's opportunity. She had a regular army of 300,000 men and 379,000 volunteers (militia). Only 22,000 were required in India. Had the home duty been assigned to the volunteers, and a British army of 180,000 men been Pitt's opportunity. assembled and sent to north Germany in September, it would quickly have decided Prussia to join the coalition with her ready 130,000 men; it was the safest side that Prussia's king was waiting to join; it would have kept from Napoleon's army at least 45,000 Germans, two-thirds of whom would have been mustered against him, and, leaving the 165,000 Austrians already in the field to take care of south Germany and Italy; it would have prevented the whole Ulm campaign, and presented an army in north Germany against Napoleon of above 450,000 men, as soon as Kutusoff's 116,000 Russians could arrive.

Buxhoven with more Russians was also coming. Additions would have come from Hungary, Austria, Prussia and Germany.

It was 45,000 Germans that raised Napoleon's 180,000 men to 225,000 at Ulm. Their absence

¹ Bourrienne ii, 303.

would seriously weaken him. Had these 45,000 been against him it is hardly probable that he could then march out of France with above 230,000 good soldiers; if more they must be recruits.

Such is the great strategy that might have been used had able, practical men, a class in which Britain is prolific, been at the head of the government.

Such was the September opportunity.

The October opportunity was still better. Napoleon was in distant Bavaria, nearly a month's march from Antwerp. The French were weak in Holland and north Germany. Of Napoleon's 20,000 veteran reserves in France, at Boulogne, one-half were seamen; his other reserves were newly levied conscripts not yet ready, and not yet as well drilled as the British volunteers, and less than one-fourth their number; and 150,000 British, led by an able commander, of which Britain had several, could have taken Antwerp. Napoleon rated Antwerp as the first port of his empire. It is now a fortress of the first class; the British could have made it as strong then. Counting on the stupidity of George and his ministry, Napoleon had left it exposed to capture. Its conquest would have released Holland and its navy from France; from it an army could have marched by way of Waterloo on France; Napoleon at Ulm could muster less than 170,000 *French*, had he marched to Antwerp's relief he would have had the whole available forces of Austria, Prussia and Russia on his flank; it was impossible without great French disaster. Instead of marching to Vienna and Austerlitz, he must have hastened to cross the Rhine followed by greatly outnumbering foes. Even were it possible that he could have marched safely against the British at Antwerp, they had the barriers of the Rhine and the Maas against him; detention there would have brought the combined armies of the allies upon him, a stronger combined force than that which overthrew him in 1813.

Had one-third of Britain's 300,000 regulars been united in Belgium with the 23,000 Swedes and Russians that were in Hanover, and the available Dutch, Danes and north Germans, without a single Prussian, when in November Napoleon was on his distant march to Vienna, they could have marched into France with 60,000 more soldiers than the 90,000 that Wellington had in Belgium in the famous campaign of Waterloo. Napoleon could not then have retired from Austria pursued as he would have been by the Austrians and Russians, and attended with the desertion of his Germans, without losing a large part of his Ulm army. Neither could he have raised a new army of French in the north in time to bar the way to France. While on the upper Rhine he might have tried to defend France against the Russians and Austrians, France would be open toward Belgium; if he marched his army in sufficient force to the north to stay this British invasion, that very movement would open France by way of the upper or middle Rhine to the armies of Austria and Russia with additions of many German troops.[1] All this, even if Prussia remained neutral, an entirely improbable event.

Instead of such effective strategy Pitt had sent a paltry 12,000 British to Hanover.

[1] Consult map of Central Europe.

VI

WHILE Mack was in Bavaria the Austrian Archduke Charles was between Verona and Vicenza in Italy with 90,000 Austrians.

The French Marshal, Massena, with 50,000 men tried to drive Charles from his position. It was an indecisive battle of three days. The loss of Mack's army caused Charles to hasten north to defend Austria. He hoped to be able to unite with the Russians. This hope failed. Archduke John escaped from the Tyrol into Styria with the remains of one of his three divisions. Of the other two, one surrendered to Marshal Augereau at Feldkirch, the other tried in vain to reach Venice, and capitulated to the French at Castel Franco. Massena followed Charles' retreat until compelled to halt by the danger of getting too far from his base in Italy.

The British and Russians landed a little army in Naples, encouraged by Queen Marie Carolina, daughter of Marie Therese of Austria, who, ruling for her worthless husband, King Ferdinand, had thus broken the truce with Napoleon. She united her troops with the Russians under a Russian general.

Napoleon vigorously followed up his success. Four days after Mack's surrender he reached Munich where the Bavarians received him with expressions of delight. The French eagles were quickly borne in triumph across Bavaria.

The first Russian army under Kutusoff was advancing by forced marches. Suddenly it found it necessary to turn back to join with the second Russian army under Buxhoven in Moravia.

During Napoleon's whole march from Ulm to Vienna only one French reverse occurred. Marshal Mortier crossed to the left [north] bank of the Danube at Linz with orders to keep near the main body, which was marching down the right bank. Mortier's three French divisions were separated, when, in a narrow way, the Russians attacked in force, and severely defeated Mortier with great French loss [November 21, 1805].

Murat entered Vienna November 11. Napoleon established his headquarters at the imperial palace of Schonbrun. Everything was quiet.

" The Austrian officials were so completely separated from all ideas of the people, and every one so completely dependent on his next immediate superior alone, that the whole machine went regularly on, and Vienna continued to be quietly governed," says the German Schlosser.

Practically it mattered little whether it was Francis or Napoleon at the head.

It was of extreme importance to the French to get possession of the bridge across the Danube near Vienna. It was the only Danube bridge within a long distance. The Austrians still held this very important passage. They had every thing ready to blow it up; 14,000 Austrian troops were there on the north bank to guard or to destroy it, their cannon covered the bridge, they were ready, artillerymen stood with lighted torches ready to fire the bridge which was strewn with explosives.[1] The loss of this bridge would shut Napoleon from the north side of the Danube for an indefinite time, until temporary bridges could be built, not an easy matter in presence of an active and vigilant foe.

[1] Bourrienne ii, 300.

Fortunately for Napoleon, unluckily for Austria, a hereditary prince was in command there; with princely stupidity this prince of Auersberg allowed the French, by a ruse, to capture the bridge. Here is Marshal Lannes' story of the affair:—[1]

"Murat, Lannes and some others advanced unconcernedly and entered into conversation with the commander of the post in the middle of the bridge. We spoke to him about an armistice which was about to be concluded. While conversing with the Austrian officers, we contrived to make them turn their eyes toward the left (Austrian) bank, and then, agreeably to orders I had given, my corps of grenadiers advanced on the bridge. The Austrian cannoneers on the left bank, seeing their officers in the midst of us, did not dare to fire, and my column advanced at quick step, Murat and I at the head of it, gained the left bank. All the combustibles prepared for blowing up the bridge we threw into the river, and my men took possession of the batteries erected for the defense of the bridge head."

This audacious act barred a junction of the Archduke Charles with the Russians.

At Vienna the French took the great Austrian arsenal with 2,000 cannon and 100,000 stand of arms,[2] almost as many cannon as Nelson had taken or destroyed at Trafalgar. On November 15, the French dragoons captured 190 cannon and an immense amount of equipments from the retreating army.

THE AUSTERLITZ CAMPAIGN.

The retreating Russians under Prince Bagration inflicted severe losses on the French in a battle near Iglau. After severe struggles and several battles, the retreating Russians and Austrians joined the second Russian army at Wischau in Moravia. This junc- *Nov. and Dec., 1805.*

[1] Bourrienne ii, 299. [2] Alison ii, 362.

tion was dangerous to Napoleon. The necessity of guarding so many points and keeping open a line of communications from Moravia to Vienna and Vienna to France absorbed many French and greatly reduced Napoleon's available field army.

Archduke Charles was approaching with a great Austrian army via Hungary. Archduke John would bring up the Hungarian levies with all speed. Prussia was preparing to descend on the French with 80,000 Prussians. It was extremely important for the allies to avoid battle till all their great strength should be available.[1]

To Napoleon delay threatened ruin. He must have not a battle only, but a decisive battle. An ordinary victory might ruin him. It would deplete his army, not easily to be recruited, while with all the probable reinforcements, his defeated enemy might renew the contest with increased prospects of success. Napoleon had ventured so far, had so diminished his field forces that it seemed that only a genius for blundering by his enemies could save him from decisive, ruinous defeat. He collected his available forces at Brunn.

What the allies needed, all they needed, was delay;[1] delay until all their supports could come up. Then they would overwhelm Napoleon by weight of numbers. Napoleon must fight before Charles and John and the 10,000 men under Ferdinand at Iglau, and the 12,000 more Russians now near at hand could arrive. He must win decisive victory before Prussia could hurl her ready 80,000 troops on his rear by way of Franconia, and, with the allies co-operating, repeat

[1] Metternich Mem. i, 35.

against him the very same strategy by which he had so recently destroyed Mack's army.

Everything was helping the allies. Even nature itself was aiding them, for the season was advancing to render the country less physically practicable and so increase the natural advantages of greater numbers and decrease the value of military art and tactics and Napoleon's peculiar faculty for that celerity of movement which, next to his marvelous power of concentrating strength on the desired point, was one of the most powerful reasons of his wonderful military successes. Winter and its obstructions to a country were against Napoleonic tactics. Napoleon was already a long way beyond Vienna, and even Vienna was in the heart of the enemies' country; his base of supplies was far off.

Although Prussia meant to play a safe game, yet the moment that he should weaken, down upon him would come Prussia's 80,000, now only a few days' march away. The 10,000 Austrians at Iglau had dangerous facilities for descending on his supply trains.

Now was again England's time. Had Pitt been a Marlborough, England would have had another Blenheim. Had even its little 12,000 men frittered away in Hanover been at hand, under the Stewart that seven months later won brilliant but useless victory at Maida, or under Beresford, Picton, Moore, Graham, then might have been another Detingen, and a dethroned Bonaparte. But George and Pitt at that moment had these great British soldiers elsewhere uselessly occupied.

Pitt was about to send a force somewhere under

the Duke of York with the Dukes of Cumberland and Cambridge as staff officers! These hereditary incapables, sons of George III, against Napoleon! It was like setting green goslings to war against the most robust of eagles! These royal ducks of dukes to be commanders of the best of troops when they had hardly been learners![1] Such was the folly of Pitt and George III.

"News from Paris of the internal condition of France was disquieting. . . . A great financial panic and bankruptcy was hovering over Paris. . . . The French treasury was mixed up with Ouvrard's speculations, the matter hung like a cloud over Napoleon during the Austerlitz campaign."[2]

About 68,000 Russians and 14,000 Austrians were at Olmutz under the two emperors, Alexander and Francis. The junction of Ferdinand's 10,000 from Iglau and the approaching Russians would raise it easily to above 100,000. Olmutz is near to Hungary; Charles and John might arrive. Charles' army was large; delay would immediately augment the allied army; delay would ruin Napoleon; Alexander would not delay.

Probably Napoleon could not make available at Brunn more than 70,000 combatants, a force less in numbers than that under the two emperors on his front already; less than Charles was expected to bring; less than the Prussians already so near and so threatening. Inclosed, in a few weeks, by these great combined armies, as he had inclosed Mack, how could he expect to escape the same fate that he had given to Mack? His chance of escape lay in the fact that leaders by birth, instead of generals by merit commanded his enemies.

[1] Martineau's Eng. i, 133.   [2] Bourrienne ii, 311-320.

The Emperor Alexander was the real commander of the allies at Olmutz. So far was this birth folly carried that this born leader of this great, superior force, about to engage in a very terrible death struggle against the greatest soldier the world ever saw, had never in his life seen a battle! Such stupendous folly could only occur in a hereditary system.

Had Russia and Austria been blessed with representative governments, like the Americas, Great Britain, France, and Switzerland of today, an able, experienced soldier like Kutusoff or Bagration would have been in unfettered command.

Kutusoff and Bagration were great soldiers. But what could these generals do when burdened with the presence and predominance of the two incapable emperors and their numerous princely staffs of boasting inpracticables, like Prince Dolgorouki, chief-of-staff?

When by waiting all was to be gained, nothing hazarded, the two hereditary emperors threw away this great advantage: just as Napoleon's necessities demanded, so decided Alexander and Francis. They resolved to give battle at once. Bagration exclaimed, "the battle is lost." The able Kutusoff they esteemed as too slow. Had the marplot emperors and their vaunting staff absented themselves and left all to the ranking general, Kutusoff, perhaps this fighter of Turks might have anticipated Waterloo by nearly ten years. But the men born to compel abler and better men to obey, were not satisfied to await an attack in their strong position as Wellington and Picton did at Waterloo, but also threw away this decided advantage by moving forward to attack

Napoleon in his chosen position. Common sense almost reels at such audacity. Battle has little respect for birth's privilege; cannon shot have no knees to bow before royalty; Kutusoff and Bagration, the able, must simply try to execute the plans of inexperienced Alexander!

Napoleon sent the astute Savary to the Russian camp with a letter complimentary to Alexander, but really as a spy. Alexander received him. Savary returned, having discovered that Alexander was surrounded by inexperienced nobles, whose presumption might mislead him into some fatal act of rashness. Napoleon acted on his knowledge of the propensity of hereditary sovereigns to be misguided. As he had arranged, when he saw the first movement of the Austro-Russian advance, he retired.

Alexander sent Prince Dolgorouki to return Napoleon's compliments. Napoleon, as if the interior of his camp, displayed scenes that he did not wish Dolgorouki to see, met him at the outpost, where the Russian saw soldiers hastily erecting fieldworks. Dolgorouki made excessive demands. Napoleon firmly refused. Ignorant of Napoleon's great military principle, "divide to subsist, concentrate to fight," Dolgorouki thought he saw preparations to retreat. He withdrew with the firm conviction, which he did not fail to communicate to Alexander, that Napoleon had lost all confidence and was trying to extricate himself from his really great peril.

Then Haugwitz came to Napoleon with Prussia's ultimatum of November 5. For four weeks had

The Prussians. Prussian measures shown decidedly hostile intent. Not only were its 80,000 troops marching on Franconia in dangerous proximity to the line that connected Napoleon with any hope from France, but a powerful Prussian army was collecting in Silesia just beyond the allies. Prussia was aroused to warlike enthusiasm; even the Berlin garrison had orders to march.

Napoleon's dangerous situation had become more perilous. He must act quickly; only complete victory could avoid destruction; defeat would crush his army and throne; even a check would turn all against him; delay was check, check was defeat, defeat was overthrow. He saw it all. To delay Prussia for a few days he recommended Haugwitz to defer offering to him Frederic William's ultimatum and to open conferences with Talleyrand at Vienna, instead of remaining in the discomforts of bivouacs. Haugwitz, the wily Prussian diplomatist, one of the ablest in Europe, not sorry of an opportunity to await events before finally committing Prussia in this great contest which he had so long labored to prevent, readily obeyed. Now Frederic William could see which is victor before taking side.

The allies knew the inferiority in numbers of Napoleon's army at Brunn, that there were but about 50,000 of them, but they did not know of the other corps, admirably placed in echelon to the rear.

Austerlitz, Dec. 2, 1805.

The Austrian General Weirother, a favorite of Alexander's, explained from a map the plan of battle to the allied generals while Kutusoff, the able, slept. Weirother believed the French were either retreating or changing position. "He has extinguished his fires; a good deal of noise comes from his camp."

The plan was to pass the right of the French, thus severing communication with Vienna and all hope of aid from Massena, and establishing more direct their own connection with Charles' large army in Hungary.

The emperors began their movement at daybreak, November 27, but instead of pushing it with all vigor and celerity and continuity, they spent the time till December 1 in desultory fighting and movements. This gave Napoleon time to concentrate; time for Bernadotte, Davoust and Mortier to come. On November 29 the allies had advanced two leagues toward the French right; the next day they retraced this movement.

When Napoleon examined the highest ground, the heights of Pratzen, he said: —

"If I wished to prevent the enemy from passing, it is here that I should station myself; but that would only lead to an ordinary battle, and I desire decisive success. If on the other hand, I draw back my right toward Brunn, and the Russians pass the heights, they are irretrievably ruined."

On the first advance of the allies Murat, Lannes, and Soult had fallen back behind Brunn.

Napoleon carefully chose his battle ground. Now he abandoned the heights of Pratzen and drew back his right as if afraid to encounter the allies. He evacuated the little village of Austerlitz, and concentrated around Brunn, waiting for the allies to make a mistake.

The French right rested on little lake Moenitz; their left on the high hill, Bossnitzberg, intrenched and crowned with artillery. On their front marshes bordered the stream, which were intersected at right angles by the great road from Brunn to Olmutz and by smaller country roads. Directly in their front, and beyond the rivulet, were the uneven heights gradually rising to the high point of Pratzen with its masses of Russians, thus conspicuously placed with intent to draw Napoleon's attention from the general movement behind that height, to turn the French right.

The French left, under Lannes, was at the foot of the hills, having a strong advance of cavalry in front of their cannon-crowned hill; next toward the center was Bernadotte's corps, and then Oudinot's grenadiers and Murat's cavalry. The Imperial Guards were behind them in the third line. In the center was Soult's corps, then unusually strong; it occupied the villages opposite the heights of Pratzen.

The French right wing under Marshal Davoust was thrown back in a semi-circle reaching the lake Moenitz, its reserves concealed behind the abbey Raygern. From a hill Napoleon could send his eagle glance over the general extent, but many parts were obscured by rising ground, copse woods and villages. On the evening before the battle the Russians still believed that the French would retreat, and Prince Dolgorouki directed his soldiers to "watch which way the French retired."

The night passed in preparation and anxious expectancy. Napoleon slept little, but went around among the soldiers explaining the plan of battle and animating them, and he issued an address.

At last the fateful morning of December 2 began to dawn; the eager combatants were ready. Napoleon perceived with delight that heavy columns were passing across his front, at short distance, toward his right. The great general battle that was to decide the fate of himself and his empire was at hand. He carefully avoided interrupting the Russian movement, but watched it with intense interest. The first allied column, under Doctorof, advanced beyond the French right; the second, under Langeron, occupied the heights of Pratzen, directly before the French right; the third, led by Prybszeweki, crowned the eminence behind that vital, most elevated point; then the fourth, under Miloradowitch; the fifth, under Prince Lichtenstein, followed, showing its column flank to the French, and stretching along the whole French front. The allied reserve, under the Grand Duke Constantine, were on the heights in front of Austerlitz. Thus about 80,000[1] men, of whom 15,000 were cavalry, arrayed in 114 battalions and 172 squadrons, were taking position for the terrible combat to decide the fate of half of Europe.

The valley, as seen from Napoleon's position, was wrapped in fog. From the wavelike surface emerged, as from a milky sea, the heights, and above these fog clouds soon rose "the Sun of Austerlitz."

The Russians had been in motion for some hours. At midnight they had received their orders. Long before the earliest beam of morning they had been drawing near to the fatal spot where the silence was to be broken by the wild crash of battle.

Napoleon had been eager, alert. He had ordered Soult to bring up his force to the very furthest front position that would still afford concealment. They now lay well advanced, but covered and concealed by the fog.

[1] Danilewski, Berthier, Alison, Lanfrey.

By the bright "Sun of Austerlitz" Napoleon distinctly saw the Russian columns descending the heights of Pratzen and disappearing into the sea of fog. They were still going toward his right. Away to his right he heard their artillery carriages.

The heights of Pratzen, the key to the allies' position, yesterday covered with a great multitude, was now seen partially denuded of its living covering. Intent on outflanking the French, the two emperors had materially weakened their force at this vital point. The marshals who surrounded Napoleon saw the advantage; they eagerly besought him to give the signal for action; he restrained their ardor; he asked Soult: —

"'How long would it take you from hence to reach the heights of Pratzen?'

"'Less than twenty minutes,' replied the marshal.

"'In that case let us wait twenty minutes; when the enemy is making a false movement we must take good care not to interrupt him,' said Napoleon."

A crash of cannon thundered toward the right. "Now is the time!" said Napoleon. The marshals galloped to their corps. The vigorous Russian assault carried Pilnitz, the most advanced village in the French right; on they came and took another village; the French right really appeared to be turned. Then Davoust's concealed reserve appeared and assaulted them; drove them back; took six cannon; was driven back in turn; the battle had opened furiously; there the conflict raged. Soult's heavy masses were quickly in motion; they scaled the height of Pratzen; they entered the open space between the Russian corps, completely severing the Russian left from their center.

The fourth Russian corps was just beginning to ascend the slope of Pratzen when they saw the dark masses of Soult's infantry emerging up from the sea of fog, while the Russians were at disadvantage in open marching columns. The Russians quickly formed in two lines. Soult's attack was impetuous; it broke the Russian front line, drove it back on the second, and took several cannon.

Another Russian corps came up the slope. There the terrific combat went on for two hours. The French carried everything; they took Pratzen; the allied army was cut in two!

The hereditary leader, the Czar Alexander, for whom the Russians were being crippled, mutilated, killed, instead of animating his troops at the points of danger like a brave man, set a bad example:—

"He found himself under fire, his men dispersed, and he himself was obliged to retire at a gallop attended only by his doctor, a single orderly, and two cossacks."[1]

In other words, the man who ruled by claim of birth actually ran away. He deserted his victims who were fighting for him. This is the man whom some writers praise as the model sovereign; he was the best monarch then in Europe; only the best of a bad, unmanly lot.

The French left also surprised the allied right. Lannes advanced according to Napoleon's system of tactics. (See next page.)

[1] Rambaud ii, 282.

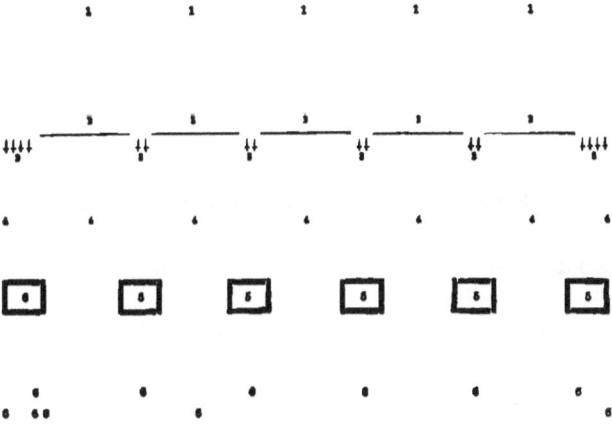

NAPOLEON'S SYSTEM OF LINE OF BATTLE.

Section of his left at Austerlitz, where occurred the tremendous collision of Imperial Cavalry.

¹ Enemy. ² Line of Infantry. ³ Cannon. ⁴ Light Cavalry.
⁵ (squares) Infantry. ⁶ Heavy Cavalry, concealed.

Napoleon's tactics were: First a line; second a line of squares of battalions (the artillery and light horse in front); then the heavy cavalry in several lines in rear of the squares. Then if a charge of horse broke the first line, as it did at Austerlitz, it met the second line with its front and side oblique fire; and if the enemy then dashed between the squares, it received in passing the side fire of the squares on both its flanks, and then was suddenly assailed, when blown and dispersed, by the heavy cavalry of the rear. If this drove them back through the spaces between the squares, flanking fires of the squares again assailed them. Such was the frightful experience of the Lichtenstein cuirassiers at Austerlitz.

The Russians were thunderstruck by the sudden attack by a host emerging from the fog of the low ground. So completely were the Russians caught unready, that their reserves were among the first on whom the French blow fell. They maneuvered quickly into line and brought their artillery into action.

The French infantry gained ground. Kellerman's cavalry were assailing even the Russian Imperial Guards themselves. Then Austrian cuirassiers charged Kellerman's, broke the French cavalry; the allied horse broke through the first French line, swept through the openings of the second line, between the squares, interposed itself between the corps of Lannes and Bernadotte, were there charged by Murat's cavalry, driven back through both broken French lines, whose flanking fire on their now disordered squadrons half annihilated them.

All the multiplied murder was still indecisive; but it so long prevented aid from the Russian right to its hard-pressed center. Kutusoff was compelled to call most of the remains of this same half-destroyed Lichtenstein cavalry to Pratzen heights to connect communication between the allied center and left.

Alarmed at the progress that Lannes and Bernadotte were now making, the grand Russian Imperial Guard itself [infantry] were sent down the slope into the low ground where Vandamme's infantry gave them furious combat until the Russian cuirassiers charged Vandamme's flank. The tremendous shock was irresistible; the French column was broken; three French battalions were trampled down; the French Fourth lost its eagle.

Then came a spectacle such as the world has seldom seen, frightful, terrific.

The Russians, after this great success, had scant time to reform their squadrons when the French horsemen were upon them; a veritable avalanche of men and horses, it struck with tremendous impetus; the Russian horsemen were driven back over the dead bodies of the French square which they had just destroyed; they lost their four cannon, they rallied, returned, they charged again; the French, too, charged to meet them; the finest cavalry in the world, the very select of France and Russia, the two splendid Imperial Guards, both renowned through the world; each a wild, thundering tornado of men and horses at full speed, met, collided in their frightfully terrific career. *Collision of great cavalries.*

The shock was tremendous, horrible, appalling; men and horses were crushed in masses, went down in squadrons; the massacre with sabers was indescribable, revolting, hideous; it continued above five minutes, it was the struggle of bloody desperation, both sides wild with frantic rage, covered with blood, cutting, slashing, stabbing at each other; a loathsome carnage; men turned to sanguinary furies; not a glorious spectacle as youth sometimes mistakenly pictures war, but a scene too bloody, too frightful, too furious even for the better class of devils: —

"It was downright butchery," afterward said Rapp, who commanded those French furies; "we were opposed man to man, and were so mingled together that the infantry of neither the one nor the other could venture to fire for fear of killing its own men."[1]

Infantry advanced on both sides to aid their coun-

[1] Bourrienne ii, 307-8.

trymen, but still the cavalry, squadron to squadron, company to company, man to man, killed each other. At last the desperate bravery of the remnants of the Russians yielded to the fiery valor of the remnants of the French; the Russians had lost their artillery, they lost their standards, they were driven in confusion; many of the very flower of the armies of Russia and Austria were dead, trampled, mutilated, on Alexander's first battlefield, from which he had hoped so much.

This desperate encounter was decisive. Pierced through the center, the allies still fought, not for victory, but for escape, for existence as an army. Their center had been driven back a mile; this, still worse, exposed their ill-fated left.

Napoleon threw his reserves and Soult's corps again on the rear of the allied left; Davoust pressed its front, both its flanks were assailed at once by impetuous cavalry and vigorous infantry flushed with success. This wing was now defeated and half its numbers soon made prisoners.

Buxhoven's shattered corps was hard pressed near a frozen lake; it resisted bravely; it was overwhelmed, 7,000 were taken or killed. A large body of Russians tried to escape by crossing the ice, the French broke the ice with their artillery and the Russians sank through it.[1]

Still on the Russian right, the sharp, hammering sounds of musketry were interrupted by the thundering crashes of artillery; heights, plateau, villages, were successively taken by the French.

At last the Russians and Austrians retreated.

[1] The French at first reported the number drowned at 20,000, but it was afterward said to be 2,000.

Suchet and Murat with infantry and cavalry pursued. They dislodged the allies from the road of Olmutz and there captured most of their baggage. The two emperors, looking out for their own comfort, left Bagration to conduct the retreat. Had they at first put him in sole command, it is probable that it would not have been a retreat. Bagration halted at Austerlitz village, encumbered with many wounded.

Thus ended Austerlitz, the greatest of Napoleon's victories, thrust on him by the folly of the emperors in not waiting till their forces could be so concentrated as to render their defeat impracticable ; by the folly of Alexander in trying to command in a campaign and in a great battle before he had ever seen a battle. How well Kutusoff knew how to command successfully is seen in the masterly strategy with which he fairly outgeneraled Napoleon in the second battle of Smolensk in 1812 when Kutusoff was seventy-four years old.

Austria was prostrate ; Russia was defeated ; Prussia was thunderstruck ; George III's policy was beaten. Pitt, the inveterate, was ended ; the shock of this great defeat killed him, the only man in Europe who, himself not a soldier, as instigator of the shedding of blood could almost rival in badness Napoleon himself, and in Pitt George III lost his pet minister. But George still remained. As evils in Europe, George and Pitt on one hand and Napoleon on the other were pre-eminent ; Napoleon for his quarrelsome and very aggressive disposition and total lack of conscience, and as a destroyer of the liberty that he should have protected : Pitt and George for their gigantic efforts to everywhere restore old abusers and abuses, the tyrannies, fooleries, and stupidities of old royalties which anywhere remained vigorous only in licentiousness and rapacity. Napoleon would have made a new privileged class ; Pitt and George would degrade men and manhood that decayed old nobility might rule.

Napoleon was the greatest soldier of modern times, Pitt was the greatest conspirator; Napoleon was a great success, Pitt was a great failure ; Napoleon robbed many foreign nations of money to make war for France, Pitt robbed England to make war for foreign nations ; Napoleon disbursed foreign wealth in France to benefit the French, Pitt and George disbursed British wealth abroad to benefit foreign kings, foreign nobles, foreign customs, manners, religions, arms, oppressions.

Napoleon was so far triumphant ; to Pitt, " almost every month brought some new disaster or disgrace."[1] Both were unscrupulous ; both trampled on human rights ; neither was worthy of the great nation in whose name he did his wicked deeds.

Napoleon was still master of a great empire ; all that Pitt had conspired for was lost, and Great Britain loaded with a great debt for ages. The highest compliment that can be paid to Great Britain is that she endured Pitt, George and Napoleon, and still survived, a vigorous, powerful nation.

The loss of the allies at Austerlitz was enormous, from 27,000 to 30,000 men killed, wounded and prisoners, many cannon, 400 caissons, 45 standards, while the French killed and wounded are reckoned at about 12,000 men. The allies were cut off from retreat to

[1] Macaulay.

Olmutz; if they were to take the road to Hungary it would expose their flank; a victorious army thundered in their front. Stunned, astounded at their great defeat, a midnight council decided that the war was hopeless. At four in the morning Prince Lichtenstein was sent to Napoleon to propose an armistice. Napoleon refused it.

But he gladly accepted an interview with the Austrian emperor the next day. Great dangers still surrounded Napoleon. He was ready to make peace. The terms were verbally agreed upon at this interview, the formal treaty would be made at Presburg. Alexander consented, but he would not be a party to the treaty.

Alexander was glad to extricate his army from the perilous situation. The Russians were to evacuate Moravia in fifteen days, and Galicia in a month. Their Army of Reserve had arrived at Breslau, only a few days march from Austerlitz.

Now that Russia was defeated and Austria humiliated, Napoleon threatened Haugwitz that he would turn his army against Prussia, wrest from it Silesia whose fortresses were not prepared for defense, and excite insurrection {Prussia, Dec., 1805.} in Prussian Poland, but that reasons of state restrained him; he would condone Prussia's conduct only on condition that it enter heart and hand into the French alliance. Haugwitz changed the whole Prussian plan. Instead of presenting a formidable war ultimatum, he signed a new treaty with Napoleon by which Prussia was to receive Hanover in exchange for Anspach, which it was to cede to Bavaria, and Neufchatel to France.

Thus the coalition that cost so much British money wasted by Pitt, was beaten in the field and dissolved in diplomacy.

Great was the indignation at Berlin when the treaty was made known. Instead of being delighted as Napoleon hoped, the honorable Prussian conscience was shocked, Prussians felt insulted. Its ratification was long and anxiously debated in council. It seemed now to be only a choice of ratification or war single handed with Napoleon. After striking out the words "alliance offensive and defensive," it was ratified with the illusory proviso that it was provisional till a general peace, and that Napoleon should procure a formal cession of Hanover to Prussia. By this treaty Napoleon hoped to produce war between Prussia and England. Frederic William tried to acquire Napoleon's consent for him to seize the free towns of Hamburg, Bremen and Lubec.

When Gustavus IV of Sweden came with his 8,000 troops to Hanover in 1805, he brought along a printing press, that he might, in imitation of Napoleon, issue pompous bulletins from the field. He began with a flaming one announcing his arrival. To his folly of engaging in a war to which Sweden had not been provoked, he added personal absurdities that rendered him odious to friend and foe, and especially to his own highly respectable nation. Not content with drawing, uselessly, the powerful enmity of Napoleon, the foolish fellow sent back to the king of Prussia, a Prussian order because it had also been conferred upon Napoleon. With his little army he threatened Prussia that he would hold Hanover

Sweden in 1805. A royal crank.

against Prussia and Napoleon and for the king of England. When the Prussian advance into Hanover almost collided with four hundred Swedes at Seerfield, they, wiser than their master, retired and avoided a rupture. He laid an embargo on Prussian vessels in Swedish ports, and actually had the audacity to blockade Prussian ports. Only the wisdom of the Prussian government spared retaliation.

The combined British, Russian, and Swedish occupation of Hanover came to an untimely end on receipt of news of Austerlitz and Presburg. Gustavus returned to Sweden where his unlucky subjects received him with regret. He tyrannically abrogated the constitution which he had guaranteed to Swedish Pomerania. Neither fully insane, nor possessed of good common sense, he was still permitted to reign and prepare great calamities for his too patient country, although schemes were laid to remove him to avert the threatened evils.

By the treaty of Presburg Austria ceded its old dominion, the Tyrol, and also the Vorarlberg to Bavaria, and that part of Venice of which it had despoiled the Venetian Republic in the treaty of Campo Formio, of 1797, to the kingdom of Italy. It recognized all the changes south of the Alps; Napoleon's two allies, the Electors of Bavaria and Wurtemberg, were made kings and each had considerable additions of territory. The Emperor Francis was required to engage not to obstruct any act of the new kings, a clause which left little of the already depleted powers of the German emperor.

Treaty of Presburg. Dec. 27, 1805.

The counter stipulations were illusory; Napoleon

guaranteed, jointly with Austria, the independence of the Helvetic Confederacy (Switzerland), which country he still held with a firm grip, and of the Batavian Republic (Holland), of which he soon after made his brother Louis king.

Austria was to pay to France 40,000,000 francs in addition to the sums already levied by the French commanders; it submitted to the loss of the vast military stores and magazines which the French had taken, which were soon sent off to France or repurchased by the Austrians.[1] Its fine altogether amounted to about $25,000,000.[1]

Austria is said to have lost by this treaty 1,331 square miles and 2,700,000 subjects.[2] Austria appears to have paid a part of her great fine to Napoleon by giving him a Hamburg bill for 7,000,000 fl of the very money that George and Pitt were sending as subsidy to Austria. George and Pitt had as usual blundered, and thus Napoleon got the very money they had taken from the British for use against him.[3]

September 21, 1805, Ferdinand, king of Naples, engaged to remain neutral, and the French troops were withdrawn. Napoleon sent them to Massena.

Naples, 1805.
As soon as they were gone Ferdinand's army was raised to a war footing. In November the queen, Caroline, broke the treaty with Napoleon, and received 12,000 Russian and 8,000 British troops. Ferdinand proclaimed his neutrality and inability to resist this force. Caroline did everything in her power to engage Naples in the war against France. She gave

[1] Alison ii. [2] Ibid. ii, 375. [3] Bourrienne ii, 331.

NOTE. After Presburg, Austria had about 25,000,000 people, and an army of 230,000 men; Bavaria had of people 3,250,000, and of army 60,000; Wurtemberg had of people 1,154,000, and an army of 20,000. Alison ii, 375.

PALACE OF FONTAINEBLEAU.

command of Ferdinand's army to a Russian. The French ambassador left Naples.

December 26, 1805, after Austerlitz, Napoleon announced from Vienna that "the dynasty of Naples has ceased to reign."[1] Massena and St. Cyr marched to execute this sentence, and, says Miss Martineau, "in a trice the Russians were sailing away from one coast and the British from the other," before the French arrived.

Ferdinand fled with the queen to Sicily. Their son, in whose favor they abdicated, surrendered Gaeta, Pescara, and Naples itself to the French, who soon after lost the fortress of Gaeta to the British and Sicilians.

Napoleon made his oldest brother, Joseph Bonaparte, king of Naples.

Splendid fêtes welcomed Napoleon back to Munich, during which his step-son, Eugene Beauharnais, son of Josephine, was married to Amelie Augusta, daughter of the newly made king of Bavaria, and the grandson of the Elector of Baden was married to Stephanie Beauharnais, adopted daughter of Napoleon. The next April [1806], Napoleon formally adopted Eugene Beauharnais to the succession of the throne of Italy in default of his own lawful issue. *Triumphs and marriages.*

A hundred days after Napoleon had crossed the Rhine he recrossed it, returning to Paris a victor. He now met triumphal arches and applauding multitudes. A hundred days full of momentous events — Ulm, — Trafalgar, — Vienna, — Austerlitz, — Presburg! *Napoleon's rapid success.*

[1] Napoleon, December 26, 1805.

On September 24, Napoleon had been still at Paris; on the 30th, he was at Strasburg; it was but sixty-four days later until he had achieved the final victory of December 2, at Austerlitz. It was October 4 when Napoleon's troops began to cross the Danube to get into the rear of Ulm; it was just sixty days later that Napoleon and the Emperor Francis agreed to terms of peace after Austerlitz. There had been but sixty days of actual collision.

The Peace of Presburg gave great impulse to Napoleon's plans of a dominant empire, as it enabled him to surround France with a great system of dependent sovereigns who should do his will.

Napoleon well knew the extreme peril from which Austerlitz and Presburg had liberated him financially, but he resolved to dazzle the world by a splendid declamation of the glories of French prosperity. Champigny made the oration. He recounted the grandeur of the victories; the magnitude of the undertakings; the navigation of rivers improved; the fortifications erected; Genoa acquired to furnish its many sailors to increase French naval resources; Italy delivered; science and art encouraged; Paris adorned; the Alps and the Apennines conquered; the roads of Mt. Cenis and the Simplon rising; harbors and docks being improved; Antwerp and Cherburg to rival the greatest naval establishments of England. The first coalition [1792] ended in the treaty of Campo Formio [1797] and gave France the frontier of the Rhine and the kingdom of Italy; the second [1799] yielded Piedmont; the third [1805] Venice and Naples. Russia owes the escape of its army solely to our generosity; Italy forms part of the great empire; the emperor, as the chief supreme, has guaranteed the sovereigns and the constitutions of its several parts.

Of his tremendous defeat at Trafalgar, the conflict in which was lost more heavy cannon than taken in any victory of Napoleon; the greatest of all naval victories, so decisive of the sovereignty of the seas; a British victory far more important and resultant than his Austerlitz — a result that placed everything beyond sea out of his reach; that protected England, America, the West Indies; that dispelled all his hopes and fond dreams of eastern conquest, Napoleon merely said to his Senate: —

"The tempests have made us lose some vessels after a combat imprudently engaged in,"—

yet he was the party who pressed his gallant, but unfortunate admiral, to engage in it.

During 1805, after Trafalgar, several other naval collisions had occurred between French and British, always to British advantage. Great Britain could defy him in sight of his own ports. A long line of brave and capable men had built up the renown of the British navy, during a series of generations; a masterly power, so complete, so skillful, so daring, so heroic, that it was beyond the power of Napoleon to overthrow, or even of Pitt and George's bad management to ruin it. Nelson and Collingwood are but the continuation of great naval commanders, illustrious in every generation of British naval history; not exceeded in numbers; not excelled in dauntless dexterity; not surpassed in enterprising success.

November and December, 1805, a financial panic broke out at Paris; the Bank of France had granted discounts to excessive amounts; extensive speculations were afloat. Then came the Austrian campaign, metal money that would pass anywhere was wanted Napoleon crippled the bank by taking 5,000,000 francs from it for public use; the public must have money, so the minister of finance advanced to contractors 102,000,000 francs in exchange for 150,000,000 francs in long bills, but this did not stop the run on the bank and on the treasury. Paper money ceased to pass, credit stopped, the government became without means of replenishing the public service. Such was the disastrous aspect before Austerlitz. The loss of that battle would have ruined the empire.

<small>Financial panic.</small>

But Austerlitz and Presburg dispelled the panic. With the close of that war the demand for the precious metals ceased, the crisis was over. Nothing but the immediate end of the war could have averted the great peril. Had Alexander and Francis refused battle, as d'Tolly did in 1812, and prolonged the war, it would have thrown Napoleon's government into bankruptcy.

The actual receipts of the French treasury had for five years been less than the expenditures, which were lavish; extravagant expenditure by Napoleon made the panic; the treasury reports had made the situation look better than fact.

Says Napoleon's trusted Savary:—

<small>"Beaten in the depths of Moravia, deprived by inconceivable imprudence of all the resources on which he was wont to calculate, he would have been wholly unable to repair his losses, and his ruin, from that moment, was inevitable."</small>

Not his own ability alone, but the blunders of Pitt, Alexander and Francis, had saved him. Instead of

UNITED STATES AND EUROPE.   165

Pitt, had an able man been at the head of the British government, and an able soldier, untrammelled, commanded the allied army, then had Napoleon ceased to reign in 1805.

Napoleon sent Molitor to take possession of Dalmatia, which Austria had just ceded to the kingdom of Italy. But he found that the Russians occupied Cattaro. Molitor charged the Austrians with having sold artillery from the Dalmatian fortresses. Napoleon wishing to march troops through Austrian territory from Venice to Dalmatia, seized the charge as a pretext to hold the Austrian fortress, Branau ; and he strengthened it as a barrier against Austria itself, and he declined to withdraw his armies across the Rhine within the time stipulated [before April, 1806]. The treaty broken.

The condition of Austrian affairs was deplorable. Confusion and disorder prevailed in civil and military. The emperor was compelled to find some one more competent than himself to conduct affairs. He appointed his brother, the Archduke Charles, to restore order in the government itself. Charles made reforms. A great number of officials were dismissed, but the incapable emperor, who had permitted such a state of things to exist, and who was responsible for the great disasters, was kept in place. Austria.

Napoleon made his minister, Talleyrand, Prince of Benevento, Italy; Marshal Bernadotte, Prince of

NOTE. In 1805 London docks were opened; the French and Spanish fleet failed in an attack on Dominica; Holkar was defeated by the British in India; Catholic petitions were rejected by both Houses of Parliament; Jefferson was re-elected President, and Paley died, æt. 62, and Schiller, æt. 46; Disraeli and Bulwer were born; Madame d'Stael wrote Corrinne.

Ponte Corvo, Italy; Marshal Berthier, his adjutant, Prince of Neufchatel, lately Swiss territory, and settled on each one-fifteenth of the revenue of his principality. Napoleon reserved large domains in conquered countries to use to bind officers and soldiers to himself. Every conquest added means for these great bribes. He created fifteen foreign duchies for his generals and ministers. These foreign titles carried foreign income to their holders.

Napoleon made his brother Joseph king of Naples. Joseph entered Naples March 30, 1806, with French troops. Insurrections followed. The reign of Joseph was disturbed. A British fleet captured Capri island. Generals Fox and Sir John Moore won honor for Britain by their humanity in refusing to attempt the capture of Naples when they could not hold it. This magnanimity was the more conspicuous as Massena was cruel.

Napoleon changed the "Batavian Republic" into the Kingdom of Holland. He required a few prominent Hollanders to come to Paris and sign a new treaty. Natives of Holland were to hold the state offices, Napoleon's brother Louis was to be king, the national debt was recognized, legislation was assigned to the king and thirty-eight deputies; to raise the present number to thirty-eight the king was to select one from each four candidates nominated by deputies and department assemblies; each member was to serve five years; all laws to originate with the king, he held the executive power, the deputies were but a council. It was a form of government to delight a despot; the deputies, not the people, ratified it. It was not submitted for popular vote. Very few Hollanders had any part in the transaction. It was a fraud of the most glaring kind.

Says the German, F. C. Schlosser, "a keen, critical and powerful writer, who judges men and events by a stern, ethical standard" :—

"The miserable, old courts, and poor souls who belong to them in Germany and Italy, but especially in Spain and Portugal, would have served the object of a universal monarchy, if Napoleon entertained such a project, far better than the new dynasties."[1]

" A Bonaparte was also forced upon the Germans, but the Germans were never consulted on the subject as the Dutch had been, because for centuries they had been accustomed to cabinet decrees disposing of their lives, properties and rights without asking them any questions."[2]

By treaties with Prussia,[3] Napoleon expected to obtain Cleves and Wesel, and he got Berg from Bavaria. He gave these countries to Marshal Joachin Murat, husband of Napoleon's sister Caroline. He further bound this new Grand Duke to him by retaining him as Grand Admiral of France. Murat instituted reforms that benefitted his German subjects.

Whenever Napoleon conferred a favor he required personal service. He was never gracious, never really generous in manner in giving benefits.

"The king of Wurtemberg, one of the worst despots, in a country whose dukes, with very few, and therefore more honorable exceptions, have been notorious as oppressors of their subjects, immediately used his sovereign power for the destruction of his people; he abolished the Estates (the legislature), which were very burdensome to him, and yet far from being models for imitation; he rioted in luxury, hunted, and in the midst of the greatest suffering and misery employed himself in collecting menageries and other costly vanities, solely for his own pleasure."[4]

[1] Schlosser's Geschichte des 18 Jahrh, vii, 453.   [2] Ibid. 459.   [3] Ibid.
[4] Ibid, vii, 468.

Pitt died January 23, 1806, just three days before Napoleon, his great enemy, victor of Austerlitz, re-entered Paris. As a statesman, a manager of campaigns, a promoter of coalition wars, a rival of Napoleon, Pitt, the orator only, was a gigantic failure. Only as a marplot, a misleader, a servile panderer to the follies of a half-witted king, was Pitt a success for the last twelve years of his life. Though he was but forty-seven years old, yet he had outlived his better self for thirteen years. His private debts to the amount of £40,000, parliament saddled upon the nation to pay.

In the efforts of George III and William Pitt to replace Europe under its old despots, they taxed Britain heavily, increased her great debt, wasted her money, risked making general bankruptcy. This fact is proof of Britain's marvelous vitality. It raises the question to what marvelous greatness might Great Britain not have reached if a real statesman, of which it had plenty, had then been at its head with a sovereign discreet enough to let the ministers and parliament control public affairs. Miss Martineau says of Pitt:—

"There was no part of his life when he was so unpopular as in the closing period, for his peculiar policy was in course of wretched failure. . . . . Friends found it difficult to press a resolution that he was a great statesman. . . . . He proved that a war administration was no field for him."[1]

Complaints against the abuses of government, during so long and so costly a war had greatly multiplied; opposition journals increased in number and vehemence. A general wish was felt for a government that should unite "all the talents," without

[1] Martineau's Eng. i, 142.

regard to party. At last George III was fairly constrained to admit into the cabinet, the ultra Whig, Charles J. Fox.

Fox was a man of tender, genial feelings, a grand orator, a very able man, but his private moral character was bad ; a fierce gambler, dissolute, he had not the confidence of the British, yet in politics Fox had often been right and his rival, Pitt, wrong. Fox had opposed war with France ; he supported the policy of non-intervention ; he loved peace ; he sought to abolish the slave-trade ; he desired to benefit the British people ; he opposed old abuses and new evils ; he was a practical statesman of liberal, generous views, of magnanimity, of humanity, but he was an intimate associate of the rowdy Prince of Wales, afterward George IV, and to this he added a too ardent admiration of the French Revolution with its bloody, tyrannical atrocities, when the British saw that despotic cruelty of Jaques is no better than despotism of Louis.

It was bad for Great Britain that, while George and Pitt were blindly, stupidly against all French revolutionary government, the Opposition leader Fox was too blindly for it. The happy medium course was lacking.

The Russian army had gone home. Napoleon had nothing to fear on the continent. Austria was prostrated, Prussia had yielded, Spain, Holland, Italy, Switzerland and Germany were his mere vassals.

The Irish Catholics were discontented, were hardly loyal ; Pitt and George had emptied the British treasury, the spirits of the aggrieved nation were depressed ; it was difficult to get money ; Lord Melville at the head of the navy had stolen navy funds and been acquitted on trial by the lords. People feared that the high army affairs were little better under the king's pet son, the Duke of York. The king and his son George, the heir to the throne, were enemies and political rivals, each knew and detested the well known badness of the other; the king was become more nearly imbecile than usual, but still stubborn, self-willed; but he was compelled to yield to public sentiment, the Whigs would not come to his aid without Fox, so he had to take Fox whom he hated. But George maliciously consoled himself that the situation to which he and Pitt had brought the country was so deplorable that the Whigs could not extricate it, but were coming in just in time to receive from the country condemnation for its disappointment of hopes of relief. In this hope George's malice was too well gratified; no cabinet could undo the gigantic misdoings of George and Pitt. From Fox the people expected the impossible, expected him to redress irrevocable wrongs that he would gladly have prevented. The great orator Sheridan, being a drunkard, could not be trusted in the cabinet, so they made him treasurer of the navy![1]

There were three parties: 1. The Whigs, who adhered to democratic principles and free institutions, led by Fox and Lord Erskine, who desired reform of parliament, so that the people should be represented, there being till 1832 only high-class representation, seats bought, sold, given away and held by a few as their private property,—there was extreme need of this 1832 reform,—they wished to repeal the acts

[1] Martineau i, 175.

which barred from civil and military offices persons not members of the state Church; they wanted to abolish the slave trade and slavery, and this alone brought against them great rancor of feeling; they loved the great blessings of peace.

2. A faction of the Whigs led by Lord Grenville, Earl Spencer and Mr. Windham, and composed of old families, with less hold on the popular feeling. They were hostile to France and to free principles, and were very aristocratic.

3. The old Tory party, conspicuous for the long term of power and the injuries it had done England. It was still powerful.

Mr. Fox, far the ablest man in the cabinet, did not take the first place; Grenville was at the head. Fox was minister of Foreign Affairs. But when persons spoke of the cabinet it was of Fox that they were thinking.

George Canning, the leading "Pittite" in parliament, bitterly opposed this new ministry.

The miserable king now insisted on right to control of the army as his prerogative, through his pet son, the duke of York, the commander-in-chief. Grenville held this claim to be illegal; they disagreed, Grenville considered himself dismissed. So the new government was obstructed at the very start by the same old marplot. George's brain, the smallest of any English king, except James II,[1] was now almost completely muddled, yet he could still stop the government. Changes in many offices were necessary, but he wished to control all these places.

Two days passed. George must have a ministry.

[1] Green.

He pretended to yield, but he required that all army changes be with his knowledge and consent. Then really Grenville yielded.

The new ministry violated English custom and law by placing a judge (Ellenborough, the Lord Chief Justice), in the cabinet. Judiciary and politics should always be separate.

Though George and Pitt were so long in power, not a single improvement in the government is due to them. Of Pitt, one of his most ardent ultra tory admirers[1] admits: —

"'Napoleon observed that he (Pitt) had no turn for military combinations, and a retrospect of the campaigns which he had a share in directing, must, with every impartial mind, confirm the justice of the opinion. He prolonged the war for an indefinite period, and ultimately brought upon the country losses and expenses much greater than would have resulted from a more vigorous policy,' .... 'and saddled the nation with the ultimate payment of one-third more than it received' in the debt."

Pitt's funding law was his own invention. In this he fairly outrivalled his king in masterly stupidity. He was pre-eminently the worst financier in Europe.

The principles of his famous funding scheme, a fraud that deceived British tories and, strange as it may seem, convinced even sane persons that Pitt was a great financier, was about as follows: Pitt borrowed enormous sums of money for the government, where for each $60 borrowed he gave the nation's bond for $100 at interest. He paid the interest partly in taxes and partly by borrowing more money on the same ruinous terms. He borrowed vastly and often.

Then came in that strangely foolish scheme, his great claim to be considered a financier. Periodically the borrower lent to himself, at compound interest,

[1] Alison.

small sums (say 1/500 of the great debt), and gravely expected those small sums at compound interest, himself against himself, to pay his whole enormous debt into which he had plunged the nation! This was Pitt's famous Sinking Fund Law of 1786, which stood till 1813.

That this folly, so incredible, could possibly be excelled in all the annals of foolishness, the ministry found a way to go to still deeper depths of absurdity, and actually sometimes borrowed the money to put into the small sinking fund — borrowed money at high rates of interest and high premium to put at interest to pay their debt!

The new Grenville government, with a head hostile to France and containing several peace members, prepared to carry on the war. Income tax was raised from 6½ to 10 per cent, and sugar tax increased. Still a loan of £18,000,000 (nearly $90,000,000) was borrowed for that year. This increase of income tax was loudly complained of as a grievous burden, and departure by the ministers from their professions before they took office. The whole expenditure that year was £72,000,000 (about $355,800,000), of which £23,000,000 were debt charges that came from former ministries. England was indignant at the higher taxes, while the king's great income was exempted from taxes. That the king, the very man who should have been the first to make great sacrifice should be excused from any tax was unlike Fox, but very like the selfish George.

The ministry secured change in enlistment laws, making the term seven years with three years more in time of war, instead of for life. It was not easy to get recruits. The new plan increased enlistment less than it would if barbarous punishments had been abolished. Still might soldiers be flogged even six hundred stripes,— such was the still cruel law of 1806 of Windham, a minister who also defended the slave trade.

In a few weeks Fox was ill. He was but a few months in the ministry. George III had hated him ever since his opposition in the American Revolution. His hatred had been often refreshed; it had been especially aroused in the late session when Fox and Grenville had again brought forward Catholic emancipation, to which George was bitterly opposed, even while George was aiding the most intolerant Catholic despotisms abroad against the interests of their people, as he once aided French Catholics against their own French government *de facto*.

Fox was a comprehensive statesman. Many measures for which he struggled against the narrow prejudices of George and his supporters, have, since his death, been enacted and are now among the vital principles of British policy and glory and renown.

PRUSSIA, 1806.

The Prussian military were arranged as if all trouble was over, while Napoleon still kept an army on the Main. Haugwitz was sent to Paris; Napoleon used to him severe language; he threatened the downfall of Prussia. After a stormy interview with Napoleon, Haugwitz received from Talleyrand notice that, as the Haugwitz treaty of December 15, 1805, was not ratified by Prussia within the specified time, it was not concluded. Another draft was laid before him still worse for Prussia. Bayreuth was added to Prussia's sacrifice to robbery. Prussia was now required to assume an attitude decidedly hostile to Great Britain; to shut the Weser, the Elbe, the Ems against English trade. England desired to hold the world's carrying trade as far as possible, but Napoleon was fast taking the position of hostility to the world's trade itself.

Until 1806 Napoleon had warred against individual nations; he was now rapidly becoming the enemy of all the world that lay outside of his own empire, as he was the despot of that within.

Haugwitz was told that if he did not sign this offered treaty the French troops would be put in motion immediately against Prussia. Haugwitz well knew that this meant not only the troops of France proper but other large forces. He saw no escape for Prussia; her armaments were on a peace footing; she was already embroiled with Britain and with Sweden; there can be little doubt that Napoleon had already used large sums of money to buy advocates in the Prussian court; what could Prussia do if Napoleon's great army of combined forces of twelve [1] countries, with the possible help of three others,[2] were suddenly let loose upon her?

Haugwitz, under this strong compulsion, signed the offered treaty, February 13, 1806. Six days later, before Prussia ratified the treaty, as soon as an order could reach them from Paris, Bernadotte took posses-

[1] France, Italy, Naples, Switzerland, Bavaria, Wurtemberg, Baden, Holland, Hanover, Belgium, Berg, and Spain.
[2] Hesse, Saxony, and Portugal.

sion of Anspach for Bavaria, and Murat took Wesel and Cleves for himself. Nothing was left in exchange to Prussia but the much-disputed Hanover. The king of Prussia again offended Napoleon by showing special honor to the Russians, and reviewing the Russian army at Stettin, March 3. On March 9, he ratified the Haugwitz treaty, committing Prussia to unfriendly attitude toward the British and Russians. This was the incapable conduct of the man placed by heredity in a place that nature never intended him to fill.

On news that Prussia occupied Hanover and closed the Elbe and Weser against English trade, the British embargoed all Prussian ships in British ports.

Thus Napoleon's cruel policy enriched his enemy, England, with the prizes of about four hundred Prussian and German vessels, and annihilation of Prussia's trading fleet, the very thing that benefited England most, by removing the Prussian and German competition to British trade.

April 1, 1806, Prussia took formal possession of Hanover, received from the French. Mr. Fox, in parliament, denounced "that worst emanation of the disorders and calamities of Europe," the transferring of people from one power to another like so many cattle. This sale of a country, so in harmony with the atrocious practice of those wicked times, so in defiance of every principle of justice or morality, was in this instance met by the Whig ministry with a declaration of war, June 11, 1806, against the rapacious king of Prussia, Napoleon's victim.

Napoleon had criminally traded what was not his own, and not even in his possession, for he held but a single town of Hanover when he sold the whole state to Frederick William who bought it and then did the actual robbery himself. Napoleon was gigantic in this species of crime. It is not certain that Napoleon would ever have made conquest of Hanover, yet he feloniously sold it to Prussia in exchange for Anspach and Bayreuth, given to Bavaria in exchange Berg and Cleves (and Wesel), which Napoleon gave to Murat, whom he made Grand Duke of Berg and Cleves.

The punishment of the purloiner of a country soon overtook Frederick William; it was deplorable that it also punished guiltless Prussians and Germans, a race whose noble qualities deserved a better king and a fairer fate.

VII

UNITED STATES AND GREAT BRITAIN.

WAR against wholesome trade is war against mankind. The enemy of innocent commerce is the whole world's enemy.

But the right of a belligerent to station before a hostile port a force to prevent entrance and egress of neutral vessels, is founded in recognized principles, but the blockade must be actual and sufficient.

George III's ministry "pretended that if a port was declared to be under blockade it must be regarded as actually blockaded." Other nations generally resisted this principle.

May 16, 1806, the Grenville Whig ministry declared all French ports from the Elbe to Brest, about eight hundred miles, under blockade. This illegal order caused great uneasiness in America. Next to Great Britain the United States had the richest commerce of any nation. As America was neutral in European wars, French, Dutch and British and Russian merchants shipped great amounts of their goods in American vessels, because the vessels of a neutral are, by international law, exempt from capture by parties at war, while their own vessels are liable to be taken by the privateers and war ships of the other side. This carrying trade had become very profitable to Americans. Any interference with it was keenly felt by the commercial districts from Baltimore to Eastport, where most of our ships were owned.

The United States and Britain had long been at controversy because British navy officers stopped American ships, searched their crews and seized and took away native British sailors, and sometimes American seamen, whom they compelled to serve in the British navy.

America often remonstrated. The power was on the British side and Britain used it. America had very little navy; Britain was the greatest naval power of all history.

British and French restrictions on American commerce excited different feelings in the two great American political parties. The southern slave-holders who dominated the democrat-republican party were then in power. They loved France; they hated England, Napoleon warred on England, he was a great soldier, they were dazzled by his military "glory," so they admired Napoleon.

During the ninth Congress, in 1805, Jefferson's

party accepted the name, till then refused by them, of Democrats, flung at them by Federalists in reproach as a charge of favoring mob rule. It did not supplant the name, Republicans, and it sank out of sight when all parties became Republicans in 1815. But it was revived on the disruption of that general party into Whigs and Democrats in Jackson's time, and the name Republican disappeared until 1856, when it was taken by a new party.

The Federalist party, out of power, was strongest in the North. It did not like Napoleon, nor despotism under any name. It could not admire George III, any more than England of today admires him. It wanted peace with England, open commerce, prosperity; it wanted a navy to protect America and our commerce. Beyond the odious George it saw the kindred British people to whom they were friendly.

While the Jefferson party saw all France in Napoleon, commercial America saw in George III only an incumbrance, a handicap on his honorable people, saw the great distinction between a nation itself and its rulers, saw that England was not George, that France was not Napoleon, that England and France were the victims of their rulers. Federalists detested Napoleon's aspirations to empire of the world; Jefferson's party admired his overthrow of thrones, though he raised new thrones as despotic.

We are not to study history to excuse our faults, so with candor we must admit that Britain had just cause of complaint that American captains shipped British seamen knowingly when Britain was in great need of their services; it was as if English vessels had employed great numbers of our men of military age during the late secession war and so kept them out of the way of our conscription when General Grant was before Richmond. Had the British arrested only British subjects on American ships in British ports it might have been tolerated rather than risk war with the mistress of the seas, but they searched our ships at sea and took away part of the crews. England asserted its right to take its subjects thus, and offered to give up Americans on their ships on demand, with proof. America regarded naturalized men as fully Americans; Britain denied that its subjects can cease allegiance to Britain, and it urged its great emergency as reason for insisting.

The eccentric John Randolph, till then a follower of Jefferson, declaimed in Congress:—

"What is the question? .... It is the carrying trade which covers enemy's property, and carries, under a neutral flag, coffee, sugar, and other colonial products, the property of belligerents. .... It is not for the honest trade of America, a trade that European peace will dispel. .... I am averse to a naval war with any nation."

Such were the Jeffersonian sentiments of 1806. News came of Trafalgar. Jefferson's party saw that Great Britain no longer had a naval rival on the seas. Randolph justly remarked:—

"Take away the British navy, and France is tomorrow the tyrant of the ocean."

It was true. But in this remark he had expressed Federalist opinion. Randolph was accused of deserting the Jefferson party. That was also true. Trafalgar had opened his eyes.

James Madison had what he called a pacific policy. Refuse British imports; nobody must buy, nobody must sell English goods. The Jefferson party seized the idea. In March [1806] Congress passed an act which forbade any import of leather, silk, hemp, flax, tin, brass, high-priced woolens, glass, hats, clothing, millinery, beer, pictures, prints, card and silver plate from England. Several of these articles were not produced in America. We had no silk, tin, brass, glass, and plate factories.

A singular feature of this "pacific" policy was it included an act authorizing the president, if he desired, to call into military service 100,000 militia or volunteers! His party had always bitterly opposed having a standing army. Now they were apparently preparing for war!

In April, 1806, Pierce, an American, was killed in American waters, near New York by a shot from a British war vessel. Excited New Yorkers called on the president for ships of war to protect their great harbor. Jefferson, always against an American navy, sent them a copy of his favorite law against increasing our feeble, miniature navy, and a proclamation ordering the offending vessel to depart, an order which he had not force to make effective. Jefferson was the leader in opposition to an American navy, yet Jefferson wrote to Monroe the great assumption, "We consider the whole Gulf Stream as our waters."[1]

Congress gave $250,000 to build fifty more of Jefferson's small, useless guncraft, but Congress refused money to build or even to repair frigates, so hostile was the South to a navy. For years war had been threatened, yet the only addition to our navy in six years had been two sloops!

Frames laid years before for six ships of the line,

[1] Jefferson to Monroe, May 4, 1806.

were actually cut up for these useless guncraft that nobody heard of when real war came. Timber bought for frigates when Adams was president was thus wasted. Most of our very few small war vessels were laid up at a time when our rich commerce was greatly exposed to pillage by England, France, and Spain — when even little Denmark seized American vessels.

All America was enraged by the British impressment of many Americans, yet America was totally unable to enforce its just claim against impressments. The great British navy contained more than 100,000 men; our navy 925 men! Their naval force was more than a hundred to our one. There was nothing for us to do but negotiate. Yet our population was one-half that of England, Scotland, and Wales. We could raise Madison's 100,000 militia, but as England had neither disposition to invade our country nor army to spare to do it, and as 100,000 militia could not meet the British navy at sea, it is hardly apparent what was to be done with them if Jefferson should call them out as Madison's law provided. (Better perhaps in all wars that each party be unable to get at the other; it would save bloodshed).

Americans had warmly sympathized with republican France. But France was no longer a republic. It was a much more arbitrary monarchy than Great Britain. It was strongly centralized; liberal views were entirely suppressed; it was not the France of liberal Lafayette. Napoleon, never a friend to anything but himself, France, and Italy, was in almost absolute power. Yet still in Jefferson and his party remained strong French sentiment. In our war of liberation the French people had won our love. All Americans remembered that; but all Americans did not give to the great oppressor of France the love and gratitude that was owed to only the French people themselves. That was a difference between the Jefferson party and the other Americans.

After 1783, the American republic was never in danger of being overthrown by any power but Napoleon, and Napoleon overturned everything within his reach. There is no reason to believe that this most arbitrary of conquerors would have spared the American republic, whose very existence was a constant menace to his throne by its facilitating the spread of free principles. Spain gave him no provocation, yet he gave her a most terribly devastating war of six years; Portugal gave him neither insult nor injury, yet he almost annihilated her, his armies utterly destroyed even the crops of her fields and the huts of her lowest peasantry; Denmark never harmed him, yet it was a bitter lot that he dealt out to her. The Prussian king was his friend, his accomplice in despoiling Germany, yet he turned upon Prussia a vengeance too horrible for one's worst enemy. The Czar of Russia was his bosom confidant, yet he wasted 250,000 human lives on his own side and a countless number of Russians, trying to destroy the Czar's empire in 1812. He was always a bitter friend, a destroying enemy to all nations that lay accessible.

It was the British navy alone that barred him from access to America. If once Napoleon had controlled the ocean, he could have sent here armies of many times the numbers of the largest that England had been able to send in our British war. As late as

1810, in his ministry, appeared a plan for the conquest of America. It is hardly likely that Fouché originated that plan without former discussion and inspiration from Napoleon.

The situation of England was critical. The admiralty dared not announce cessation of seizure of British seamen on neutral ships, lest American vessels be asylums to British deserters and wholesale desertions should denude, not only its merchant vessels, but also that navy on which England's safety from invasion by the French depended. They showed a disposition to be willing to let impressment quietly cease without public notice and gradually, but Jefferson was unwilling to wait. From time immemorial Britain had obtained men for its navy by the outrageously wicked system of impressment. Now that it was in a stupendous struggle for very existence, it must husband all its resources of recruitment. With peace the practice of invading American vessels would cease of itself. The war depended on the one life of Napoleon, which he freely hazarded in war. All human life must end, a successor was impossible, then probably nobody could hold together his empire, not the ablest French marshal, the most influential statesman, certainly no other Bonaparte. Then England's great trial would end.

Fox was sick. Lords Auckland and Howick (Grey) acted for him. They proposed to the American envoys at London, Monroe and Pinckney, that England make it penal to impress Americans, and America to refuse certificates of citizenship to British. The Americans declined. This project would interfere with the American doctrine that any man has a

ONE SIXTH OF JEFFERSON'S EFFECTIVE NAVY.

right to expatriate himself, that America will always allow foreign born persons to become American citizens, and will then protect them.

The British proposed that Britain would stringently instruct British officers not to molest Americans, and would promptly redress any cases of molestation. Monroe and Pinckney understood them to intend a quiet abandonment of seizure of men from neutral ships, without risking the dangers and damage of its announcement on their own army and navy; an expressed willingness to do anything but to renounce it might cause wholesale exodus of British seamen from their own to our flag for shelter from naval service. Should they neglect this opportunity? Monroe said "no," Pinckney said "no." They made a treaty, somewhat like Washington's Jay treaty of 1795; trade between the United States and Britain on entire reciprocity; American vessels in the East India trade limited to direct voyage to India and back; no British concession in British West Indies; Britain's blockade recognized as in the then existing Jay treaty, but no American vessel to be visited or seized within five miles of the American coast. Britain made the concession, extremely important to Americans, that our vessels might, during the present hostilities, carry to any port not blockaded by force, any European goods, or colonial produce, not contraband, if it was American property, previously landed in the United States, and had paid an American duty of at least one per cent above drawback.

This treaty did not mention impressments. News came of Napoleon's famous Berlin Decree, and then the British negotiators asked assurance that America would resent any interferences with our trade by France. Our envoys refused to give this assurance; they would not quarrel with France to benefit British trade. The treaty was then signed, the British declaring in a separate paper their right to retaliate the Berlin Decree.

This treaty seemed all that could be had. England would yield no more till peace with France. It is all that the war of 1812 obtained. The power at sea was so strongly British that she could withhold what she pleased.

The Franco-Prussian campaign of October, 1806, came and ended, and Napoleon made a wicked retaliation for England's blockade order of May, 1806. By his infamous Decree of Berlin of November, 1806, he declared the whole British islands under blockade. To call such a declaration a blockade of Great Britain was absurd. He sent not a single ship, not a gun, not a man to enforce it before any British port. It could therefore claim none of the sanction that international law gives to blockade. It was an arbitrary act, outside of law of civilized nations. Therefore no one had moral duty to respect it. By this illegal Berlin Decree all communication between the French empire and England was forbidden; no letters in English nor parcels addressed to England or to an Englishman were to be sent from post-offices; every British subject found in any country occupied by the French was to be prisoner of war. All property of any Englishman was to be made prize, one-half to go to

Berlin Decree.

French merchants whose vessels were taken at sea by the British. All vessels coming from England or its colonies, or having been there after date of this decree, were refused admission to any French port.

Says the Frenchman, Bourrienne: —

"This is what was called the 'Continental System,' which in plain terms was nothing but a system of fraud and pillage . . . . extorted exhorbitant prices for articles which the habits of three centuries had rendered indispensable to poor and rich. It was in revenge for the English very extended system of blockades which after Trafalgar put it out of his power to keep the seas.

The hurling of twenty kings from their thrones would have excited less hatred than this contempt for the wants of nations."[1]

Napoleon caused Denmark to adopt it October 31, and Russia, November 7; only Turkey and the islands of Sicily and Sardinia rejected it, though Spain and Portugal opposed it. All other ports of Europe were thus closed against British vessels. Says Rotteck (German): —

"These measures were mainly the result of the general discontent which the British government had caused by its illiberal views and its acts of violence."[2]

The arbitrary Napoleon issued his Berlin Decree like an order of the day, and his servile Senate ratified it. France itself had no hand in it. It was simply the arbitrary act of absolutism, entirely regardless of what might be the opinion or the wishes of France.

"Its execution did most harm to France, and to band all Europe against it."[3] By it he practically blockaded his own empire. It was savage hostility toward all mankind, but it seems to have caused

[1] Bourrienne ii, 361-65
[2] C. Von Rotteck's Allgemeine Weltgeschichte, iv 176.
[3] Bourrienne ii, 366.

most suffering to his own subjects, from whom it barred articles of prime necessity. That was an epoch of bitterness, of lack of mercy, of want of equity, of public injustice. So dull was the public conscience that some persons even defended as justifiable Napoleon's conquest and plunder of Prussia, and George's piratical raid on Copenhagen. There were even men who regarded those two unworthy rulers of honorable nations as good monarchs!

January, 1807, British "Orders in Council" declared that no vessel shall be permitted to trade from one port to another of France or her allies, or possessions, or ports so far under her control that British vessels may not trade thereat, "on pain of capture and condemnation."[1] This order applied in its terms to France, Spain, Holland, Italy, Naples, Belgium, Denmark, Prussia, Germany, and Russia, and the French colonies.

As Napoleon's Berlin Decree injured Americans, George's ministry hoped by adding the British injury contained in their "Order in Council," to arouse the Americans to resent the French injury alone! This was reasoning worthy of George himself.

Napoleon was no champion of human rights; he was champion only of his own power and his avarice. His Berlin Decree was war on all commerce. For a time he pretended to exempt Americans from its effect, but American vessels in the West Indies were seized by French on pretense, perhaps true, of having British goods on board, and English manufactures in Europe, owned by Americans, were "sequestrated" to await Napoleon's decision.

[1] Official Document.

Jefferson and Secretary of State Madison rejected this treaty. Congress was in session. The president did not submit it to the Senate. Not even a cabinet consultation was had.

They objected that it did not end impressments of Americans; that it appeared to leave to England the power to ignore our neutral rights if France were permitted to ignore them; that this might leave Britain unbound and America bound for ten years to pass no embargo or "take any other measures to restrain the unjust pretensions and practices of the British."[1]

But Congress might have approved it with the proviso that any violation of its terms by England should release America.

Monroe at London responded that impressments were left open for future discussion. Jefferson instructed Monroe and Pinckney to negotiate further and not conclude without abolition of impressing from our ships, and not to allow England to treat neutrals as France might treat them. Jefferson indicated willingness that practice should conform to the basis of this treaty. To manifest his wish for conciliation he proclaimed suspension of the non-importation act till the next November. But Fox died. It was Perceval's Tory ministry that received Jefferson's own refusal. Perceval was not conciliatory. The great opportunity had passed. Jefferson had failed to follow the example set him by Washington in accepting the Jay treaty in 1795. The Chesapeake affair followed.

Had Jefferson accepted the treaty, taken the easily

[1] Jefferson to Monroe, March 21, 1807.

paid duties on our imports to build frigates, and allowed merchant ships to arm and defend themselves, he could have commanded foreign respect and spared his embargo and the American distress it caused. But while we were without means to resent or redress English insults and injuries, England would hold to its advantages of deriving strength to its navy by taking its deserters and subjects to impressment from our vessels; she must have seamen; she could not afford to let hers escape in our ships.

With similar grievances, Washington, in April, 1794, nominated John Jay as special envoy to Britain. Washington stated that he hoped to honorably prevent war.

What Washington did in a similar case.

But in 1794 he was opposed by the large Jefferson party in Congress who wanted to stop all trade and intercourse with Britain, to attempt to coerce its Pitt ministry to deal more gently with us. Madison, prompted by Jefferson, who had retired from Washington's cabinet, introduced resolutions with that object. It was thought that embargo would so distress the English common people and laborers that its ministry would yield to relieve them; they little realized the hard hearts of George and Pitt. Jefferson's party vigorously opposed Washington's wise measure. In the House the matter was violently discussed; it was contended that embargo was better than conciliation, and the foolish idea was held that conciliation is sign of weakness. The friends of Washington, with better knowledge of human nature and of British nature, represented that an embargo is almost war without war's compensations; that it would only irritate rather than coerce the ministry; that Britain's vast resources could sustain her without our trade; that our own commerce and prosperity would receive a severe blow, and our revenue fail to pay our debt; that negotiation might succeed and war be averted; it was not best to throw away the chance. All this in the House which had no vote to confirm or to reject the nomination of Mr. Jay. In the Senate, after a hard struggle, the Jefferson party failed to get a majority to vote against Washington's measure, and Jay's nomination was confirmed. In the House was still a small Jefferson majority against Washington's policy; they refused to sanction Jay's mission; they held it to be humiliating. Peace between Portugal and Algiers had left the Algerine vessels free to depredate on American commerce; they took several of our vessels, held the crews as prisoners and confiscated the cargo. The jealous idea was started that George's ministry had procured this peace for that very object, to annoy our commerce. The ministry disavowed it.

Mr. Jay made a treaty. It contained all that the British cabinet would yield; it did not end impressments, and, to the Jefferson men's special aversion, it required honest debts due to British or to royalists who had left the country, to be paid, and it restricted entry of our vessels to British West India ports, to those under one hundred tons burden and with cargoes from the United States. This restriction to vessels too small to trade across the ocean was aimed at France and Spain; England had defeated their trade with their colonies; it would be throwing away the reward of victory if she allowed them to recover this trade by using American vessels.

Tranquility was rudely broken by the boisterous conflict for and against this Jay treaty. Public meetings were held in towns to protest against it. The fight was very earnest, animated, bitter. William Corbett has described the scene when Washington came to make his annual speech to Congress, December, 1795.[1] The Congress was in grave silence, the gallery was crowded with spectators. The tall form of Washington entered the hall. His manly figure was well set off by the old style of dress, his powdered wig, his long blue coat with buff facings, his silk hose and buff waistcoat and breeches; and then his bright, florid face and his mild blue eyes evinced trouble today; he was not assured of welcome; he saw before him numbers of men who wished to thwart his measures. It was the first time Washington had ever met a Congress that was opposed to him; he felt the changed situation; he "spoke in a timid manner;" when he spoke of the British treaty he cast those mild blue eyes "with a look of injured innocence toward the gallery" where sat sympathizers with his policy. Not a murmur of dissent was heard; all was silence — cool, calculating silence. When he had retired the House refused to adopt its answer to his address because its draft contained an expression of "undiminished confidence" in Washington.[1] The Senate ratified the treaty, but it was conditionally and without a single vote to spare. Only one more vote against it and Washington would have been defeated in his measure. Then, with a strong memorial against the British order to its naval officers to seize all food in American cargoes

[1] Peter Porcupine's Cong. Gallery, 21.

JEFFERSON OPPOSING WASHINGTON IN THE FIRST CABINET.

destined for French ports, Washington sent his approval, the British ministry soon revoked their odious order, and there was peace.

But the Jefferson party in the House still tried to defeat the Jay treaty by refusal to appropriate money to execute it. It was only after long and angry discussions and unjust reproaches of Washington, the bitterness of which he was made acutely to feel, that some few of the opposition, knowing that a ratified treaty is law, and that its violation would disgrace our nation and dishonor our good faith, voted with Washington's supporters and made the appropriation needed. I explain this here in order that the different courses of Washington and Jefferson under similar circumstances may be compared. The first resulted in peace, the second, we are to trace to its culmination in war after causing terrible distress to both countries.

The horror excited by the Sedition law passed in John Adams' term, with its only six trials, powerfully aided in 1801 to place Jefferson's party in power. But under Jefferson in 1806 several libel suits were brought. Such suits were in violation of the principles professed by Jefferson before his election. They were notably Doane's case in Pennsylvania, Reeve's, and the Courant newspaper cases in Connecticut. They failed, and the press had less to fear. The Courant case brought the important decision by the United States Supreme Court that Federal courts have no criminal jurisdiction not expressly given by statute.

VIII

NEGOTIATIONS for peace between Fox and Napoleon dragged heavily. Napoleon, as usual, protested that he desired peace, but he was not willing to be just or honorable.

Negotiations. 1806. The basis for these negotiations was for each party to hold its conquests. After much difficulty, Napoleon was brought to offer to restore Hanover to George, although he had already sold it to Frederick William. The retention of Sicily by its king, Ferdinand, was the grand *sine qua non* of Fox. And Fox was right; Napoleon consented, but he fell away from his promise; he demanded Sicily; he had never conquered it; Sicily was out of reach of his conquest; it, like England, was protected by the surrounding sea. Yet on this point Napoleon, the unjust, made a stand. The secret of his falling away from his own terms was soon apparent. News came to England that he had deluded the Russian ambassador, d'Oubril, into making a separate peace with him. The almost dying Fox learned this fact July 25.

There were great obstacles in England to peace. Nobody could trust Napoleon; he was ready to break a treaty whenever he saw chance of conquest and spoils; he had broken many treaties; who could confide in his pledged word? England believed that a peace would be only a truce until it suited Napoleon's grasping rapacity to renew war by some new, sudden advantage. England did not believe that he would relinquish his desire for universal dominion. He could not tolerate freedom ; he hated the voice of the people.

It was believed that he had formed the design to invade England, less to destroy its power, than to extinguish the liberty of the British press, as he had silenced the French press and French speech. A free people within six leagues of France was a seductive example to the French.[1]

January, 1806, the British completed conquest of Dutch Good Hope. Talleyrand urged that the possession of Good Hope for commerce, the restitution of Hanover for the honor of the British crown, the retention of Malta for the honor of the navy, ought to satisfy the British.

Napoleon's desire to obtain Sicily was in itself a threat to England. He hoped to sometime gain control of the Mediterranean, clear the way to Egypt, and thus on to India, there to disturb British possession.

For the King of Naples in exchange for Sicily, the greedy Napoleon offered the Hanse towns, never his, but which were free, independent cities, each with its own government.

Of course Fox refused this dishonesty. Then the dishonest Napoleon offered Dalmatia, a province of Turkey, but held by Italy ; the Balearic Isles, which belonged to Spain ; Ragusa, which was an independent republic ; not one of these belonged to France ; but that made no difference to the man devoid of conscience ; he made no scruple of taking, using, trading, or trampling the property or possessions of

[1] Bourrienne ii, 326-27.

others ; he was constantly doing deeds that, done on a small scale by a private person would, in any civilized or half-civilized country, have quickly brought the doer to a felon's fate richly deserved.

Mr. Fox was not a villain, so he did not, like Frederick William, trade for others' possessions and then commit high felony to get them. With honorable British manliness Fox refused these offers so like that made by the devil on the mount. Fox insisted on *uti-possidetis*.

September 3 came news that the Czar refused to ratify the D'Oubril treaty, and therefore France and Russia were not yet at peace. Then Napoleon was willing that George should recover Hanover; that the British retain Malta and Holland's Good Hope and Spain's Tobago and Indian Pondicherry; and that Spain should give to Ferdinand her own Balearic Isles, and that Ferdinand should give his own Sicily to Napoleon! Still a trade in other peoples! It would not have been at all singular in this trader in human beings and countries that he did not possess, if he had offered the American states to England as his minister, Fouché, did in 1810. There can be no doubt that he would readily have done it, if he had seen any chance for his own personal advantage in it. He wanted Cattaro, a spot on the Turkish border that might be made a base for aggressions against Turkey. Fox insisted on a guarantee of Turkey's security from his attack. British honor was safe in Fox's hands; he refused to give British sanction to the monstrous trade in peoples and countries. Great as were Napoleon's frauds they never gave him Sicily.

June 6, on Fox's motion, the House of Commons

voted to act with expedition to abolish the African slave trade. This was the last motion that Fox ever made. He was stricken with dropsy and marked for death as long before as March, early in his ministry.

A great statesman's last motion.
The slave trade, 1806.

It is hard to realize how great and virulent was the opposition for many years to the abolition of this odious trade. Many supported slavery and the slave-trade as having the sanction of the Bible.[1] The royal family were for slavery and against abolition. Many defended slavery as property not to be ruined. For many years Fox, Wilberforce, and others had struggled almost hopelessly for the prohibition. The Lords passed the bill to prohibit export of slaves from British colonies after January 1, 1807. It was not then generally known that the only way to abolish the slave-trade was to abolish slavery; that the demands for slaves would continue the trade illicitly, but enormously, for many years longer.

The Calabrians rebelled against their new king of Naples, Joseph Bonaparte. Sir John Stuart, with about 5,000 British and foreigners, crossed from Sicily into Calabria.

July 4, the French General, Regnier, with about 6,300 men, left his strong position at Maida and attacked Stuart in the plain. The French believed that no troops could stand their bayonet charge. They tried it. The British sustained the charge and completely routed the French, who retreated beyond the Apennines.

Maida.
July 4, 1806.

Stuart's force, like George III's usual expeditions,

[1] Martineau i, 181-84.

was too small to hold the country or drive out the French. Reduced by fevers, its remains went back to Sicily.

The expedition was almost useless,[1] but it showed what British troops could do if given a chance. What they might have done at Eylau to have rendered Napoleon's defeat there a complete overthrow.

Admiral Popham captured Buenos Ayres and made prize of $1,200,000, which he sent home to the British government. He also took quicksilver to double that value. Of course this property was pirated from private individuals. This piratical success produced a wild delirium of mercantile ideas in England; endless markets, boundless fields of wealth were in the English visions; great preparations were made to realize those visions; but in two months the South Americans expelled the British intruders after a bloody contest.

British attack Buenos Ayres June, 1806.

IX
"CATECHISM OF THE EMPIRE."

In 1806 Napoleon procured the signature of the pope's legate, Caprara, to the "Catechism of the Empire," which contained these blasphemous answers:—

> "Because God, by loading our emperor with gifts, both in peace and war, has established him our sovereign and his own image upon the earth, ... In honoring and serving our emperor thus we are honoring and serving God himself .... he has become the anointed of the Lord by the consecration which he received from the sovereign

[1] Martineau 1, 189-90.

pontiff .... those who fail in their duties towards our emperor will render themselves worthy of eternal damnation."

Thus Napoleon conscripted religion, and the Catholic Church into his own service!

Another answer acknowledged that: —

"We owe him (Napoleon) especially love, respect, obedience, fidelity and military service. ..... We ought to pay the taxes ordained."

X

NAPOLEON, the dishonest, still kept his army in Germany and compelled the Germans to feed and clothe it. He also continued to hold as prisoners 30,000 Austrians that he had pledged his word to liberate long ago. He was trying to compel Austria to submit to some new robbery on account of alleged popular insult to the French consul at Cattaro. *Germany. 1806.*

On July 12 a new "Confederation of the Rhine" was formed. It comprised Bavaria, Wurtemberg, Baden, Darmstadt, Berg, and several small states. The Archduke Ferdinand, formerly of Tuscany, who had escaped from Mack's army at Ulm, and had received the present of Wurzberg, was admitted. *Confederation of the Rhine. July, 1806.* It declared its states separated forever from the German empire, and placed under the "protection" of the emperor of the French. Any hostility against any of them was to be considered as war against the whole. The military contingents were fixed, for France 200,000 men; for German members, 58,000 men.

The Emperor Francis, no longer head of the German empire, nor German ruler, saw that the German empire had ceased; he renounced the Imperial crown and absolved Germans from duties to it.

Exit German empire, August 6, 1806.

Thus passed away the crown of Charlemagne which had endured for a thousand years and had accomplished an incredible amount of harm to human rights, happiness, and liberty. It is to Napoleon's credit, though he did it from the most selfish motive, that he destroyed that despotic, illiberal crown that for centuries had held so many millions of people in bondage and darkness. The Germans possess great merits, and had been greatly wronged by their rulers and their noblesse.

The Rhine Confederation was a vast increase of Napoleon's power, so it greatly offended the other great powers, especially Prussia, from which it was concealed until accomplished. Napoleon practically ruled the Confederation. Great was the consternation of Prussians when they saw this formidable, solid power appear at their door.

To conciliate Prussia, Napoleon intimated that if Frederick William wished to form a league of the north German states favorable to Prussia, he would not object. But he did object to including the Hanse towns in a Prussian league, or Saxony without its consent, and he tried to bring Hesse into his own Confederation. What was there left for Prussia's league? Prussia was thus again offended. Germany received some relief by abolition of several petty rulers. German rulers were hard masters. Now there was much union of public service with private servitude. The reign of Napoleon in Germany, as in many lands, was the period of plunder, of exaction rivalling and sometimes even surpassing that of their hereditary princes.

It was a generation fruitful of immorality, injustice and cruel exaction, misery, devastation, want, death. Acts of the enlightened nations were fertile in dishonor to the Christian name; of discredit to pure, noble, and generous Christian principles.

The Confederation being in complete vassalage to Napoleon, he afterward drew from it many more than the stipulated 58,000 soldiers.

Thus far, in Germany, Italy, and Austria, Napoleon had contended with rulers, often bad ones, not with the people themselves. Each of those countries was several states loosely held together, or actually disunited. The day was coming when he would meet the people in arms.

Carl von Dalberg, archbishop of Ratisbon, was an admirer of Napoleon; he adopted Napoleon's uncle, Cardinal Fesch, as his co-adjutor, thus making him primate of the German Catholic clergy.

Not content with the cheat and insults that he had put on Prussia, Napoleon took possession of the abbacies of Werden, Essen, and Elten, claimed by Prussia. German bitterness against him was fast increasing. People wondered what high robbery Napoleon would next commit. He did not long leave them in doubt. He demanded from the Hanse,—free cities,—the sum of 6,000,000 francs for his "protection;" what they needed "protection" from except his own rapacity, is what his own ambassador, Bourrienne, who made the demand and collected **the** robbery, confesses that he could not perceive. He really wished to destroy the long enjoyed freedom of those three towns, reduce them to all the evils of his arbitrary despotism, and take their cash from precisely the same motive that any other burglar takes property, to gratify himself. He compelled them to pay him roundly in money for the damage that he would do them. "I really had no advantage to offer in return to the Hanse towns," says Bourrienne (vol. ii, 328). These Hanse towns, Hamburg, Bremen, and Lubec, had then a population of 200,000; they carried on an extensive commerce on many seas and to many lands. As Napoleon was an enemy to trade and commerce, and really made war on it, he was the last ruler in Europe that could be likely to favor their prosperity, and the one that least deserved to rule or dictate them.

The brave, honorable, Prussian people were very angry; they saw with rage the insults by Napoleon, and with shame the unworthy character of their own king. Publications full of indignant eloquence issued from the press; the people became inflamed with patriotic passion.

Prussia. 1806.

Had the king possessed the wisdom and ability of the average Prussian, affairs would never have reached this stage of insult. Already grossly insulted before Austerlitz, Prussia should have thrown its forces upon Napoleon in the heart of Austria, and exacted ample security for the future from the man who disregarded human rights, nation's honor, common custom and comfort, and freely broke his own treaties and violated his own honor, and indulged the most testy, restless, quarrelsome temper in all

Europe; the man whom many admired as a marvelous soldier, but whom none loved; the most eminent man in the world, but without personal friends.

November, 1805, was Prussia's opportunity, a moment which an able man like Stein, Blücher, or Scharnhorst would have used to hurl Napoleon from his throne, to have secured safety and liberty to Germany and Prussia, to have left France to govern itself in its own way; and the old tyrannies of Europe would not, as they did in 1814-15, have re-enslaved the people of central Europe. Had Prussia had its own choice then, the ardent patriots, Stein and the gay, warm-hearted Blücher, would have led them. Prussia had the power in November, 1805, to soon place herself at the head of a confederated free Germany, and Stein and Blücher knew how then to do it and were ready. But the king in politics was too great an incumbrance. A republic, or a monarchial republic like England today, with the king excluded from politics, in the then existing state of Prussian public sentiment, would have had the great Stein at its head, supported by Blücher and Scharnhorst.

Prussians themselves, in spite of the king's restrictions of the press, saw all this; they had long seen the deplorable situation; they foresaw war as inevitable; they clamored for it in the right time for it, the autumn of 1805, yet then the king was weakly trying to be a friend to Napoleon, and expected a friend's reward from the man who bound men to him only by interest and did not deal in sentiment or ideal friendship. In 1805 the king held back his people when he ought to have obeyed their wishes; in 1806, when

Napoleon had goaded the Prussians into an enthusiastic madness for war, and the king ought to have held them in check until the Russian army, still a long way off, could come up to aid Prussia; the king, at this worst possible moment, decided for war.

When the king of Prussia learned that Napoleon was negotiating to give back Hanover to George III; that while urging Prussia to look to robbing Sweden of Pomerania for indemnity; that Napoleon had signed the D'Oubril treaty with Russia which would guarantee Sweden's possession of that same Pomerania; that while professing friendship for the king, Napoleon had offered not to oppose Russia's seizing Poland, including Prussian Poland, and establishing it under the Russian Grand Duke Constantine; that Napoleon was, as usual, still doing acts so criminal in their nature that such in commercial life would not only be disgraceful, but would soon consign the doer to a felon's fate, then Frederick William's small brain was utterly confounded.

The Confederation of the Rhine not only vastly increased Napoleon's power, but was a direct blow at Prussia. The foolish king had hoped to elevate his incompetent self to the head of the German Empire. It was now in Napoleon's power. One petty prince who was brother-in-law to the king, was now become tributary to Napoleon. This family matter, of no moment to Prussia, irritated the king more than a great insult to Prussia itself.

A writer has carelessly asserted that Napoleon was not immoral,[1] and Theirs says that the only cruel act

[1] Crowe I, 187.

of his career was the murder of his 4,000 helpless prisoners at Acre.

Napoleon's tendencies were all immoral, wicked. He was filled with pride, envy, cupidity, avarice, anger, revenge, greed, lust of power; he was faithless, rude and uncivil in manners; he lacked both honor and honesty; was very ungentlemanly in deportment; was very arbitrary; he wanted only servile instruments, who would not mind being frequently insulted; he was the champion liar of Europe; gigantic, cylopedian in intellect; he was in morality a very dwarf, a moral idiot; he was false to French liberty; he promised it but suppressed it; false to his marriage vows (his Polish lady of 1806-14 was not his only mistress); false to his most sacredly pledged word, for the treaties that he broke or evaded are many; utterly false to those who tried to be his friends, for never did man try harder to be a friend than did poor Charles IV of Spain, yet Napoleon dethroned him and detained him many years in France; than Frederick William did, yet we are now to see that the cold-hearted, ingrate Napoleon, treated him far worse than he treated his enemies. As to cruelty, his whole career is full of it. Not only his murder of the three hundred Russian police at Moscow, of which Napoleon boasts in his own letter of October 28, 1812, to the Czar Alexander; and the inhuman seige of Saragossa; but his whole Spanish war, his whole Russian war, his reckless exposure of his troops in the Eylau campaign to the terrible effects of northern winter, the fiendish campaign of murder and torture by Ruffo *vs.* Ruvo, under his auspices at

Real character of Napoleon.

Naples in 1798-99, and his brutal sacrifice of men's lives and limbs and health by compelling them to fight his aggressive, and frequently unprovoked, and sometimes entirely useless wars, all were cruel. He caused the loss of many hundreds of thousands of lives; he filled every land of Europe with cripples and invalids; scarcely a home in many lands but he deprived of some loved one; individuals he impoverished; countries he devastated; hearts he blighted; prosperity he blasted; yet he was all, all self.

In crime he was so gigantic that he has dazzled many good men into admiring him. To such I merely say, please analyze his real character coolly, impartially as you would weigh the evidence in a case if you were a member of a jury in a court of justice. I am not writing this history for the purpose of decrying any man or any country, nor for the object of lauding them, but only to represent facts as they exist. I do not propose to either spare or to excuse either Europe or America, or their prominent actors; that would not be real history.

Napoleon signalized his accession to German power by a cruel murder. Palm, a bookseller of Nuremberg, sold, as did other booksellers, a pamphlet in which resistance to French aggression was inculcated. Napoleon caused him to be seized, carried to the Austrian military post, Branau, which Napoleon had not restored to Austria as he had pledged his word to do, and there, at a long distance from the scene of the book sale, with the least possible chance of presenting evidence, among strangers and men foreign to him, Palm was put through the hasty forms of a military court that had been convened to condemn him; on Austrian soil, Palm, a German, of a free city, was, by French officers, sentenced and shot. This atrocious violation of the laws of God, of man, of nations, and of decency made profound sensation in all Germany, one of horror. Germans saw that no hope remained for public or private liberty or security, but in resistance to the grand murderer. The honorable, humane, and peace-loving Prussians became terribly in earnest for war. The war enthusiasm was everywhere.

When Pitt began the war in 1793 it was against the French republic, against what was called democracy; now all that was changed; it was now tyrant against tyrant, with small chance for the people. It was not till 1813–14 that the people of Germany came to the front for a little while, and Napoleon went down.

In August, 1806, the miserable Prussian king began to arm. His bad care had left the army unready and unfit for war. Some of the best troops in the world had only old favorites in command. As many a Prussian peasant had more natural ability than his king, so Prussia possessed many sub-officers far more capable of commanding her armies than her noblesse generals. Blücher and men of his sort were unpopular with the king.

The beautiful queen of Prussia was patriotic; but what could woman do when incumbered with so incompetent a husband and king?

The absurd king wanted the British to subsidize him while he tried to hold on to George III's Hanover![1]

[1] Scott i, 107.

The British withdrew their blockade of Prussian ports. Had the Prussian king been a respectable business man he could, no doubt, have procured valuable aid from the British.

> "The idea of peace was hateful to Prussia. Her measures, till now sufficiently moderate, suddenly assumed a menacing aspect on learning that the king of England had declared in Parliament that France had consented to restitution of Hanover. The French ministry intimated to the Prussian government that this was a preliminary step toward general peace, and that large indemnity would be granted in return. But the king of Prussia was well informed . . . . considered himself trifled with, and decided on war."[1]

October 1, 1806. The Prussian king's ultimatum was presented at Paris. It was:—

1. That the French troops forthwith evacuate Germany.

Ultimatum. 2. That France cease opposing a counter league of all the German states not in the Confederation of the Rhine.

3. That negotiations open for detaching the fortress of Wesel from France, and for the restoration of the abbacies which Murat had seized as a part of Berg.

With these terms was a long letter severely criticising Napoleon's encroachments; very just, perhaps, but very much out of place in that document. Sir Walter Scott remarks that the first two articles in that singular ultimatum:—

> "Were subjects rather of negotiation than grounds of an absolute declaration of war, and that Wesel and the three abbeys were scarce of importance enough to plunge the whole empire into blood. Prussia, indeed, was less actually aggrieved than she was mortified and offended. She saw that she had been outwitted by Buonaparte in the negotiation of Vienna; that he was juggling with her in the matter of Hanover; that she was in danger of beholding Saxony and

[1] Bourrienne ii, chap. xxx.

Hesse withdrawn from her protection to be placed under that of France; and, under a general sense of these injuries, though rather apprehended than really sustained, she hurried to the field. If negotiations could have been protracted till the advance of the Russian armies, it might have given a different face to the war; but in the warlike ardor which possessed the Prussians, they were desirous to secure the advantages which, in military affairs, belong to the assailants, without weighing the circumstances which, in their situation, rendered such precipitation fatal. Besides, such advantages were not easy to be obtained over Buonaparte."

The king should have known that to obtain any advantage as an assailant, would require that he quickly invade south Germany with an efficient and large army, and with superior celerity attack the greatest master of military celerity, in detail, before he could concentrate, which, had it not been absolutely impossible, would certainly have roused the princes of the Confederation of the Rhine, as well as the French troops coming direct from France, to fall upon the Prussian long line of base which was necessary to the existence of the Prussian army so far from Prussia. So advantage was impracticable.

Napoleon put in motion a 100,000 disciplined veterans from Branau, the Inn, the Neckar, against Prussia.

September 13, 1806, Charles J. Fox, the illustrious leader of liberal principles in Europe, passed from life into history. *Death of Fox.*

Says Gibbon:—

"I admired the powers of a superior man as they were blended in his attractive character with the simplicity of a child. No human being was ever more free from any taint of malignity, vanity or falsehood."

He was a great leader of the friends of the human race. The oppressed and the destitute saw in him their great champion. Says Chateaubriand:—

"Ever on the side of suffering, his eloquence acquired additional power from its gratuitous exertion in behalf of the unfortunate."

But his habits were too desultory, his indolence too great, his love of pleasure too powerful. He was peerless in debate; powerful in defending right; fascinating in winning affection. His great objects triumphed after he was dead; the abolition of the slave-trade and of slavery; emancipation of Great Britain from intolerance; reform of representation; a free republic in France; these were among his great hopes.

Charles Grey (Lord Howick) took Fox's place as Foreign Secretary.

In George's war department, under his pet son, the Duke of York: —

"Abuses which might match those of the navy were brought to light . . . . gross frauds of various kinds were exposed . . . . men of family and of fashion who did not know how to take care of themselves, and to maintain their station otherwise than by holding offices which they turned over to deputies, were placed in positions of trust which should have been filled by men of business . . . . millions of the public money for intervals of time without interest had been lent; there had been cheat in coal and in blankets, while soldiers shivered for want of them."[1]

Spain, unwillingly, had been drawn into the war by Napoleon solely for his purposes, not for hers. Now with her navy crippled, her harbors blockaded by his enemy, Great Britain; her intercourse with her many valuable colonies cut off; war made on her because she was domineered by him; she saw him exclude her from taking part in the common negotiations for peace, and learned with surprise that he had proposed to trade away her Balearic Islands for his own benefit; that he was assembling an army at Bayonne

Spain. 1806.

[1] Martineau's Eng. i, 199.

on her border, ostensibly against the independence of Portugal, but really where it might threaten Spain.

Godoy, indignant at these outrages, no sooner heard that peace had failed and Prussia was in arms, than he raised more troops and watched for a chance to free Spain from Napoleon's alliance.

Britain and Prussia easily resumed friendship. The madcap king of Sweden was pacified by allowing him the childish privilege of holding Lauenburg for George III. The Czar promised to aid Prussia with 70,000 men. Prussia strongly urged Austria to take part with her, but as no reliance could be placed in the vacillating king of Prussia, and Austria was not prepared financially or otherwise, she declined. Prussia was in 1806, strangely enough, repeating the great mistake of Austria of 1805. The Elector of Hesse Cassel armed 20,000 men for neutrality.

Though Napoleon soon had more than 180,000 men rapidly approaching Prussia, supported by strong reserves, the Prussians were in excess of war enthusiasm. But their important fortresses were uprepared, almost unprovisioned, Prussia not ready. hardly were the guns mounted. The strong places likely to be the first scenes of combat were in deplorable state; depots were not formed; no central rallying point was prepared for chance of disaster or defeat, although the great fortresses of Magdeburg, Wittenberg, and Torgau lay at the right spots just in the rear of the probable theater of the war.

Frederick William and his brother kings were combatting common rights everywhere. He would not give command, as Napoleon did, to men who had military merit alone. None but nobles could command his troops. This was a source of frightful calamity to his people. At this great crisis, when about to risk the fate of Prussia against the ablest commander of Europe, the king foolishly gave the command to the Duke of Brunswick, the very man who lost the decisive Cannonade of Valmy in 1792, a noble weak in mind, infirm, obstinate, and generally disliked. The king took to the field as his own mentor, old Mollendorf, who bore the weight of eighty-two years. It was Prussia, unprepared, with her 9,500,000 people against Napoleon, prepared, with his 40,000,000 subjects.

These incapables took as their plan the very same system which they had seen prove so disastrous to Austria the previous year. Prussia had not even the advantage of numbers.

The war plan.

Prussia's policy should have been delay till a Russian army and British aid were at hand.

But sagacious policy was beyond the capacity of Frederick William. Men like Von Stein and Haugwitz were then kept in background.

Extreme prudence was needed; but the Prussian army was rashly thrust forward in a long, scattered, ill-connected, badly supported line, in a place not well situated to support a great army. To crown these follies, their magazines and depots of provisions were wrongly located at Naumberg, on their extreme left, exposed to risk of being cut off by the French.

Saxony, in 1806, like Bavaria in 1805, desired only to be neutral. But Frederick William resolved to force that peaceful people to fight on his side.

He succeeded. The Prussian army entered Saxony uninvited. They treated the Saxons more like tributaries than like allies. The united Prussian and Saxon army was a very large one, probably about 150,000 men. Saxony had suffered too severely from Prussia in the eighteenth century to be very friendly.

The Prussian army threatened Franconia. But Marshal Bernadotte quickly seized all the mountain passes of that route.

October 9, Napoleon's army moved from Bamberg. On the right Soult and Ney marched from Bayreuth via Hof on Plauen; on the center moved Murat's cavalry, with Bernadotte's and Davoust's corps from Bamberg, via Cronach on Saalbourg. The Prussian commander, Brunswick, neglected even to guard the passes through the forest.

Napoleon begins the Prussian War. Oct. 9, 1806.

The French caught the Prussians at disadvantage, and easily turned their badly exposed left wing, and moved on their left rear to cut them off from their stores at Naumberg.

The Prussian general and king had managed so badly that, in presence of Napoleon, who was remarkably quick to take advantage, they were thrown into a change of position and complicated cross movements, with their flank exposed to the French, an extremely perilous position.

The men performed their evolutions with remarkable skill and precision, but they had already been marched and countermarched till they had lost confidence in their incapable leaders, who in a council of war so late as October 6, had been unable to settle on a plan of campaign!

The king and Brunswick saw that they must concentrate. It was their left that was turned. Instead of concentrating in that direction, they made the astonishing blunder of concentrating toward their center, precisely the certain way to allow Soult and Ney to pass through their left and get between the Prussians and their supplies.

The Prussians lost at the very outset, the moral advantage of advance, and, on the very first day the French captured important stores that the Prussians much needed.

October 9 the Prussians at Schleitz were defeated and driven with loss. October 10 Murat captured five hundred wagons and a pontoon train. On the same day, Louis, who, because he was a prince, held himself above orders, disobeyed and caused the serious defeat of the column that he commanded in the Prussian front. The French took from him 1,200 prisoners and thirty cannon. This serious defeat greatly dispirited the badly led Prussian soldiers and their excellent line and regimental officers.

Then Prussian headquarters fell back from Erfurt to Wiemar. Jena being evacuated the French seized it. The Prussians might have taken position at Domberg, the highest ground near Jena, but the king neglected it. The bad management caused food and ammunition to become scarce among the troops. Royal incapacity destroyed alacrity.

Their line was broken in several places; concentration interrupted; their supplies in part lost; their march intercepted; dejected columns without fixed rallying point were wandering about; while the French, led by officers who had risen to command by soldierly qualities were taking the badly led Prussians at great disadvantage. The Prussians became despondent. They saw the helplessness of bad command. In deep dejection, they were assembled with difficulty in two bodies, one near Wiemar under the king, the other near Jena under Prince Hohenlohe, who was placed in command not because he was a good soldier but because he was a prince.

The advance of the French on Naumberg cut off the Prussians from retreat to Leipsic; the French had gone beyond the Prussians, turned around, and now faced toward France; the Prussians had faced about toward Prussia, just as sixty-four years later their two armies were again placed at the defeat of the French at Gravelotte.

On the night of October 12 Prince Hohenlohe's command of perhaps 55,000 men was formed on the heights; his advanced post was a steep hill (Landgraffenberg) from which his whole line could be seen. Over this hill lay the only road by which to attack him.

The king and Brunswick had concentrated about 65,000 men above a league in the rear.

Bonaparte sent proposals of peace, which the king did not receive until after the great battle.

These two great bodies of Prussians of whom 18,000 were superb cavalry, with 300 cannon, urged by lively patriotism, supported by ardent hatred of Napoleon, animated by the warm prayers of Prussians, charged with the dearest national hopes of Prussia, men who had come with warmest blessings from loved homes of fatherland to protect their own nation from foreign conquest, these 120,000 choice young patriots of Prussia were to measure strength with the French grand army, already veteran victors over some of the best armies that Europe had yet ever seen. It was a day momentous for Europe, thrice doubly momentous for Prussia. Not a man in Prussia, not the highest noble, not the humblest peasant but had a tremendous stake in that day's doings. Not a person in all Germany but had great interests in the result of that day's great battles. Prussia's independence or fate, Germany's liberation or vassalage were to be decided. Germany was to be freed from Napoleon's oppressive grasp, or Prussia, too, was to fall.

No better people existed. She was threatened with terrible disaster; her people were generously brave; her great need now was a general. Incapacity in the government had brought her to this frightful danger. Her soldiers were ready to die saving her. Oh, for one day of her great soldier, Frederick II! Had her own Blücher organized that campaign and commanded that patriot army, then subsequent history of central Europe might have been different.

Each army having passed its opponent cut off the other's communications. But the French still had a line of retreat to the Main via Hof; the Prussians, separated from their supplies of food and amunition, had no resource but victory.

At this moment of tremendous interest, when fate of Prussia was to be quickly decided, the Prussian king made a hazardous flank march of ten leagues and arrived at night at Aerstadt. Surprising folly! Instead of fighting Napoleon with all his force, the king left less than half to receive the shock of Napoleon's terrible legions. Napoleon, unaware of this strange move, prepared to fight the whole Prussian army.

The French light troops dislodged the Prussian advance guard from a steep hill directly in front of the Prussians. Napoleon went there. He saw the Prussians quiet in their strong position on the opposite ridge. Not doubting that their whole army were there awaiting attack, he stationed Lannes' infantry to hold this important hill. The Prussian prince now saw his great mistake in not holding that hill. He prepared to retake it, but desisted. Its possession enabled Napoleon to see the Prussian movements, while the hill masked his own. The French made a road up their side of this steep hill and brought up artillery and cavalry.

<small>Jena. Oct. 13, 1806.</small>

Napoleon ordered Soult and Ney to march all night by the right in order to turn the left of the Prussian position; he ordered Davoust toward Naumburg to threaten the Prussian rear; he sent Bernadotte to Domberg to cut off retreat.

The two hostile armies were near each other; each could see the night gleam of the other's bivouac fires. The firelight of the Prussians illuminated the night over a broad space, and threw a great glow into the heavens; those of the French were more contrated. Thus passed this eternity's eve of many thousands of brave men.

At early dawn, Napoleon, on horseback, rode among his advance troops. He addressed them: —

"Soldiers: The Prussian army is turned as the Austrian was a year ago at Ulm; it no longer combats but to find the means of retreat. The corps which should permit itself to be broken would be dishonored. Fear not its renowned cavalry; oppose their charges in squares with bayonets."

Loud cheers responded.

Hohenlohe was not expecting an attack. He intended to give his weary men a day of rest. The Prussian position was strong; its flanks were secured; in front were steep, narrow defiles, bad for French manœuvering.

The early morning came, dim, misty, a fog covered everything. The French descended into the front low ground. On their right a sharp fight began.

Low down the morning mist began to rise. The Prussian advance guard were astonished when they saw the grand army in force advancing right on them. Yet these surprised Prussians made a gallant resistance, so vigorous as to indicate what Prussians might have done with a good general. They were driven back on the main body with the loss of twenty cannon. The French emerging from the defiles, extended their line from right to left. Still Hohenlohe, the prince, not at the front, believed this affair to be only a skirmish. He said "his troops should remain quiet in camp till the fog had risen." The incessant discharges of musketry and the breathless messengers demanding aid, soon convinced him that it was attack in force.

On the heights the mist was still so thick, so almost impenetrable, so favorable to such attack, that the combatants could see each other only at a very short distance. The prince had failed to secure the defiles; he lost the precious moments when he should have held the great advantage of keeping his enemy in the gorges. A commander like Wellington or Sherman or Bagration would have made those defiles a scene of frightful loss to the French.

At last the sun dispelled the fog. The Prussians were startled at sight of their deadly peril. The French grand army no longer struggling through steep, narrow, and dangerous gorges where they might have been terribly repulsed, now stood before them, magnificently deployed, with their cavalry and artillery upon the broad expanse to which the gorges led them. In front a large French force had taken the villages at the foot of the Prussian position. They were preparing to ascend to close conflict. To right and left were other great bodies of French in battle order. Another mass was pressing forward to turn the Prussian right. Murat's splendid cavalry stood on the slopes in reserve. 135,000 men were about to join in tremendous battle. 80,000 healthy, vigorous young men led by Napoleon were about to make deadly attack on 55,000 of the physically best young men of Prussia.

There will be bitter tears of mourning shed in Europe for the bloody deaths of this fearful day. 135,000 men, each one of whom other persons love, the active, most choice young manhood of many nations. The gay-spirited men from far off Catalona, and from the soft climes of farther Andalusia; the grave men from the mountains beyond the Pyrenees, lent out by the foolish king Charles IV of Spain; dark-faced men from Rome and Genoa; sons of the sunny south of Naples; liberty-loving Piedmontese; bright, active Milanese; men from all shores of the distant Adriatic; men from the high Alps; steady Dutch from flat Holland; sprightly, vivacious, Walloons from the Meuse, and sober men from Flanders; men from almost every state of Germany; men of several languages and races, of diverse civilizations, religions, manners; men from all the lands from the North Sea to the far south Taranto; men from the Elbe to Gibraltar; such was the strange medley combined with the French to form the grand army.

To defend their country against this variegated horde of sudden invaders were only the Prussians aided on compulsion by Saxons.

Men of every nation of the continent west of Russia and Austria and south of Denmark, were killed, torn, mutilated, or crippled for life, that day at Jena and Aerstadt.

Those were all men of Christian lands, and so-called Christians mutilate, cripple and kill each other on far grander scale than do benighted savages. Christians on both sides were imploring a merciful God to fight on their side; calling on the highest Holy to take part in devil's carnage, to bless Satan's work.

What was all this war for?

Their imperial and royal masters had disagreed — well, what was it all about? I have, in previous pages, described the "causes" of this un-Christian Christian war; but really what it was all about was to decide just which of two sets of oppressors should tyrannize over and wrong these very prime young men, and the very families, fathers mothers, wives, children, relations and countrymen of these gallant youths who now stood ready each to do all that a devil's malice could do, "to welcome with bloody hands to hospitable graves" the opposing gallant youths.

These young men had no quarrel with each other; they were there to fight and die merely for masters who practically owned and disposed of their lives and limbs as personal property; living, loving, hating, armed men, but still, to every practical intent and purpose, held as property, fought as property, dying as property of their rulers.

Many battles have been glowingly described; yet nobody sees a battle in detail; the volumes of rolling smoke hide it; frequently the nature of the ground is such that it is masked from view.

My own observation in battles is that by a rattling fire where a moment ago you heard great rolling vollies; by the confused noises where you just now heard the steady tramp of regularly moving columns; by the sudden cessation of field artillery here and its prompt reappearance farther advanced or more retired; by the changing position whence come to you through the thick driving smoke, the sounds of cheering over points won; by the rising and eddying, the storming and receding of sounds; although you can see but little at once, still you know how the battle is going.

The Jena battle-ground disappeared under smoke; the terrible conflict raged in this semi-darkness; at length the sounds told Napoleon on the hill in the rear, that the Prussians were yielding.

Then advanced Murat's splendid cavalry; 12,000 horsemen, fresh and in fine array, rode into the smoke, the blazing of the great combat; they galloped upon the wearied, yielding Prussians.

The Prussian cavalry, that morning, brilliant, effective, dashing, now wearied by eight hours of fighting, once again made gallant resistence, were broken now at last; horse, foot, cannon pressed in wild tumult together, hurried to the rear, followed by the French bloody sabers; all Prussian order was lost; in confusion blended men, horses, cannon, caissons; no longer is it a battle, it is bloody, fierce, horrible massacre.

A little later all gave way; the Prussian army, reserve and all, a broken army; a defeated, rushing torrent of fugitives, poured from the battle-ground, pursued by the victors as far as Wiemar, six leagues away. Why had not the other 65,000 Prussians been there to save Prussia? Because the king had marched them away!

But Jena was not the main battle of that day. The decisive contest was fought by Marshal Davoust at Aerstadt with about 30,000 men against the king with all that he could bring up of his 65,000.

Aerstadt. Oct. 13, 1806.

The Prussians were in open column and straggling as all troops will straggle when not well commanded. They were advancing toward the Elbe, when suddenly they were met by the vanguard of Davoust on the summit of Aerstadt. So dense was the fog that neither saw the other till very near. Each mistook its enemy for only a detachment. Each fell back to collect force to clear the way; the Prussians to drive the French down the defile which they had just ascended.

Speedily reinforced, each side attacked; neither yielded; both were obstinate. Davoust threw forward Gudin's division; the king ordered Blücher with 2,500 cavalry to clear the plateau of the French. A body of French cavalry were overthrown by the suberb Prussian horsemen; they in turn were shattered against the French infantry.

Then the fog disappeared; the sun shone out; it revealed to each side that an army was facing it. There were the splendid regiments and regular lines of the Prussians, and there the French squares, and behind hedges and garden walls of a village stood their lines.

The Prussian infantry and dragoons came on in a dashing charge. The French fired continuously and murderously.

The king's general, the Duke of Brunswick, fell mortally wounded; the second in command, Schmettau, was shot; the king's mentor, old Mollendorf, was killed.

The Prussian attack, not in column, but in line, began to waver; the terrible musketry fire blazed continuously; the artillery fire swept through both sides.

Gudin's French division was terribly depleted; nearly one of every two had fallen; they could hold out alone but little longer; it would be ruin to yield the ground. Under that awful devastation they held together till two more French divisions arrived.

The narrow defile of Aerstadt would not admit of bringing up the overwhelming Prussian force at once. The opposite defile of Koessen would not permit the French to arrive more rapidly.

A powerful body of Prussian cavalry surmounted a height and struck the French left. In squares the

French received its repeated impetuous charges. These intrepid horsemen dashed up to the very bayonets of the French; they rode around the steady squares, trying to break them; the fast flashing fire, streaming from these flaming human walls, over an impenetrable hedge of gleaming bayonets which the kneeling front rank presented, compelled even this desperately brave Prussian cavalry to recoil; in disorder it fell back; the cavalry charge had failed; infantry had beaten this celebrated cavalry; this was a notable event in military science.

Now on their right the French assumed the attack; they were pressing for the heights of Sonnenberg, whence their guns could command the area of battle, and make untenable the position of the Prussian reserves. The Prussians saw that French possession of that height would decide the battle; to prevent it they made a tremendous charge; the French met them; for minutes the balance trembled; then the French began to gain; still the contest raged; then the French artillery, which they had dragged up to the summit of the height of Eckartsberg, opened its destructive fire into the Prussian ranks; that decided it; the French had won that part of the bloody field.

These heights of Eckartsberg commanded the line of Prussian retreat. The engaged Prussians were forced back on 15,000 Prussians that had not been engaged, crowding and embarassing them with a crush of men, guns and horses. Taking advantage of this jammed condition of the Prussians, a great attack of the French in force defeated and drove this reserve. Aerstadt was lost; Prussia was lost; all was lost.

"THE PRUSSIAN CAVALRY CHARGED."

That day at Jena, Napoleon, with 80,000 men, had, with difficulty, defeated 55,000 Prussians and Saxons. Davoust, at Aerstadt, with 30,000, had crushed the king of Prussia with 65,000. Yet common fame gives Napoleon the military credit, and incorrectly calls the great victory that prostrated Prussia — Jena. It was Aerstadt. Napoleon[1] gave Davoust but little credit, and meanly represented that he had fought 80,000 Prussians at Jena, and Davoust but 50,000 at Aerstadt!

The extent of mismanagement of the high-born Prussian commanders is astonishing. They had ruined Prussia. The number of the Prussians killed and wounded is believed to be about 20,000. They lost nearly as many taken prisoners[2] and 200 cannon and many standards. The amount of the loss of the French is uncertain as Napoleon's report is entirely unreliable. It was large. Alison estimates it at 14,000.

A general panic ensued. The cross tide of fugitives from Aerstadt and Jena intersected each other in the retreat. Infantry, cavalry, artillery dispersed, leaving horses, guns, carriages, ruin in the roads, and fled across the fields without appointed rallying point and in any direction.

The retreat.

In one day these two battles prostrated the Prussian monarchy that had withstood the power of Austria, Russia, and France in the "Seven Years' War." The next day Napoleon assessed Prussia 134,000,000 francs, Saxony 25,000,000.[3]

Erfurth contained the Prussian grand park of artil-

---

[1] Lanfrey iii, 167. [2] Koch-Schell ii, 218. [3] Nearly $30,000,000 in all.

lery, stores, and camp equipage. Two days after these battles it surrendered with 14,000 men, 120 cannon, and immense war stores. More than 7,000 of these prisoners were wounded men.

"The carelessness, the unskillfulness, or the treachery of their commanders, and the want of means of defense, were the causes why several fortresses and whole bodies of troops surrendered after slight resistance."[1]

October 27, the Prussian reserve, also commanded by a prince, Eugene of Wurtemberg, was beaten near Halle by Bernadotte, who took about 4,000 prisoners.[2]

The French crossed the Elbe, marched into Potsdam, took the strong fortress Spandau, and they entered Berlin, October 25 [1806.]

Prince Hohenlohe surrendered near Prentzlau, October 28, with 17,000 men and 6,000 cavalry capitulated at Passewalk, October 29. The great fortress of Stettin yielded, October 28; Kuestrin, October 31.

To the astonishment of the world, the almost impregnable fortress of Magdeburg, a main fortress, the great bulwark of Prussia, capitulated with 22,000 men.[3] Hamelin followed with 6,000 and Nieuberg with 4,000.[3] Near Lubec, Blücher's 21,000 men laid down their arms.[3] In six weeks from Aerstadt and Jena, nearly all Prussia to the Oder had fallen into the power of Napoleon. He ruthlessly seized neutral Fulda with which he had no quarrel. He regarded whatever he could seize as good prize. He declared the neutral Elector of Hesse an enemy and seized his territories in alliance. He occupied the unoffending free Hanse towns, for nothing was sacred from his rapacity. Later he took possession of

[1] Koch-Schell ii, 218.   [2] Schlosser vii, 512 : Coote, 131-133
[3] Anl. Reg.: Koch ii, 48; Scott, 115; Rosteck, 171.

Mecklenburg, Brunswick, and of the Czar's uncle's duchy of Oldenburg. But he dismissed the Saxon prisoners with only their promise not to serve against France. The Saxon Elector recalled his troops from Prussia, accepted first neutrality, and then alliance with Napoleon.

But Napoleon delayed definite peace with Saxony till December, while he plundered it.

Says the German, Schlosser: —

"The officials, accustomed to serve those from whom they had their living, served the French as they did in Hanover and other occupied countries, and afterward in Prussia: official life and tax-gathering remained precisely as it was except that Frenchmen or half Frenchmen, were placed at the head of the extorting machine." [1]

Napoleon robbed Leipsic and Wittemberg of 6,000,000 francs each. Elsewhere he laid heavy robberies.

His treaty of December 12, 1806, with Saxony, conferred the title "king" on the Elector, which was useless and increased Saxon expenses.

The newly made king was required to join Napoleon's "Confederation of the Rhine," a vassal, that the blood and property of his unlucky subjects might swell the strength of Napoleon. He gave the French a military road through Saxony. Napoleon forced him into the war against Prussia, to furnish at first 5,800 soldiers, and then more than 20,000.

Negotiations began October 21. Napoleon proposed: —

1. That Prussia cede all her possessions between the Elbe and the Weser.

2. That Prussia shall pay 100,000,000 francs.

3. That she refrain from interfering in German affairs.

[1] Schlosser vii, 511.

4. That she unconditionally approve all the changes made or to be made.

The Prussian answer was delayed nine days; events had progressed; then Napoleon gave no reply to the Prussian note signifying that the king would accept these terms.

Napoleon visited the tomb of Frederick the Great at Potsdam. With his own hands he robbed the tomb of the cordon of the Black Eagle, and the sword and scarf of the great Prussian soldier. Shameless in this sacrilege he sent them to Paris.

A brilliant, triumphal procession, headed by Davoust, was made into the Prussian capital.

"Under Clark's government, at Berlin, the inhabitants were subjected to all kinds of oppression and exaction."[1]

October 21, 1806, Napoleon issued his famous "Berlin Decree," which will be explained elsewhere.

Attempts to make a treaty failed; Napoleon asked too much.[2]

Napoleon advanced toward the Vistula with fresh forces following in the rear. He awed the Prussian states.

He required a fresh conscription of 80,000 from the boys who would reach the military age the next year [1807]. He pressed the troops of Hesse into his service.

His offer of armistice on very severe terms by which the strong places, Breslau, Glogau, Colberg, Graudenz, and Dantzic should surrender to him was refused by the king.

A Russian army of 90,000 men arrived in Poland in November. The Prussians collected 40,000 troops. It was with difficulty that artillery could be moved.

[1] Bourrienne ii, 358.   [2] Bourrienne ii, 371.

Both sides suffered severely from bad roads, bad weather, and all sorts of privations.[1]

After repelling the Russian advance guard, Murat reached Warsaw. The French found the passage of the river Bug sharply contested, but they succeeded in passing it.

The Czar had been active in repairing his losses of the previous year in the Austrian war. New regiments were formed and old ones filled. A great conscription was made. He called for 600,000 militia to aid to defend Russia, their homes, and their religion. He summoned students and young nobles with promise that they should be officers after six months' service. The priests were ordered to proclaim that Napoleon is a relentless foe to Christianity; they were called to defend their faith. Alexander's effort to excite a religious fervor for the war, was generally ridiculed in Europe, but it greatly aided to arouse peasants to become soldiers.

Forty days after the French crushed the power of Prussia at Aerstadt-Jena, Alexander sent a Russian army, unwisely, aggressively, into Moldavia. Indeed to invade Turkey at that moment was an act of extreme folly. He had time to have recalled his orders to again attempt to rob the Turks of two provinces. It was an ill-chosen time for such greed. An able government would have concentrated all the Russian available forces for protection against the terrible foe that was approaching and threatening Russia, and left the Turks to enjoy their own in peace.

As Prussia had made the same blunder at the beginning of her campaign of 1806 that Austria had

[1] Bourrienne ii, 379.

made in 1805, so "during the Prussian campaign Austria played the same waiting game which Prussia had played during the campaign in Austria."[1] She assembled 40,000 men in Bohemia as near the scene of war as was prudent. If Napoleon should meet with disaster she could fall upon him at the right moment; if he should be successful she could keep aloof and quiet.

Napoleon, acting as a great bandit, made enormous demands. Hamburg, the free city, had never been at war on either side; it had given Napoleon neither insult nor injury; all it asked was to be let alone; yet of Hamburg Napoleon demanded 50,000,000 francs. It escaped that time by the immediate payment of 16,000,000 francs and 50,000 overcoats.[1] Lubec, Leipsic, and other neutral towns he also robbed of large sums.[2] Thus by robbery he obtained clothing, magazines, and stores. By December he had eight corps on the Vistula ready for service. After guarding his strong points, he had 100,000 men for the field, and more were coming.

Napoleon arrived at Warsaw December 2. With patriotic ardor the Poles hailed him as their prospective deliverer. A provisional government of Warsaw was formed "until its fate should be settled by a general peace." The Poles were animated with hope; the national dress was resumed; national music was again heard; several regiments of horsemen were quickly enrolled; before the campaign ended 30,000 Poles were enrolled in Prussian Poland. Napoleon encouraged it in Prussian, but not in Austrian or Russian Poland.

[1] Bourrienne ii, 379.   [2] Bourrienne.

Europe had not been accustomed to war in winter. This Napoleon had done at Austerlitz, as Pichegru had successfully done in Holland in 1795. Now Kamenskoi, the Russian commander eighty-one years old, made the active advance.

With severe fighting the French succeeded in crossing the Ukra, and separated the Russian forces into two parts; one part moved for Golymin, the other toward Pultusk.

The continuous forest, the deep mud, the roads cut and ruined by the many wheels, offered difficult obstacles.

Old Kamenskoi ordered a retreat with great sacrifice of artillery stuck in the mud.

Benningsen, with his corps, disobeyed the absurd orders of the old chief and resolved to hold Pultusk to gain time for the artillery and equipage to pass on to the rear. With about 40,000 men and 120 cannon he made a stand. Three other Russian divisions were too far to the rear to assist.

The French plan was similar to that of Ulm. Its right was to cut the Russian retreat; its left to interpose between them and the Prussians, under Lestoc.

The vigor of the Russian retreat, its celerity aided by Kamenskoi's sacrifice of seventy cannon; the heavy rains; the very short days and long, dark nights; the obstructed nature of the country, that so impeded the French advance, enabled the Russians to reach both Pultusk and Golymin a few hours before the French, instead of being, as Napoleon intended, cut off from those points.

Battle of Pultusk. Dec. 26, 1806.

A terrible conflict ensued at Pultusk. The fight

was in the midst of nature's horrors. Winter, disturbed by these ardent warriors, was angry. A wild storm was sweeping over the gloomy north. In the midst of the thunders of cannon and the crashes of musketry, heavy snowfalls filled the air and obscured everything; men fought without seeing each other; the mud was, in many places, knee-deep; the maneuvers were difficult; men fell to be trampled deeper in mud, while still alive; wounded, crippled men were crawling in snow and mud; the battle-ground was a pandemonium of human suffering, a very carnival of misery. The darkness of night came and added to the frightful horrors. Still, carnage, frightful death, human tortures, most dreadful, everywhere. Nature's wild, wintry storm, quite late, renewed its fury. As if angry, indignant at man's horrible doings, its blasts at last separated the fierce combatants.

In the intense darkness of this northern winter's night, on that terribly storm-swept, war-mangled and battle-torn spot, more dismal than Plutonian shore, in the deep snow-covered mud, lay nearly 5,000 Russians, and between 6,000 and 8,000 of Napoleon's conscripts of many nations, — called French, — the wounded, the mutilated, the dead, all together.

And for all this neither side was decisively victorious. The Russians had the advantage. The French plodded their weary way a few miles in retreat.

The Russians held the battle-ground till midnight; then, in the deep darkness of a sixteen-hours night, they resumed their retreat to Russia, "leaving in the mud of Poland eighty field pieces and nearly 10,000 men,"[1] including the loss at Pultusk.[2]

[1] Rambaud ii, 287; Lanfrey iii, 214. [2] Napoleon's 47th Bulletin says 12,000.

Another battle on the same day at Golymin was not decisive. The French took twenty-six cannon and a large train of army wagons, but they suffered severe loss. Here again the Russians held their ground till midnight, and then retired. The French extreme left, under Ney and Bernadotte, drove the remains of the Prussian army, under Lestoc, into Konigsberg. Battle of Golymin. Dec. 26, 1806.

Could Soult, according to Napoleon's plan, have reached the rear of the Russian army that had fought and retired from Pultusk and Golymin, and so barred their retreat, they must have been compelled to surrender; but the depth of mud, the fierceness of the weather which deluged the troops with drenching rains, pelting sleet, and driving and melting snow, and the activity of the Russians, completely defeated his plans. "Men fell in great numbers without a battle."

It was a very cruel war, made, as the eminent Frenchman, Guizot, says: —

"In the service of a senseless ambition, as fatal to the sovereign as to the people, both foolishly dragged along by a vision of glory toward injustices and crimes.[1]

The war had no necessity; peace was long ago at Napoleon's call; his useless, awful continuation of needless war was excess of cruelty.

Rest was necessary. The aggressor ceased to advance. Both armies went into winter quarters.

Sickness swept over devastated Prussia. It was a winter of misery, of general robbery, of moral dishonor to Napoleon and his troops of many nations.

[1] History of France vii, chap. ix.

Both parties claimed the victory; the Invalides cannon roared triumph at Paris; with better reason *Te Deum* was chanted at St. Petersburg. But Napoleon was in a struggle unlike anything he had before experienced. His winter campaign had failed. The Russians were not defeated. To the folly of Alexander in sending an aggressive army against Turkey when he ought to have concentrated all his strength against Napoleon's hordes with a vigorous commander instead of old Kamenskoi, it was that Napoleon owed his escape from crushing defeat.

Napoleon tried to stimulate the Poles to rise in great numbers. Says Guizot:—

"In their turn the Poles, long crushed down by harsh servitude, asked for guarantees from the conqueror, who had only delivered them in order to subjugate them afresh."

They knew too well his character for falsity. They dared not trust him. A spurious address with the unauthorized name of Kosciusco was circulated to arouse them. Kosciusco declared it false.

The Prussian fortresses in Silesia yielded one after another to the invading French. The surrender of Kustrin furnished abundant war material for the reduction of Glogau, which, in its turn, furnished from its vast stores the needed armament for the reduction of Breslau, which yielded 6,000 prisoners, 300 cannon, and immense stores. Brieg and Kosel fell. Jerome Bonaparte was made governor of Silesia.

The Czar now saw what all the world had seen, his great blunder in making the war with Turkey. He ordered 25,000 men from there to the Neimen. Napoleon took measures to stimulate the Turks against Russia. Ever vindictive, he tried to rouse Persia to attack the Russians.

Old Kamenskoi was far in the rear of his army, and if not actually insane was mentally unfit to command. So Buxhowden and Benningsen each commanded his own corps, and each was jealous of the other whom he would not obey.

At last Alexander saw the folly of this situation and gave the chief command to Benningsen. But the armies did not long stay in winter quarters. Benningsen opened the campaign again in February. Bernadotte with 55,000 men was away off to the left of the other French. Ney was next. Benningsen came on with 75,000 Russians and 500 cannon, hoping to get between Bernadotte and Ney and attack Ney's scattered forces. But winter's frozen ground did not enable him to arrive soon enough, and he was too hesitating. The move caused several severe contests, with varying fortunes.

Napoleon put the grand army in motion. He sent an order to Bernadotte to decoy the Russians as far as possible, that he might fall upon their flank while in march. This order fell into Benningsen's hands; it warned him of Napoleon's plan.

Benningsen fell back. After serious fighting he concentrated from 55,000 to 65,000 men at Preuss-Eylau. He must have lost already 10,000 men in this movement since January 4.

February 8 came the bloodiest battle that Napoleon had yet seen. *Battle of Eylau. Feb. 8, 1807.* Eylau was a town in a hollow between the two armies. Mistaking their orders, the Russians who were to have defended it, fell back; the French seized it; the Russians soon retook it by a fierce attack. It is said that the Russians had 400 cannon on their front.

The forces of Napoleon were about 85,000 men. Stronger in cavalry, they were weaker in artillery than Benningsen.

At the first the Russians gained advantage; but they did not press it with sufficient rapidity, and so gave time for French corps to come up and greatly outnumber them.

Napoleon made a violent attack on their right and center; Marshal Augereau advanced in heavy force; Soult, with 150 cannon on his front, marched against their center; 40 more guns thundered against the Russian central battery.

The Russian cannon shot ploughed fearful gaps through the mass of advancing French; 200 guns were there working with frightful rapidity; Napoleon was meeting heavy losses.

Then heavy snowfall darkened the heavens and filled the air so thick as to shut out the combatants from each other's sight.

But the deadly storm of bullets and cannon shot continued to destroy those devoted men in the wintry gloom.

When shaken, terribly torn and shattered, Augereau's division, on his left, suddenly saw, at only a few yards' distance, the long lances of the Cossack horsemen emerging from the thick falling snow screen. Almost at the same instant Russian cavalry dashed and crashed against his right almost unseen.

Here in torrents of blood ended the career of Augereau's corps. The fight was terrific. It was brief;

it was quick; the slaughter was appalling; the French were broken; they gave way; in shattered fragments they fled in confusion.

The Russian sabers and Cossack lances were quick after them; the great corps of more than 16,000 French, so intrepid a few minutes before, Napoleon's own warriors, were sabered and trampled in great numbers; the great corps was annihilated; it never again appeared as a corps.

The Russians pursued the fugitives so closely that they were near taking Napoleon himself a prisoner. The Russian pursuers were disordered by success, and before they could reform their ranks the French were upon them on both flanks, and almost a whole division were slaughtered.

Soult's attack on the Russian center was repulsed. The French were beaten. Had the army which Alexander had so foolishly sent against Turkey now been at Eylau, it was the moment to crush Napoleon. Or had the erring British ministry but sent there only 30,000 men in time for Eylau! As neither of these rulers were wise, neither worthy of its country, so Benningsen was fighting greatly superior numbers at Eylau. Often in his career Napoleon owed his escape from ruin to the faults of his enemies' sovereigns.

Then came Napoleon's grand attack. An enormous array of cavalry, — 14,000 horsemen, the pride of his army, and a great throng of 25,000 infantry advanced.

It was snowing so thick and fast that the Russians could not see this great multitude, this army of 39,000 men, as, with 200 cannon at its head, it came thundering up the slope.

The fierce onset of this enormous mass of men and horses was terrific; the shock was almost irresistible; the Russian front line yielded ground, but though broken it did not fly; it still maintained the awful conflict with tenacity in such bodies and knots as could hold together. Men died rather than retreat. Prodigious numbers on both sides were destroyed. It was a marvel of desperate fighting.

Then came forward the Russian reserve. Regardless of the storm of shot from many French batteries that rapidly thinned their ranks, they united with the remains of their first line, and with loud shouts, they charged the charging French.

It was one of those most awful scenes of war, a great charge meeting a great charge in full career.

Essen's Russian division was crushed. A French regiment of cuirassiers swept through the gap and were all killed but eighteen.

With bloody bayonets the Russians drove back the French and captured several eagles and cannon; the battle seemed gained; the French center and left were defeated with extraordinary loss.

Still the Russians were unaided; the Prussians had not arrived; they had been constantly expected; now they were needed to complete the Russian victory.

But the French right had succeeded; there Davoust's corps made a terrible attack; the Russian extreme left gave way before the fierce onset; the Russians lost the village on which their left rested. Thick masses of smoke which the wind drove rolling down the Russian line showed that the village was burning. Friant's French division had got in the rear of the Russian left and was pressing hard toward its center.

With great loss the Russian left was driven back. Still it did not fly, but re-formed at right angles with the center toward the rear. The battle now bore the singular aspect, the Russians victorious on their right and center and badly defeated on their left, and still both armies in position, each partly victor and partly vanquished!

At this critical moment the Prussians appeared on the extreme Russian right; they moved quickly across the position in rear of the Russians, refraining to fire till they arrived close to the French; then they charged bayonets with energy and effect. Davoust's French were there in force, but in a vigorous contest they were driven back, losing about 3,000 of their numbers on the hotly disputed ground.

Night came; those still living paused. The bloodiest battle that Napoleon had ever seen seemed ended. The groans of the snow-clad wounded were heard in place of the roar of cannon and the crash of musketry. Almost as many men as the entire Russian army engaged, lay mangled and bleeding in the winter darkness. It was a night pre-eminently memorable for human suffering.

Checked and beaten, Napoleon, the cause of all this needless suffering, ended the destruction of men for a moment by ceasing to attack.

Now innumerable bivouac fires were lighted; the living needed rest; the wounded wanted aid; it was time for humanity to begin its work.

But even at that terrible moment both armies were suddenly startled by sharp vollies and loud shouting that broke out on the victorious Russian right.

Napoleon saw himself poorly prepared to meet a

new attack. He gave orders to prepare for retreat. He ordered his heavy artillery and baggage to retire toward Landsberg. He directed Davoust to retreat to the position that he had occupied in the morning.

Napoleon saw that his great army was defeated, and he, evidently, feared a great disaster was upon him. Neither his skill nor his greatly superior numbers had saved him.

But the firing was made by Ney's corps which had just arrived and taken a village to interrupt the Russian communication with Konigsberg.

Benningsen saw this danger and sent a Russian division to storm that village and drive back Ney's corps, which they very gallantly did late at night, with loud cheers. Then the very sanguinary battle of Eylau had at last closed.

A Russian retreat was expedient. Ney had brought a strong re-enforcement to the defeated Napoleon; Bernadotte with his large corps of fresh troops was expected; Benningsen already knew that not less than 20,000 Russians had fallen; he knew not how much was Napoleon's loss. The Russians were short of ammunition, in need of food, and must maintain communication with a source of supply. So at midnight the Russians began to move to a new position. They halted three leagues toward Konigsberg and food. Their last division did not leave Eylau till morning, but Napoleon was too badly beaten to molest it.

Eylau was a battle of unmitigated horror; fought amid cold and storm, in a bleak, northern climate, at dead of winter; it was extremely bloody and obstinately contested; a disaster to Napoleon; a cruel

BATTLE OF EYLAU IN A SNOW STORM.

sacrifice of men for no decisive result. Had the Russians been in numbers equal with the French, it is very possible that Napoleon's power might have been overthrown, his throne destroyed, and the period of the greatest conflicts of modern times ended.

The sight of the battle field the next morning shocked even the strife-hardened Napoleon. The snow was filled with an immense multitude of the dead and the wounded, men and horses, with broken guns and all the debris of battle.

About 55,000 men lay there weltering in blood in the cold, frost and snow ; 25,000 Russians and more than 30,000 followers of Napoleon ; 10,000 more had scattered, and they struggled for days.

Few prisoners had been taken ; the fight was too fierce for that. The wounds were very severe ; the deadly cannon shot at close range had terribly mangled Napoleon's bloody victims on both sides.

The piteous cries of the great host of mutilated and torn men, still alive and suffering, on that cold, winter morning, everywhere exposed without shelter and without help in the snow, were heart-rending.

Everywhere were cries for help, cries of dying men to be put out of their misery. Men were still breathing and conscious, under heaps of dead men and horses, and their smothering groans of agony still failed to turn the relentless Napoleon from his cruel love of war.

Tamed by suffering, exhausted by the loss of blood and by lack of nourishment, the many thousands of foemen lay side by side among 6,000 fallen horses.

Great numbers perished by cold, want and excessive exertions. It was an immense aggregate of the most acute and terrible suffering. Many of the wounded, less fortunate than the dead, must through life continue to endure the most agonizing suffering, undeserved tortures, hapless victims of Napoleon's callous ambition.

"What a massacre!" exclaimed Marshal Ney, "and without result!" He might have added, "and without cause except Napoleon's depraved war madness."

Eylau was indecisive. After all this cruel murder, this devastation, this mutilation of men, the war was still to be fought as before. What for? Nothing but further aggression by Napoleon.

The Russians had taken twelve eagles, the French fourteen standards and 6,000 Russian wounded and 16 guns were left at Eylau. Napoleon announced his terrible check as a victory, and, with characteristic meanness, he gave the credit for it to his own brother-in-law, Murat, although many others had fought as well as he.

Benningsen marched away; Napoleon remained, his army crippled, hardly able to march away. He ordered up all his available strength, but when these great re-enforcements came up by forced marches, so great had been the havoc in his army that he did not venture to attack the Russians though they were still waiting within striking distance. He sent his heavy cavalry forward, but they were soon beaten with severe loss. The Cossack horsemen scoured the country and brought in great numbers of Napoleon's men as prisoners, especially cavalry.

Napoleon had expected to beat the Russians, capture Konigsberg, and there with its great stores, make his army comfortable at Prussia's expense. But defeated in his designs, he was left out in the severe northern cold.

Napoleon hoped that Russia would offer terms. Four days went by and no terms came. Then seeing his own dubious situation, he wrote to the king of Prussia, in tone almost entreating : —

"I desire to put a period to the misfortune of your family, and organize as speedily as possible the Prussian monarchy, whose intermediate power is necessary for the tranquility of Europe. I desire peace with Russia, and, provided the cabinet of Russia has no designs on the Turkish empire, I see no difficulty in obtaining it. Peace with England is no less essential to all nations, and I shall have no hesitation in sending a minister to Memel, to take part in a congress of France, Sweden, England, Russia, Prussia, and Turkey. But as such congress may last many years, which would not suit the present condition of Prussia, your majesty will, I am persuaded, be of opinion that I have taken the simplest method, and that most likely to secure the prosperity of your subjects."

The king refused unless with the concurrence of Russia.

Nine days after the great battle Napoleon retreated from Eylau. The Russians re-occupied it. Both armies again went into winter quarters, both claimed the victory; 30,000 human lives had been wasted; almost every country of the continent had a great quota of cripples.

The battle of Eylau made a great sensation in Europe. Martineau says : —

"Fifty thousand men could at any time be furnished for a great continental expedition."[1]

Yet the feeble ministry, not worthy of that energetic nation, let the Eylau opportunity escape.

Had England instantly reinforced the Russians

[1] Martineau's History of England i, 199.

with 60,000 British soldiers, such as won Salamanca, and with needed supplies, it might have also decided Austria to throw her force into the scale, and Napoleon must have been quickly overwhelmed. Germany, already indignant at his pitiless exactions, wished to join against him, and might have risen as she did in 1813.

The public sentiment of Great Britain demanded vigorous action; the nation was ready; but, unfortunately the present British system of exclusion of the sovereign from active public policy did not prevail, and George III was at the head of British affairs. Nothing was done till the favorable time had passed, and then, by 80,000 sterling advanced to Russia; and with 100,000 more of Great Britain's money, and a large amount of stores, the embezzling George bought of Prussia a solemn renunciation of all rights to Hanover, of which George was hereditary Elector, but which was not England's at all!

Eylau excited great consternation at Paris. The public funds fell; a great mourning gloom was spread over France. Strange, and even exagerated stories of Eylau floated about. A report spread that Napoleon was killed. The sad gloom was deepened when Napoleon's message arrived, demanding of the servile senate, a fresh conscription of 80,000 men in March, 1807, that were not due till a year and a half later, in September, 1808. This was the third levy of boys for the Prussian war; 240,000 young men in seven months! What terribly frightful havoc war had made! So powerfully was France shocked that Napoleon equivocated that he wanted this new levy only for army of reserve.

So badly had Eylau defeated Napoleon that he suspended field operations for about four months.

Napoleon wanted army clothing; he caused it to be imported from England. Says his Bourrienne: —

" Thus I procured these articles in a sure and cheap way . . . . . otherwise French troops might have perished with cold . . . . my cloths and my leather arrived; cloaks, coats, boots, were promptly made." [1]

This when Napoleon's Berlin Decree had forbidden imports from England. Thus he broke his own decree while he enforced it against his subjects and subject nations.

Baron Hardenberg, on behalf of Prussia, laid the basis for a new coalition between Russia and Prussia, in which Austria, Sweden, Great Britain, and Denmark, were invited to join. This absurd treaty, made when Prussia was prostrate, read as if the allies were at Paris as conquerors, viz. : —

Re-establishment of Prussia as in 1805; the Confederation of the Rhine to be dissolved; Tyrol and Venice restored to Austria; Hanover aggrandized; the House of Orange restored in Holland; absurd "indemnity" to the kings of " Sardinia " and Naples.

Prussia agreed with Sweden to send troops into Swedish Pomerania. Francis II of Austria did not know his own mind; the Archduke Charles was arranging Austrian affairs; he said that the state of Austria's finances and her army advised him against intervention.

The immediate pretext for the war of Russia against Turkey was that the Sultan had dismissed the hos-

---

[1] Bourrienne at Hamburg furnished 50,000 cloaks, 16,000 coats, 37,000 waistcoats, and 40,000 pairs of boots. So England clothed the grand army. Bourrienne ii, 385.

podars of Roumania, friends to Russia, and appointed in their places men friendly to French alliance. The British ambassador was indignant and threatened Turkey.

<small>Russia, Turkey and Britain.
February, 1807.</small>

The Russians, 40,000 strong, had invaded those countries with military success.

The British ambassador demanded that Turkey withdraw from French alliance, and ally herself with Britain. Turkey refused. The British threatened to bombard Constantinople. Turkey declared war against Britain.

A British fleet forced the passage of the Dardanelles and appeared at Constantinople. The Turks were unprepared. Guided by the French ambassador, Sebastiani, they prolonged the exchange of notes till the aroused masses of Turks, aided by French engineers, mounted guns and made ready the defenses. Then a heavy cannonade compelled the British to retire through the battery-lined passes. Turkey adhered to France. The Russians beat the Turks in a naval fight in the Black Sea.

When England ought to have sent troops to aid the Russians and Prussians near Konigsberg, a useless and hopeless British expedition went to Egypt. It met disaster, and soon retired from Egypt after loss of one-third of its numbers.

<small>Great Britain, 1807.</small>

British Admiral Popham had wantonly attacked Montevideo and robbed it of a great sum: instead of punishing his piracy, the Grenville ministry sent another expedition to Buenos Ayres, commanded by George III's favorite, Whitelock. It resulted in another serious and shameful disaster. All was lost.

A court-martial, when too late, found George's favorite "totally unfit and unworthy." The great naval force and the 15,000 soldiers of these two ill-starred expeditions would have been sufficient to have saved Dantzic with its great fortress which unaided, capitulated [May 24], and thus released for the field the 40,000 of Napoleon's troops that besieged it.

What George's government was doing at the crisis when vigorous wisdom would have destroyed their great enemy, Napoleon, was this: —

By Irish act of 1793 a Catholic in Ireland could rise as high as lieutenant-colonel; out of Ireland, to no rank in Great Britain.

In Parliament, the minister, Lord Howick (Charles Grey) moved for leave to bring in a bill to enable persons of every religious creed to serve as officers in the army or navy without condition except an oath not repugnant to any religious belief. In England a Catholic could not be even a subaltern, because barred by a test oath. Many men fighting Britain's battles were not members of the English established church. It was even open to suspicion that they were not every one pious men.

Why should not Catholics, or even sinners, hold commissions to fight? Is fighting a trade that requires sanctification, the thirty-nine articles, confirmation? The witty Sidney Smith compared George's wretched folly to a ship attacked, and being shattered while its captain, instead of uniting all for defense, at that critical moment claps into irons his thirty prime Catholic sailors, under guard of thirty Episcopalians; tells the Episcopal gunner not to trust the Presbyterian steersman; examines his men in the catechism and the thirty-nine articles, and forbids to sponge or ram, any who have not taken the sacrament in George's own church.

The king objected to the measure. On explanation he gave way; the bill was prepared; Grey brought it in; then ultra Tories alarmed the king; he betrayed his word; he opposed the bill; he required that it be withdrawn and that the ministers sign away their right to ever again propose concession to Catholics or give him advice on that subject. The ministry, more manly than Pitt in 1803, refused to sign the humiliating paper, so George dismissed the Whig ministry. For the next twenty-five years Great Britain had Tory ministers. For this Irish affair George had lost sight of great Eylau, of England's great opportunity.

The Duke of Portland was infirm, diseased, exhausted; "kept up in busy times only by laudanum and cordials, and apt to fall asleep over the most important letters." [1]

George's New Ministry March 25, 1807.

It was this half-dead man that George called to form a ministry. Perceval was the real chief.

The Ministry that came in 1807 were: —

Duke of Portland, Premier Perceval, Chancellor Exchequer; George Canning, Foreign Secretary; Lord Hawksbury, Home Secretary; Lord Castlereagh, War and Colonial Secretary; Lord Eldon, Chancellor; Lord Mulgrave, Admiralty; Duke of Richmond, Viceroy of Ireland.

A debate in Parliament on the extraordinary demand of the king resulted in sustaining the new min-

[1] Martineau i, 209.

istry, by a vote of 258 to 226, a small majority for momentous times. No sound lawyer would, in our day, defend the demand for such a pledge. It is abhorrent to the British constitution. Ministers must be free to advise. Perceval was leading minister. He was : —

"An enemy to all relaxation of religious tests. From this time [1806] his rigid, narrow mind, honest and unphilosophical, his temper, amiable toward friends and bitter and arrogant toward opponents; his manners simple and affectionate to his connections and ludicrously presumptuous and offensive to all persons whom he considered heterodox . . . . one of those apparent mistakes of fate which make statesmen of very small personages."[1]

George caused parliament to be dissolved. The Eylau crisis was passing. Napoleon would soon recover from his great check; such an opportunity to assail his power might never recur; but foolish George, instead of doing the patriotic duty that every British interest demanded of him, took this very time to plunge into an exciting parliamentary election.

The new ministry raised again the old cry, "No popery."

"At the most critical period of the century we had a king with an infirm brain, and a prime minister dying of torturing disease and opiates."[2]

Six thousand pounds each were paid for seats in parliament. The new ministry bought all there were to be had;[3] it is supposed that the king furnished money.

"The people did not look to parliament to reflect the mind of the nation.[4] Now was Cobbett read in a hundred thousand homes; now was Burdett worshiped in the streets."[5]

The new parliament, selected by the corrupt system abolished in 1832, a system in which seats were

[1] Martineau i, 197.   [2] Martineau i, 216.   [3] Martineau i, 219.
[4] Martineau i, 220.   [5] Ibid.

sold so freely as to have a regular quotable price, and when few British had the great privilege of voting, sustained the new ministry by about 200 majority. But the new ministry avowed that the king had acted without their advice. So the election can hardly be said to have indorsed George's illegal demand. The hereditary House of Lords was, of course, with the king.

Those were dark times. The spirit of justice, equity and humanity, did not rule in Europe.

But the progress of improvement in England since then has been greater than has usually occurred in whole ages.

The new ministry agreed with Sweden to send 20,000 British troops to unite with 18,000 Swedes in Pomerania. Britain had about 80,000 men on home stations. George's ministry ought to have done at once one of two acts: either made peace or else sent a British force to Dantzic to save it from falling and so rendering available for the field the 40,000 French engaged in its seige, and they should have strengthened the Russian army before Konigsberg; they omitted to do either.

After Eylau Napoleon used the greatest activity. He drew re-inforcements from every available source. Massena brought him 36,000 men from Italy. He demanded and received 16,000 fresh troops from the king of Spain who dared not refuse. He had a large force of Poles. He directed the Polish provisional government to set apart 20,000,000 francs to recompense Poles who should distinguish themselves in his service.

<small>Battle of Heilsberg, June 10, 1807.</small>

Austria offered mediation but it came to nothing.

The Russian army was re-inforced to more than 110,000 men. Napoleon had now a much larger army.

Benningsen made an advance hoping to destroy Ney's exposed corps. But Ney fought two bloody contests at Gutstadt and Aukendorff. In danger of being surrounded by Napoleon's superior numbers, Benningsen retired to his intrenched camp at Heilsberg. Here, on the night of June 10, occurred a hard-fought, bloody battle. It began with French success but ended in French defeat, "not dangerous but sanguinary."

The useless slaughter continued far into the night. The French lost from 8,000 to 10,000 men, the Russians scarcely half that number. The next day, instead of again attacking these intrenchments, Napoleon attempted to turn them. He marched on Eylau, hoping to cut off Benningsen from his source of supplies at Konigsberg. The Russians fell back and took position at Friedland.

Benningsen was on the east side of the river Alle. The French corps of Lannes and Oudinot appeared on the west side. Benningsen sent a Russian division across against them; that not succeeding he sent more troops to its aid, across the long bridge and the three pontoons. Napoleon coming up with the grand army caught the Russians in the bad position of having a river at their back. The Russians had crossed to the west side in force. There was danger that the French would seize a bridge some miles below and cross and get between

Battle of Friedland, June 14, 1807.

the Russians and Konigsberg. Benningsen sent 6,000 men to hold it, so much weakening his main force.

The battle raged long and hard. Then Napoleon made a tremendous attack in heavy force. The Russians weakened relatively by their heavy loss, began to retire. The French reached the bridge and the pontoons and set fire to them. The Russians seemed lost, their retreat cut off, but they retreated by two fords, with loss of several cannon. They rallied their scattered corps without further molestation from the shattered French army.

Benningsen retired to Tilsit and soon crossed the Niemen into Russia, and the French took the important fortress of Konigsberg together with 100,000 muskets sent there by the British government.

Napoleon arrived at Tilsit.

The Emperor Alexander asked for armistice. It was agreed to June 21. George's treaty of London of June 17, giving to Prussia a million sterling of British money, came too late.

Napoleon and Alexander met on a raft moored in the middle of the river Niemen. Their interview lasted two hours. It began with Alexander's remark, "I hate the English as much as you do."

The raft on the Niemen. June 27, 1807.

Alexander was a mystic, a visionary. He reverenced his favorite men and women for a time and then turned to others. He had held a sentimental friendship with the king of Prussia. Now the king was not admitted to the conference.

Prince Metternich, for many years intimate with Alexander, thus describes his character:—

"He certainly possessed mind, but his mind, refined and keen as it was, had no depth; he was easily led astray (by distrust or) by erroneous theories. His judgment was always influenced by fanciful ideas .... these systems did not assimilate, they followed one another in rapid succession. Devoted to the system whose term it was, he arrived at the exact opposite .... this policy followed in measures of about five years: two years an idea grew: the third he was faithful to it; the fourth his fervor calmed; the fifth saw it nearly extinct. In 1805 he was broadly a liberal, a bitter enemy of Napoleon; in 1807 changed in his mode of thinking; in 1808 an admirer of Napoleon; in 1812 again changed; in 1814 his old philanthrophy and free-thinking took fire from the spirit of the times; in 1815 he had given way to religious mysticism; in 1817 he took a new turn; in 1818 I found him a zealous champion of monarchial conservative principles, a declared enemy of every revolutionary tendency." [1]

Napoleon and Alexander made the terms. The town of Tilsit was made neutral ground, and there the two emperors often met. They were very intimate. They passed "in a moment from open war to the most friendly relations," said Napoleon.

Peace of Tilsit. July 7, 1807.

The king of Prussia, with kingly lack of common sense, appointed the aged Count Kalreuth to conduct this most momentous negotiation for Prussia. Hardenburg said: —

"The choice is made, and our dearest interests are committed to an old, frivolous talker, altogether destitute of vigor or ability."

So the French negotiator dictated the Prussian terms to poor old Kalreuth and to Goltz. And fearfully Prussia suffered for the next seven years for the king's stupidity in trusting Prussia's case to feeble Kalreuth.

The treaty between France and Russia was signed July 7; that between France and Prussia on July 9, 1807.

[1] Metternich's Memoirs.

Alexander was willing to take the spoils of his ally, Prussia, and to wrest Finland from his own brother-in-law, King Gustavus of Sweden.

Napoleon pretended that it was from "respect for the emperor of all the Russias, and desire to unite the two nations in the bonds of eternal friendship," that he consented to restore to Frederick William old Prussia, Pomerania, Brandenberg, and Silesia.

Napoleon took all of Prussia's late possessions west of the Elbe, with Magdeburg and its great fortress.

From the Elbe to the Rhine he made the kingdom of Westphalia, including Brunswick and Hesse-Cassel.

He restored the dukes of Oldenberg and Mecklenberg, who were relations to the Czar, but he continued to occupy their territory to enforce the Continental System against import of British goods.

He compelled all the German rulers to join the Confederation of the Rhine, of which he was practically dictator. Thus they were all vassals of his great empire, and obliged to furnish him with troops.

Of Prussian Poland he made the Duchy of Warsaw, with the king of Saxony as its Grand Duke. He reserved a military road through Prussia from Saxony to Poland.[1] He donated several valuable Polish properties to some of his own officers.[2]

Russia had incurred great expense of blood and treasure, and of exertion for Prussia; in compensation Alexander took from Prussia Bialystock,[3] with about 350,000 inhabitants, for which he ceded Jever to Holland, which also got East Friesland from Prussia, but Holland had to cede to Napoleon Flushing and Bergen.

[1] Bourrienne ii, 390-91.   [2] Lanfrey iii, 278.   [3] Rosteck iv, 174.

Russia and Prussia acknowledged Joseph Bonaparte as king of Naples; Louis as king of Holland; Jerome as king of Westphalia, and the Confederation of the Rhine, and thus the dominion of Napoleon over Germany; and all states organized by Napoleon and the treaty mutually guaranteed the possessions of France and Russia.

The king of Prussia was not to receive back his remaining part of Prussia till after full payment of a war indemnity, amounting, with that already paid, to over 600,000,000 francs.[1] French account, 604,227,920; Prussian estimate, 739,800,000 francs.

Prussia lost nearly one-third[2] of her territory, with 4,236,040 inhabitants, while her remaining territory held only 5,034,504 persons.[1] Dantzic was declared a free city, but it had a French governor till 1814.

A second treaty between France and Russia, with secret articles, gave Cattaro and the Ionian Isles to France, and stipulated that if Ferdinand were deprived of Sicily, he should have no compensation but the Balearic Isles, or Cyprus, or Candia, and then Joseph Bonaparte should be acknowledged king of the two Sicilies; that amnesty be granted Montenegrins and other Turkish people lately revolted at the call of Russia; that if Hanover be united to Westphalia, Prussia should receive in exchange territory west of the Elbe with 300,000 to 400,000 people.[3]

A third treaty, offensive and defensive, provided that an ultimatum should be addressed to England, and if it had no results, war should be declared by Russia in December; that unless Turkey should make peace with Russia within three months, the

[1] Alison ii, 544.   [2] Schlosser vii, 552.   [3] Rambaud ii, 294.

two emperors should arrange to withdraw all the Ottoman provinces in Europe from Turkey except Constantinople and Roumelia; that Sweden be summoned to break off with England, and if it refused, Denmark was to be invited to take part in a war against her, and Finland to be annexed to Russia; that Austria, Sweden, Denmark, and Portugal be invited to join the Continental System.[1]

Napoleon justified his articles concerning Turkey because a revolt of the Janizaries had slain his friend, the Sultan Selim III, on account of his European innovations, and the new Sultan, Mahmoud, was not bound to France.

Mediation of Russia between France and England, and mediation of France between Russia and Turkey were to be attempted; the Russian troops to be first withdrawn from Turkey.

Napoleon gave a constitution to Warsaw similar to that of France. It abolished Polish slavery, 1807.

XI

AS long ago as 1780, to prevent France and Spain from obtaining ship timber and naval stores from northern Europe, England seized neutral vessels. To protect all but actual war material, Russia, Sweden, Denmark, Prussia, Portugal, and the two Sicilies, formed an "Armed Neutrality." France and Spain applauded. England made war on the Dutch on this question. The unanimous voice of Europe, except Britain, had opposed such search.[2]

[1] Thiers vii, 627-33.   [2] Cooper's Naval History, ii, 14.

JOSÉPHINE.

PRUSSIA'S QUEEN LUISE AND HER SISTER HONORING SOLDIER'S GRAVES.

Five seamen deserted from the British ship, Melampus. They enlisted on the American frigate, Chesapeake, Captain Barron. Two of them again deserted. The British consul at Norfolk requested the local naval officer to return them; the officer refused. The British agent applied to our government, which ordered inquiry and found that the men were born in America. Two of them were impressed colored men; two had notarial certificates that they were Americans; their surrender was refused. June 22, 1807, the Chesapeake sailed from Norfolk for the Mediterranean, with her equipment in great disorder, entirely unprepared for action and expecting no hostility. She passed two British vessels, and further out two more.

The Chesapeake Affair. June 23, 1807.

The British frigate, Leopard, hailed and asked Captain Barron to take dispatches. An officer came on board and demanded the deserters. Captain Barron denied knowledge of any deserters on board and forbade muster of his crew. The officer returned to the Leopard.

Captain Barron saw hostile signs; he quietly ordered his decks cleared for action. Before this could be done the Leopard began a close, destructive fire. Surprised, unprepared, much damaged, three men killed, sixteen wounded including Captain Barron, the Chesapeake surrendered. The British Captain, Humphrey, refused the surrender, but he took the three men and another, claimed as a runaway from a British merchant vessel. The British orders did not require Captain Humphrey to fire on the Chesapeake.[1]

[1] Cooper's Naval History ii, 14.

This outrage excited tremendous indignation in America. It united Americans in support of Jefferson, who was unfriendly to England. The President issued a proclamation ordering all British armed vessels to leave American waters, and forbidding them to enter until satisfaction be made for the Chesapeake indignity. But by Jay's treaty of 1795, between America and Britain, the war ships of either nation had a right to be in the other's ports. So Jefferson's proclamation was violation of that treaty. He called Congress for a special session. Captain Barron was court-martialed and punished for negligence.

Our minister at London, Monroe, demanded satisfaction and security. Only Britain among civilized nations had, in recent times, claimed the right to take its deserters from the war ships of a neutral.

Some British ship owners favored despoiling the rival American commerce. George III and his minister were resolute to steal British seamen at home in England and to kidnap them on sea for the British navy. Hard George III and immoral George IV differ from that best of British sovereigns, Queen Victoria, as John Bright and Disraeli differ from Pitt and Perceval; as the old age of this century differs from its cruel, bitter, vengeful early youth. Barbaric impressments were the methods then used to fill the British navy. In British ports armed parties waylaid and kidnapped any British seamen they could find, and sometimes landsmen; they violently seized men, forced them on board British war vessels, and held them to forced service for unlimited terms, a service then enforced by free and cruel use of the lash.

They invaded British streets and went into British vessels to kidnap their best men.

It was atrocious man stealing. British war vessels sometimes actually gave exciting chase to British privateers in order to steal their British sailors!

This is the very odious system that George III practiced against American sailors, of which America so much complained.

Canning, Foreign Secretary, expressed to our envoy, Monroe, regrets for the Chesapeake affair. He said: —

"If the British officers shall prove to have been culpable, the most prompt and effectual reparation shall be afforded."

But he cavilled that the President had ordered away British vessels, retaliatory, without awaiting explanations; that he would not consent to connect in negotiations the Chesapeake affair and the general subject of impressments, if Monroe's instructions so insisted he would send an envoy to Washington to arrange the Chesapeake affair. Admiral Berkeley, at Halifax, under whose orders Captain Humphrey had made the outrage, was recalled, and Humphrey was never again employed afloat.[1]

Jefferson required an apology, restoration of the men, and compensation for the families of the killed. Canning was willing to comply with this, except that one of the men was already hanged; but America insisted that visits to American vessels to search for British subjects should be totally relinquished. Canning refused.

In October, 1807, King George's proclamation ordered navy officers: —

[1] Lossing, 1812 war, 158.

"To seize upon, take, and bring away all his native-born subjects found serving in merchant vessels of any foreign state, and to report all such serving on any foreign armed vessel, that reparation might be demanded."

George III's Grenville's ministry, by "Order in Council" of January, 1807, interdicted passage of neutral vessels between any ports not open to British ships. Napoleon damaged neutral commerce; then by adding further British aggression to the French aggression George's ministry hoped to arouse neutral countries to resent French aggression only, a plan worthy of stupid George himself.

As this strange plan produced effect contrary to George's desire, his Portland ministry, hotly opposed by the British Whigs with an effort for a more enlightened policy, adopted a new aggression.

November 11, 1807, in retaliation of the Berlin Decree, a British "Order in Council" appeared, requiring all neutral traders proceeding to France, or to a French dependence, to stop at a British port and pay a duty of twenty-five per cent on the cargo; and all ports from which English vessels were excluded by France were subjected to the same restrictions as if actually blockaded, and neutrals with French certificates showing that the cargo is not of British product, should lose both vessel and cargo.

Regnier, French minister of justice, interpreted the Berlin Decree as making liable to seizure all British goods or products of colonies even on neutral vessels, and the cargo of the American ship, Horizon, stranded on the French coast, was confiscated, and extensive seizures followed. Spain and Holland made similar decrees because they dared not oppose Napoleon's imperious will.

This British order would exclude from our American trade all Europe, except Britain and Sweden, for all the rest were allies of France. *Embargo.*

The British bombardment of peaceful Copenhagen and destruction of the fleet of Denmark, might well awe our nation, which had hardly a vestige of a war navy. But prompted by Jefferson, Congress passed an embargo on all American commerce. All sailing of our vessels was to cease! The House vote was 82 to 44. Josiah Quincy's reasonable motion to except our fishing vessels on their giving bonds failed, 82 to 45.

Except foreign vessels already in our ports, this suicidal act forbad any merchant vessels to sail without the President's permission; our vessels might conduct a coast trade under high bonds to deliver their cargoes only in our own ports.

This death sentence to American commerce was passed in night session, almost without debate; Jefferson's party majority would not permit it to be debated, would not allow the public to know that such a bill was proposed; all was secrecy until it was enacted. It struck the active business part of America with the most painful surprise; it was a deadly blow at industry and labor, at means of living. Seldom or never had a nation dealt such a terrible blow at itself. Its dire effects were felt for half a generation; it was war upon ourselves by ourselves.

It would be great error to believe that Jefferson's majority were held together by his foreign policy; far from it; the famous Alien and Sedition laws, the House Tax, the Stamp Tax and the Naturalization law of the Adams term, and abhorrence of Hamilton's preference for aristocratic government, had driven many honest men from adherence to hostility to the Federal party; so intensely did men hate these ideas that they joined with the slave power to support Jefferson, right or wrong. In politics, not unfrequently it is not love of one party but hatred of the opposite party that makes bitter partisans. The price of common labor from 1793 to 1800, under Washington and Adams, had averaged but $65 a year, while sailors struck for $14 a month. Many land laborers envied these sea prices and hoped to obtain wages under a new and strange policy that should ruin the sailors. Producers in the South regarded sailors' high wages and the prices at which farm products were sold abroad more than was paid to the farmer, as so much abstracted from the producer. Among them this was a popular idea, almost a party notion.

Jefferson's party were for close alliance with France, for abrogating Jay's treaty with England; they were unfriendly to England: the Federalists were for neutrality, for the treaty, and for braving France; they were meek toward England as the Jefferson men were toward France. In 1807 Jefferson wrote that he "rather have a war with Spain than not." This was because he desired to seize Florida, which belonged to Spain, and was an asylum for runaway slaves.

Before embargo Americans had the richest, most profitable, and extensive ocean shipping trade of the world except that of the British. As early as 1789 our China trade was opened. Business was good; the people were busy; labor had fair reward; employment was ample; the national revenue more than ample.

Although buying yearly [1805-7] an average of $82,300,000 of imports, and selling but $44,866,000 of exports, we received also duties and profits on $57,701,000 of foreign goods imported and re-shipped. The treasury received in 1807 almost $16,000,000, paid $4,000,000 of funded debt, and had $17,000,000 surplus. Jefferson hardly knew what to do with the constantly increasing surplus. It was a bugbear, a nightmare to him.

Only with France and its allies did any pretense of blockade exist; All of the rest of this somewhat large world was not closed by British orders or French decrees. The British taxed our cargoes, but they rather invited than repelled them, and they gave profitable employment to many American vessels, carrying British cargoes at the risk of British merchants.

Around part of the French dominions the blockade was not strictly enforced. To Spain, Portugal, Turkey, China, South America, Africa, Canada, trade was open; Russia and the north of Europe and the Mediterranean and the Indies gave lucrative business to fleets of American shipping. Much trade, generally belonging to Russian, Swedish, German, Dutch, Spanish, French, Italian, and even British ships, was now carried on by the neutral Americans. Our import trade from the British Isles alone was almost $50,000,000 a year. Americans were carrying vast amounts for foreign merchants. Our shipping trade was remarkably flourishing. It gave ready market for American produce and goods; it made the whole country prosperous.

Why not then let prosperity remain? Why fling contemptuously away this immensely valuable trade? If the British king and ministry had insulted us, why reward them by flinging this wealth of prosperity to their subjects? The withdrawal of all American competition would of course enrich British revenue. It was a singular means to use toward an enemy, to give him that which makes you prosperous, and see him enjoy it and laugh at the poverty which your folly brings you. But so it was; then came that strange delusion, Jefferson's bad conflict with American commerce.

In supposed retaliation of the British Orders in Council, laying burdens on our commerce, and for the impressments and seizures of men from our vessels, Congress passed this embargo to keep all our ships in port!

Jefferson's embargo was not constitutional. Congress may "regulate commerce," but where is the authority to prohibit it? His non-intercourse acts were neither war nor peace; they irritated, wasted, crippled like war, but without war's privileges. The country needed as president either an Andrew Jackson or a William Penn; Jefferson was like neither.

Jefferson was a very able politician, a shrewd wire-puller, a manufacturer of public sentiment. He not only threw on all his opponents the stigma of the odious Alien and Sedition acts, but he impressed his party with the false idea that those good maxims of free governments, our liberty and equality,— common sentiments of all Americans,— were his own peculiar doctrines, opposed by all his opposers. His party accepted that simple deception.

In the Revolution he had been in favor of giving all the power to the people, yet as president he was the most arbitrary, he exercised more doubtful or unconstitutional powers than any other president of that generation. He had been the special champion of strict construction, of limited powers of the president and of Congress; he was the Calhoun of that period, the "States Rights" declaimer; but as president he excelled so far in using illegal authorities that every prominent measure of his administration was either unconstitutional or doubtful; acquisition, embargo, constraint of state governments in trade matters, non-intercourse, the stopping of trade between states, and between home ports, all are un-American, undemocratic, unrepublican, unconstitutional. And these were the essence of his administration.

The death of Hamilton and the disgrace of Burr, in 1804, left the opposition without a leader. This was extremely fortunate for Jefferson. The Federalist party ought then to have dissolved itself, as the Whig party did after its great defeat of 1852. That it did not dissolve was another good fortune for Jefferson. Had they dissolved then a new party might have arisen, led by such men as DeWitt Clinton and John Randolph, including a part of the best elements of the Republican and all of the Federal party, and, freed from the odium of the acts of the Adams Congresses, Alien, Sedition, House Tax, Whisky Tax, and increase of the Judges Acts, would have been supported by the patriotic good sense of the country, and probably have gained the elections in 1809, on a declaration of sound, practical principles, and by governing less than Jefferson governed. His greatest fault was too much government, too little of leaving men to manage their own affairs. But the dishonored Federal party remained alive and divided, discordant, and in helpless discredit. Thus Jefferson had opportunity.

Jefferson's policy was not always the same; he governed too much: he opposed the United States bank, yet he approved the bill for the branch at New Orleans; he favored the ordinance of 1787 that excluded slavery from the Northwest, but he held to slavery, and in his letter to Holmes he advocated its extension in the Missouri question; — Whitney's gin had made it more valuable since 1787; — he believed internal improvements were unconstitutional, but he signed the Cumberland bill for a national road in his own Virginia; he appears on both sides of the tariff protection system question; he was chief executive, yet he censured the co-ordinate branch, the Judiciary, in the affair of Burr, his own late competitor for the presidency, whose conviction he sought, a dangerous kind of interference in free government whose guarantee of liberty is, largely, the freedom of courts of law from political influence; he talked of liberty, yet never was there so little American liberty; he talked of good government, yet he wished that judges might be accountable to the president and subject to removal by him, and thus exposed to all the dangers and corruptions of party favor. The great security of British liberties, from which we have inherited ours, has been the free courts, their untrammeled judges and juries. Jefferson declaimed about free opinions, but he denounced newspapers thus: —

"The man who never looks into a newspaper is better informed than he who reads them," and "Nothing can now be believed which is seen in a newspaper."[1]

Jefferson loved to rule and he did the thinking for his party, and they followed him with canine docility. Down to 1860, it was somewhat fashionable for party men to claim to be his disciples, but no party now exists on basis of his principles or his practices. The world has progressed; he is as much one of the by-gones of our politics as is stupid George III in that of England; his party policy is as dead as his embargo. In 1812–15 and later, his party even claimed the credit for the brilliant glory acquired by our navy, to whose very existence they had given deadly hostility; it was as if Herod had claimed to be the special protector of young, small boys.

This embargo was put in force December 22, 1807.

No civilized nation ever before tried embargo like this. It was Jefferson's original invention; none other ever tried to starve itself in order to injure another nation. Napoleon regarded Jefferson's embargo as timely aid to himself in his barbarian war against all commerce.

While Jefferson thus tried to smother all American ocean trade, even that to the West Indies, and fettered our coast domestic trade, England still kept a great commerce with half the world; so while embargo was ruin to American ship-owners, seamen, and merchants, it was only damage but not ruin to their British rivals, and it was expected to be harmless to southern planters. It was the South and their northern allies, willing to sacrifice, not their interests, but those of Maryland, Delaware, and the North, in order

[1] Jefferson's Works.

to try to starve England to terms. Unfortunately it was the poor and the common people of Britain, not their rich rulers, who felt the starving attempt, with what effect will be seen in 1810-12, in the almost civil war of the English starving in those years, to whose distress the ministry, well fed themselves, did not yield. Because Delaware wanted business, and objected to the embargo folly, Jefferson, incensed, mentioned Delaware as merely a county of England conquered indeed and held by force.[1]

American opposition was violent, incessant; men resist their own ruin with vigor. Many men feared that Jefferson would make alliance with Napoleon, and they saw that Napoleon's allies soon became his subjects. The excitement was intense; the indignation was animated. Wild talk was freely made by both parties. Nothing could be further from the states' rights principles of which Jefferson had been the great leading advocate before his election to the presidency than this embargo by the general government; it was exercise of central, federal power, far beyond the boldest ideas of the old Federalist party. The epithets, "French party" and "British party," were bitterly used.

Non-intercourse with French countries, and allowing merchant vessels to arm and defend themselves, would, probably, have secured every object aimed at and lost by the embargo, and would have left open to our trade all the non-warring nations.

England encouraged our vessels to evade the embargo. On April 8, 1808, the ministry ordered British naval officers not to molest our vessels sail-

[1] Jefferson's Works iv, 56.

ing with lumber and provisions to the British West Indies or South America, even without regular clearances. This aided our trade while Jefferson opposed it.

In Congress a motion to repeal embargo and permit our vessels to arm and defend themselves was voted down by a large Jefferson majority. Yet embargo brought far greater harm to Americans than to our rivals abroad.

Embargo was a far greater blow to American commerce and to our home business than all the outrages of the British and French governments together. Not only did it damage trade, but it threw away great markets for the produce of American farms. It was an astounding delusion, a strange mania that possessed politicians, the idea that to stop all intercourse with Europe would bring England to terms. It was the mania of egotism that held frightful possession of Jefferson and his party; he influenced Virginia and Virginia's influence ruled the nation.

The House, after a bitter debate, refused, 80 to 50, to a third time suspend the act that forbid import of certain English goods. So beside themselves as to throw away a very rich commerce, so that British vessels immensely profited, to the ruin of many Americans; these violent legislators forgot to attach any penalty to breaking this strange law! Coasters took cargoes and ran for the West Indies, pretending to be blown off this coast, and suffered no penalty. The mortified Congress passed a new act with penalties. It required, also, that coasters give bonds to land their cargoes in America.

Merchants were to see their ships decay at the

wharves or evade the law. Many thought that they better lose some by French or English seizures than lose all the rich commerce and let their ships perish in idleness, with their crews out of employment and suffering from want, and American trade destroyed, and universal business stagnation where had been such lively prosperity; they sent their vessels to sea. Then Jefferson, to support his pet theory, set American armed vessels to preying on American commerce by chase and captures at sea. Like foreign enemies our own cruisers made prize off American ports of our own merchant vessels that persisted in business.

Asperity between the friends and the opponents of this strange policy, grew more bitter. But the Federalists, greatly reduced by their "Alien and Sedition" laws, libel prosecutions, House taxes, Judiciary Act, the odious bearing of some former Federalist judges, the supposed aristocratic tendency of some of their leaders (Adams and Hamilton), had given their party its finishing blow by their dishonest effort to obtain the choice by the electoral college of Burr for president, when the people had expressed by their votes that they wanted Jefferson. So honest Republicans, however much they might regret the embargo, found no opposition party with which their abhorrence of these Federal measures would allow them to rally; Jefferson's faction was solid; opposition was divided.

Three days after this strange embargo, a British envoy, Mr. Rose, arrived in America to treat respecting the Chesapeake affair. The embargo embarrassed him, so no treaty was attempted

Jefferson alleged that the embargo was intended to preserve our ships and seamen. Then why also forbid export of our products in foreign ships? Why not allow American merchants each to take the risks if he so desired, for the sake of the great profits of the commerce? The Embargo was to rob many merchants of their business, many workingmen of daily employment for their bread. While it damaged England by stopping our trade, it rewarded England with our great trade between foreign ports, made it a donation of this vast source of wealth.

No doubt Jefferson disliked England, but giving it a gratuity of our valuable trade with all the accessible world was a strange means to try to bring England to terms. Trade with Turkey, Sweden, China, Brazil, all Spanish America, Africa, the Eastern Islands, Canada, everywhere, thrown contemptuously at England in order to spite and damage her! It was like throwing down all your gold at your rival's door in wish to distress his business.

The embargo that can stop commerce must also stop the public revenue derived from trade. Then if war should follow? How embarrassed must America be without money! Loss of revenue meant loss of public credit. Had such an embargo been put on America by any foreign power, then all America would have risen in arms against it.

Eight weeks after embargo came another oppression. Not to be outdone in severity, Napoleon issued his Milan Decree, *Napoleon's Milan Decree. Dec. 17, 1807.* that any vessel which shall suffer a visit by an English vessel or submit to a voyage to England, or pay a British tax, is by that denationalized, has lost the guarantee of its flag, and is become English property, and good prize. The British Isles are declared in state of blockade on sea and on land.[1]

If a neutral vessel took a French certificate, or proceeded direct from America to France, Holland, or Italy, British cruisers must capture it; if to escape British seizure it paid tribute to Britain as required, confiscation awaited it at its continental port.

Jefferson said in his message October 4, 1807:—

"Under this new law of the ocean, our trade on the Mediterranean has been swept away by seizures and condemnations, and that in other seas is threatened with the same fate."

But Lord Ashburton (English) said in 1807:—

"American trade with the continent of Europe has, at the same time, since November 21, 1806, been doubled and even trebled."

Both these statements had a basis, though they appear to conflict. Jefferson saw only official reports; Ashburton took note also of the business of vessels that run the embargo and those that staid abroad and traded between foreign ports.

These Orders in Council were strongly condemned by Lords Erskine, Grenville, and Auckland, and by Mr. Whitbread and other able British statesmen. They argued that the pretended submission of neutrals to the Berlin Decree had not been proved; that it was unjust to punish them as if they had grossly

---

[1] Versions so various of this famous decree are given in different histories, that I here place a copy of the original:—

ART. 1. "Aucun bâtiment de quelque nation qu' il soit, qui aura souffert la visite d' un vaisseau Anglais, est ou se sera soumis a' un voyage en Angleterre, ou aura payé une imposition au gouvernement Anglais, est par cela seul déclaré denationalize, a perdu la garantie de son pavillon et est devenu proprieté Anglaise.

ART. 2. "Les dits bâtiments sont déclarés de bonne et valable prise. Les iles Britaniques sont déclarés en et at de blocus sur mer comme sur terre."

violated the law of nations; that the effect would be as injurious to Britain as to any other state. British trade with the United States was very large.[1]

Eight weeks after embargo came news of Bonaparte's Milan Decree.

Three courses had appeared open :—
1. To side with France.
2. To side with England.
3. To be neutral.

In attempting to be neutral by means of embargo, Jefferson had really joined in with Napoleon's bad policy to try to stop England from trade and sale of the products of her industry; to war on the workers of England. It was the slave owners who made the embargo policy, that warred on British labor.[2] The many Southern planters regarded trade and commerce as fraud, and the difference between prices of producer's sale and consumer's purchase as so much abstracted from themselves. They expected the merchants and sailors and ship owners to be almost the only sufferers by the embargo, that it would not harm planters, for they owned no ships. It was not till their own crops had, unsaleable, accumulated on their hands, and their much needed credit with those same merchants was gone, that they found themselves suffering, that they saw that they had made a mistake. But this was not till long afterward.

Foreign vessels were allowed in our coast trade; later in 1808 they were excluded. American fishermen on coming home were required to state on oath

[1] The United States average export for 1803-7, was $102,500,000, of which $44,863,517 were domestic produce. The average imports were $140,000,000, much of which was re-exported to the West Indies.
[2] Hildreth iii.

whether they had landed any fish abroad, which was a penal offense.[1]

Jefferson and his party had always opposed having an army. They denounced our little army as a Federalist abuse. Williams of South Carolina said "he would go a great deal further to see it (our little navy), burned .... it was a curse: he thanked God that he could vote against it."[2]

Now Jefferson asked for 6,000 regular soldiers; he wanted gunboats; his party Congressmen were puzzled by such federalist proposals from the great antifederalist. But against their own prejudices they voted both by a large majority. They would have opposed them with all their might had any Federalist proposed them.

Jefferson made his war on American trade still more active. He ordered customs officers to refuse clearance to American flour or rice laden vessels. Boston needed flour from Baltimore and elsewhere, for its own food; the governor of Massachusetts made complaint; authority was given him to issue permits. He did it so freely that his permits were bought and sold and used in Southern cities.

Then came a mandamus from Judge Johnson, himself a Jefferson Democrat, which compelled the Charleston, South Carolina, collector to grant such clearances, on the ground that the president had no legal authority in the matter. This was an able judicial rebuke to Jefferson's disregard to law.

A motion in Congress to repeal embargo and let merchant ships arm and associate for convoy and

---
[1] Hildreth iii.
[2] Ibid 61.

defense, was voted down by a large majority of devoted Democrat-Republicans.

In the British Parliament Alexander Baring, Henry Brougham, and others, attacked the Orders in Council. Petitions from London, Liverpool, and Manchester, asked their repeal.

But Parliament, led by the ministry, confirmed the odious orders. American cotton must pay 18 cents and tobacco 3 cents a pound duty to Great Britain, before an American could be permitted to take it to the continent, there to risk its confiscation under Napoleon's decrees; and cotton and tobacco came from the South. Carolina and Virginia could easily bear the loss of Boston and Baltimore's commerce, but though embargo covered cotton and tobacco, they could be shipped only by smuggling, yet a British tax on such smuggled cotton and tobacco influenced Jefferson's planter friends.

Napoleon was doing his utmost to destroy English prosperity. It was Jefferson's aim to so injure it as to compel England to terms.

How plainly Napoleon's keen insight took in the extreme fallacy of Jefferson's embargo policy; that it was producing precisely the opposite *Bayonne Decree. April 17, 1808.* effects from what Jefferson intended, is seen in his response to the embargo, which came in his Bayonne Decree of April 18, 1808, which ordered the confiscation of every American vessel in France, or to arrive!

The American envoy remonstrated. Napoleon cynically answered that as the embargo forbad American vessels to come abroad, those in France must be

English or denationalized, and the Bayonne Decree would give friendly aid to America to enforce the embargo. What could Jefferson reply?

Many American vessels, driven by the embargo either to decay at the wharves, or stay abroad, took British licenses, under the Orders in Council, in hazardous, but lucrative traffic. The French seized many. The British helped American merchants to extensively evade the embargo by omitting to notice lack of American clearances.

Thus, while Napoleon warred on all trade, British indulgence left open to Americans who evaded the embargo, a very profitable commerce;[1] merchants who obeyed Jefferson's embargo were being ruined; the many who evaded it were reaping wealth.

But embargo withheld the American market and some of its supplies from England. This was direct aid to Napoleon to starve England to his terms. Next to American war on England, embargo best suited Napoleon.

He saw that he soon must lose the last French colony; that France must forego, or seek substitutes for, colonial produce; the continent must use beet sugar, chicory and Italian rice.

Spain had begun its great struggle for independence of Napoleon, but Jefferson refused to receive a Spanish minister, though he admitted that: —

"If as is expected Buonaparte should be successful in Spain,[2] however every virtuous and liberal sentiment revolts at it."[3]

Jefferson said we must exclude a foreign navy as we do a foreign army, or keep an armed force in every port to restrain it, the expense of which would

[1] Hildreth iii, 85.   [2] Hildreth iii, 85.
[3] Jefferson to Monroe, Jan. 28, 1809.

be too great, — a well-taken ground had we possessed any means of such exclusion. The British vessels remained in our waters. Jefferson's illegal proclamation to exclude all British public vessels, instead of the offending squadron only, till England should have time to make reparation, was imprudent, and was looked upon by both countries as unfriendly. In Europe and America he was censured for not giving orders against harboring British deserters or enlisting British seamen; this would have been fairness. "France," was the cry, "has insulted and injured our citizens and our nation; he does not so retaliate on France." The accusation of partiality was heard alike in England and America, and the ministry felt and expressed this charge.

The embargoes of the Revolution and of 1794, were limited to thirty and sixty days; this one was unlimited; a majority in Congress could not remove it unless the president approved the repeal; it gave arbitrary war powers to the president, to that very Jefferson who had once hardly liked the Union because it gave so much power, though far less than he exercised, to the central government! He was unwilling that ship owners and sailors should be the best judges of the dangers they would risk. England and nearly half of America thought they saw in embargo the influence of the French emperor. He had expected the embargo. Jefferson meant it to coerce England.

The enlisting of British deserters and sailors were real offenses, the very pretext for the Chesapeake crime; England disavowed that crime; she was ready to do all that could be done to repair that particular deed ; she sent a special envoy to make apology and reparation ; a great public in both countries wished it settled ; it was not statesmanlike to refuse to adjust it, even separately from all other questions ; it was wrong to keep it open.

Partiality for Napoleon did exist in Jefferson's party; it was there a strong influence. But reflection must show us that if America wished that Europe should be many independent nations instead of becoming but one solid military power, then none of our people should have wished his success.

Bitterly the opposition canvassed the charges against Jefferson ; his early dislike to the constitution ; his undue attachment to France ; his fondness for French ideas ; his former censure of Washington and Adams and their policy and measures ; his removals from office of Revolutionary heroes appointed by Washington ; his hostility to a navy ; his absurd gunboats, regarded as caricatures on a navy ; his theory that judiciary should not be independent of Congress, president and party ; his professing before his election to believe that the Constitution gave too strong powers, and then in office, stretching these powers as they had never been stretched before, as the liberal constructionists had never dared to stretch them. His latitude in both respects fostered the Calhoun party that "nullified" the laws of the United States in 1832, and rebelled in 1860.

War is made by governments, not often by peoples ; often a majority or a very numerous minority oppose it. All France, with little exception, — the French marshals, the people, — were opposed to Napoleon's Russian war in 1812. His government made it all the same. Those who make wars ought to be required to do the fighting themselves. Embargo is making war against the poor, but the poor were intensely opposed to the embargo. Starvation is a horrible weapon. It was not Jefferson nor George III who were hungry because of embargo. Intense suffering of the politically powerless poor of Britain was no relief to the distress of the poor sea-faring people of America. Embargo is a mean method of hostility; nothing brave or heroic is in it, but the ignorance and semi-barbaric spirit of the times in the slave states, and in part of the North, controlled votes enough to sustain the party of slavery by a continued majority in Congress.

To be an editor now is one of the highest, most honorable of callings. Newspaper men now almost rule the nation; they form and foster much of the best sentiment; maintain honor and sunny courtesy; instruct the great public, and march with the van of advancing progress. But in Jefferson's time the press was narrow, bitter, vindicitive; editors, instead of being suitable teachers were, themselves, sadly in need of being enlightened. Peter Porcupine and his class were rough fellows compared with fourth-class editors of today.

Christianity, too, now full of humanity, good deeds, amiable, blessed courtesy, and loveable charities, and in noble, manly influence on all classes of society, was then far behind the exalted position of that glorious religion at this later day. Men might then be church members in good standing and still carry on trades that now extremely grieve all good Christians; might be rumsellers, distillers, slave-owners, raisers of slaves for market, privateers, duelists. So a representative man of those times is hardly to be expected to be the representative man of the twentieth century's more enlightened morality. Here Jefferson may claim some lenity.

Where in the Constitution did he find embargo authorized? Nowhere. It was not to "regulate commerce," — that was constitutional, — but to prevent it. Non-intervention irritated, wasted, crippled like war, but it acquired nothing, there was nothing for it to acquire.

Aaron Burr left the vice-presidency March, 1805, a ruined man in fame and fortune, as he was already bankrupt in morals. Indictments for murder of Hamilton hung over him. He formed *Burr Conspiracy. 1806-7.* a plot to separate the West from the Atlantic states, an idea that, no doubt, Hamilton, too, had entertained; another plot to invade Mexico, unite it with the West and form a vast empire from the Alleganies to the Pacific. He claimed to have contracted for a large tract of land near Nachitoches, ceded by Spain to Baron Bastrop, and pretended an intention of settling it. In the autumn of 1806 he was joined by armed men, formed a military camp on Blennerhasset's island in the Ohio, collected stores, prepared to move down the river in light boats to seize New Orleans. Government tried to intercept his expedition. A part of it — about one hundred men — eluded this vigilance. Defensive operations were made at New Orleans. Learning of this, Burr formed a camp just above Natchez. Militia were called for, but Burr seeing his plans failing surrendered himself. A grand jury discharged him and censured the government proceedings. Burr fled; was soon taken, carried to Richmond, tried and acquitted, because the acts charged were out of that court's jurisdiction; but he was held to bail for acts in Ohio; he fled to England and forfeited his bail; he lived a disgraced man.

Jefferson, in his next message to Congress, strongly hinted censure of this court which tried Burr. It is not for the executive to censure the judges; they must be free from political party influence.

XII

THE navy of Denmark was 20 ships of the line, 16 frigates, 9 brigs and many gunboats. The British ministry feared that Napoleon would invade Denmark and seize its navy. Long afterward it was pretended that the regent of Portugal had notified the prince of Wales that Napoleon would use the Danish and Portuguese navies for an expedition to invade the northeast coast of England. Of course this was a great absurdity; Napoleon did not confide his plans in advance to such men as the regent of Portugal, and the regent could hardly have communicated it to the ministry through the prince of Wales, for the prince was then in bitter opposition to his father's government.

The Copenhagen affair. Sept. 2-5, 1807.

Although Napoleon had written to Bernadotte [Aug. 2, 1807]: — "Denmark must declare war on England or I declare war on Denmark," yet the British ministry could not have known the existence of that letter. No doubt the ministry merely guessed Napoleon's intentions. Knowing him to be always ready to rob, they believed the situation of Denmark would tempt him to spoliate her.

Profound peace existed between England and Denmark. Denmark was not cordial to England because the British infringed her neutral rights, seized her ships, took away men from her crews, and otherwise insulted and injured Danish commerce.

Secretly the ministry prepared a powerful fleet of warships and transports, with 27,000 soldiers. This force suddenly appeared, surprised Copenhagen. The peaceful Danes were unready for war. The British envoy, Jackson, a coarse man, demanded that Denmark surrender all its navy and naval stores to the British Admiral, to be kept "till the conclusion of a general peace." The Danish government refused the great humiliation.

The British army landed. For four days the British bombarded that populous, peaceful city. The Danes made a vigorous resistance; great damage was done; about 2,000 persons lost their lives — 2,000 murders! 500 houses were burned — 500 cases of arson! For this was in time of peace! It was a city filled with homes that they bombarded.

This horrible affair aroused the indignation of the civilized world: —

"It would be difficult to find in history a more infamous and revolting instance of the abuse of power against weakness,"

said Bourrienne. The government that did not relieve Dantzic, nor re-inforce the Russians after Eylau at critical moments when as much force and energy as was put into this affair might have been sufficient to ruin Napoleon, and spare the whole careers of Moore and Wellington in Spain and Portugal; could send a great expedition to despoil a peaceful capital, and bombard women and children in their quiet homes: merely because they expected that Napoleon would invade Denmark and try to seize its navy, in which he might not succeed George Canning, would rob Denmark with bloody hands for fear another might rob her! Why not have proposed to assist to defend Denmark and its navy instead?

Copenhagen.

The British people were shocked, horror-stricken. That honorable people deplored the dishonorable affair. An Englishman says: —

"But this extraordinary spectacle was not hailed by any shouts of gratulation. This was a victory which caused no exulting emotions. The long glories of Britain disdained an association with such an exploit and the question was pointedly asked. — What words would have been strong enough to express the national abhorrence had this been the act of the blood-stained tyrant of France?"[1]

Sir Walter Scott said: —

"The Czar complained with justice of the manner in which Britain had conducted the war [1807] by petty expeditions conducive only to her own selfish ends: and the attack on Denmark was treated as a violation of the rights of nations. He therefore annulled every convention entered into between Russia and Britain and especially that of 1801."[2]

The Briton, Dr. Coote, said that only imperious, ruinous danger could excuse it, and such danger did not exist.

George's ministry not only robbed the Danes of their navy, but committed the further crime of treacherously seizing a great number of Danish private vessels, which, in fancied security of peace, were in law-

[1] Belsheen's George III, iii, 261.   [2] Scott's Napoleon.

ful trade, surprised in English ports; certainly a villainous hospitality. It could not be pleaded that the ministry took these to keep them from Napoleon.

George Canning and Lord Castlereagh seem to have been the leaders in this great crime. The crime had its regular result. It drove Denmark to aid Napoleon; from that time Denmark gave full effect to Napoleon's hostile decrees against English trade, ships, property and persons.[1]

In May, 1807, the British sent Sir John Moore with 10,000 troops to aid the half-crazy king, Gustavus IV of Sweden; but Moore found him so foolish that he returned with his troops to England.

Sweden. After peace between France, Russia, and Prussia, Gustavus continued hostilities against the colossal power of Napoleon. He was advised to make peace, but he seems to have been incapable of taking good advice. He refused to prolong his armistice with the French beyond July 13, though entreated by the Czar and by the king of Prussia. Napoleon wished to win the favor of the Swedes; but he drove Gustavus into Stralsund. Then Gustavus asked suspension of fighting. The French refused unless he would surrender that place. He could not hold it and he would not surrender it, but allowed it to be bombarded. He took care not to expose his own person to shot. He exhibited neither ability nor courage. He escaped from Stralsund with the most of his troops. The French entered it; then the miserable king bombarded his own city!

Disdaining the wishes of the people of intelligent

[1] Schlos-er vii, 572.

and patriotic Sweden, Gustavus put his confidence in something that he found in the Apocalypse. He provoked Russia further by giving a great fête to the actors in the crime against Denmark. The Czar demanded that Sweden close her Baltic ports against England. For once Gustavus was right; he refused. Russia prepared to seize Finland from Sweden simply because the Czar wanted it. Denmark, affronted by the fête, prepared to invade western Sweden. Gustavus made a new alliance with George III, for 100,000 sterling monthly. The Russians invaded Finland in February, 1808. Denmark soon declared war against Sweden. It was under pretense of aiding Gustavus that the Danish expedition had been organized and sent.

Although for months it was publicly apparent that war was coming and the Russians were assembling on his frontier, the foolish Gustavus made no preparations for defense. Before Gustavus got ready the Swedish army and navy, Finland, as far as Vasa, and Aland, Gothland, and the Swedish fortresses, were taken by the active Russians.

The Swedes made a gallant struggle; but who could prosper with such a ruler? The British sent him 12,000 British troops, but speedily recalled them because the conduct of the haughty fool was intolerable, even to his allies.

That excellent nation had long been patient, enduring; now they must save the nation. With the unanimous willingness of Sweden, a popular movement arrested the king in March, 1809, and he was declared incapable of reigning. His uncle, Charles, became regent March 14. On March 29 the king abdicated, and the regent became King Charles XIII. Every Swede was rejoiced at Gustavus' downfall. His reign cost Sweden dearly, and his incapacity to reign ought to have been declared long before.

Sweden so changed its constitution that, while the new king held the executive power, a Council of State decided the important affairs.

March 25, 1809, the Czar declared Finland united to Russia. Thus was a great province lost by trusting power to foolish King Gustavus.

XIII

SERVIA lay in what appeared to be the heart of Turkey. Its territory now, 1890, is 18,816 square miles, its population, nearly 1,700,000.

Servia and Turkey. "The Servians present the first example of an ancient Christian people revolting successfully against Mohammedan oppression."[1] For eighty years with one brief interval they have been independent.

They revolted fifteen years before the Greek revolution. After their early conquest by the Turks, they remained an unarmed, oppressed people, living by themselves in retired villages, while the Moslems, who were mostly not Turks but apostate Servians lived in the towns. Many a Servian never entered the nearest town in his life.

The Moslem oppressors were: —
1. High officials.
2. Janizaries, a powerful military caste.
3. Moslem landlords, mostly slaves.

[1] Clark's Races of Turkey, 279.

After the conquest Servians had been obliged to surrender their faith or their arms. Many had yielded the faith and were now landlords. It was their extortion that caused insurrection as late as 1875. The common people were Christians.

In 1878 the German emperor Joseph attacked Turkey. He armed a body of Servians. He defeated the Turks and tore from them part of Servia. The people awoke to hope. But the French wars came on and Austria dropped Servia to oppose France. The Moslems came back.

The enlightened Sultan Selim III of Turkey attempted to supersede the Janizaries by regular troops disciplined and armed like Europeans. But the Janizaries were formidable tribes. In Barbary they had already denied allegiance to the Sultan under their own leaders. Now the 150,000 in Servia revolted against Selim.

Osman Pasvan Oglu was their famous champion. At Widden he had made himself independent from 1797.

This division of the Moslems gave hope to the Christians. The Turkish commander took the before unheard of step to call the Christians to arms against the fierce Janizaries. They responded quickly. The Janizaries found more than their match; they were repelled.

But all Moslemdom was shocked. Believers beaten by Christians! Intolerable; it must not be. Selim could not stand against this fiery prejudice. He was compelled to order the return to Belgrade of these expelled warriors. They did return, fierce, furious. Mustapha was slain. Four Janizary leaders divided the provinces.

Then followed so terrible a reign of terror and blood as Servians had never seen. People fled to the mountains and fastnesses; everywhere there they rose in arms. The Pasha of Bosnia came with aid. The revolt spread like conflagration. Resistless, swiftly the Christians swept down from the mountains; gallantly they drove the Janizaries from Servia; they were masters of the country.

Tzerni[1] George was chosen Servian commander in 1804.

"This man," says Dr. Croly, "was one of the bold creations of wild countries, and troubled times — beings of impetuous courage, iron strength, original talent and doubtful morality."

Although the Christian leader, his moral sense was dull.

In 1806 he defeated a Turkish army, and in 1807 drove the Turks from Servia.

Servia was now free; George was at its head. A Senate of twelve members, one for each district, came together without election. They used legislative and executive power. Afterward George called them at his pleasure. No regular legislative elections were held till 1848. Each district had a military governor, each village its head-men; each chief town a court of justice. Public schools were founded. Old leaders were refractory; George banished all his rivals. From 1810 to 1813 George was absolute ruler. The local leaders had each his mounted followers, often lawless; but this singular George, always in peasant's dress, could rule though he could not write; he was eccentric, untrained, rough but forcible.

Early in this century power in Turkey was much

[1] Black George.

divided. Nominally subject to the Sultan; Djezzer Pasha at Damascus ruled the two Syrias; Ali Pasha reigned in Albania; Pasvan Oglu in Widden; and British and then the Begs and Mehemit Ali in Egypt, and paid tribute when they pleased. Thus Turkey was weak.

The enlightened Selim III attempted reforms. The Ulemas, who are theological lawyers and advisers of the Divan (State Council) opposed, they conspired against him, aided by Russia. Napoleon sent him officers to instruct the Turkish army like modern troops. Russia and Britain threatened war unless Selim should break off his French alliance.

Selim became Sultan in 1789. His reforms were greatly hindered by Russia and Napoleon. In 1791 Russia robbed him of his territory beyond the Dneister. Bonaparte's attack on Egypt brought him a war. Sad examples of robbery for Christians to set to Moslems.

His European army system roused up fanatic bigotry. After many dangers a fanatic revolt in 1807 overcome his new army and compelled him to resign. Mustapha IV was put in his place.

Bairak-dar, his chief adviser, an energetic, able soldier, marched on Constantinople to re-instate Selim. On his approach bigots strangled Selim. Enraged Bairak-dar destroyed the murderers. He deposed Mustapha and proclaimed Mahmud II, and became Grand Vizier.

He took energetic steps to destroy the power of the Janizaries, but[1] they attacked the Seraglio and demanded restoration of Mustapha.

[1] Metternich's Memoirs.

Bairak-dar made a brave defense. But when flames were destroying the palace and he in danger of becoming a prisoner he strangled Mustapha, threw his head to his beseigers, and blew himself up with the place.

Murder and robbery reigned for days. The life of Mahmud was spared. The Ulemas and Janizaries compelled him to allow all the power to them. He ruled only in his harem.

Turkey shrewdly accepted the Tilsit offer of French mediation. But Russia would not withdraw from Roumania as the Czar had pledged at Tilsit. So the mediation fell.

Between 1805 and 1809 Napoleon repeatedly discussed with Alexander and with Metternich the proposed conquest and division of Turkey by Russia, France, and Austria.

XIV

OCTOBER 5, 1807, the great Von Stein re-entered the Prussian ministry. He began the Stein system of reforms. He issued a royal decree that gave to burghers and peasants the right, hitherto confined to nobles, to acquire and hold land, and he permitted nobles to engage in commerce and industry; lands might be sold in parcels, and he abolished serfdom.[1] Six weeks later another of his decrees gave to burghers councilors of their own election to regulate local affairs.

The German Patriots.

[1] Schlosser.

The wise Stein found many difficulties. The host of 7,000 civil employés of the ceded provinces called for relief. The country, just conquered, and still firmly held by the French army, which Prussia was compelled to feed, clothe and pay, in addition to the immense indemnity exacted by Napoleon ; the drain of the metal money; the evils of a paper credit, added to the other distresses of the luckless war, rendered Prussia really very poor. Napoleon's Continental System and the blockade by England completed the misery of Prussia and the Prussians.

Napoleon objected to Von Stein. It was not the good of the Prussians or of any people that Napoleon desired. The king must dismiss Von Stein. The king, to please Napoleon, did dismiss the patriot. But Stein had the friendship of the people of Prussia ; he had many friends. His influence remained a power in the Prussian cabinet, though himself an exile.

Scharnhorst, a military patriot, became minister of war. He, too, applied just reforms. He opened to merit promotion to the higher grades, from which all but nobles had been excluded. It was an army led by nobles that had lost Prussia. He abolished military flogging ; he removed class exemption from military service. Henceforth all classes must be liable to be called into the army. Noble birth must not exempt from aiding to protect the country.

By the terms of the peace Napoleon had bound Prussia not to keep an army of more than 42,000 men. He meant to keep the Prussian army weak. But the able Scharnhorst had his plan. No sooner were soldiers well-drilled than he sent them home and replaced them with recruits until Prussia had a great number of drilled and disciplined men that could be called, and the military spirit became strong.

Societies were formed secretly for deliverance; rich and poor joined this tugendbund. From beyond the frontier Stein aided and stimulated this patriotic association that was destined to play a great part in all Germany. Napoleon complained, but Stein was busy, and Russia and Austria did not oppose his great scheme, that was to be so long in developing, and which we saw in 1870 ripen into a United Germany.

The treaty of Tilsit did not mention the exact amount that Prussia must pay to Napoleon; the stupid king had trusted this to old Kalreuth, who was too weak minded to see to it. This fault of the king was taken advantage of by Napoleon, who himself fixed the sum, 601,200,000 francs, so high that Prussia could not pay it; Tilsit allowed him to hold Prussia till it should be paid; so a French army held it till after 1812. Napoleon now claimed to own Prussia's Silesia. Russia objected. Napoleon was ready to give the Czar for his consent, Turkey's Roumania. It was always somebody else's property that Napoleon was ready to give. He frequently traded away countries to which he had no more of right or claim than to the North Pole.

The first few months after Napoleon and Alexander had agreed at Tilsit, Napoleon sent armies to take and hold Portugal, Rome and Etruria (Tuscany), neither of which had provoked this conquest: his attack was purely aggressive; and he tried to trade away a part of Turkey that was beyond the reach of his armies.

Without justice he was secretly preparing two aggressive expeditions to seize Sardinia Island and Sicily, neither provoked except by his own avarice for wealth and power, and justifiable only on the highwayman's plea, — that he wanted them. Both failed.

"Peace" had come, but it was a Bonaparte peace — everything was held only by force, everybody was suppressed, robbed, all liberty was held down by the throat.

Bonaparte always seized every country, every province, every power, everything within his reach. America escaped his invasion because he did not control the passage of the ocean. That was in Britain's power. For this he would always hate England and the English. For Trafalgar Americans should always be grateful.

August 18, 1807, Napoleon changed the French constitution. It was not France that changed it. France was powerless in his hands.

He entirely suppressed the Chamber of Tribunes. *He erased every trace of the Republic.* His despotism French Liberty further suppressed. was more consolidated than that of Turkey, for even the Sultan was obliged to allow ministers then to rule. Napoleon placed the already fettered press under still closer restrictions of censorship. Literary talent was compelled to take only such direction as he desired. So enslaved was the press that instead of being a bulwark of freedom it was a powerful aid to despotism both in France and in Germany.[1] It is only a press that is free that can protect liberty or oppose wrong and outrage. In France was no liberty.

[1] Bourrienne.

By decree of the servile Senate, Oct. 12, 1807, judges were not to receive their life commissions till after five years of service,—a probation of their adhesion to Napoleon and despotism.

Napoleon was extremely arbitrary; yet his power was so great that all ranks, classes, and parties were compelled to pay assiduous court to him, and sought places under him. There was no other means for any persons to advance their own interests, or to rise in the State; he was the center of favor, the only way to success in France. A Frenchman must be a Bonapartist or be a blank. With few exceptions old noblesse were slavish to him. Napoleon could easily ruin an enemy; he could reward an adherent. The liberal Lafayette; the heroic Carnot who in the government in 1800 stood alone against despotism, were noble monuments of French democracy, but they were out of power. Yet the French were better off than under the Bourbons, for by their Revolution they had won their own land and now owned and cultivated it free from the extortionate rent gatherers of Bourbon times. Thus the French people were immensely more prosperous than under their late kings and noblesse. But this prosperity came from themselves and not from Napoleon. But Napoleon's system of robbing other nations of immense sums of money, like any bandit, and his compelling other nations to feed, clothe and pay large parts of the French army, kept the taxes down in France to a supportable rate.

Revolution had its benefits as well as its damages. It brought Napoleon, but it banished hunger; it brought military despotism, but it abolished the far more onerous noblesse tyranny; it brought conscription, but it also brought the Code, framed by great lawyers. Napoleon abused the Revolution's results by his odious, hard disposition to quarrel with every people, and invade every accessible country. It was alone the quarrelsome, bitter, avaricious, domineering and blood-hardened disposition of the individual, Napoleon himself, that detracted from the rich fruits of the Revolution that France would have enjoyed under a peaceful government. It was not the Revolution's fault that wars were made with Prussia, with Russia, with Spain, with Portugal; all these were purely aggressive wars on his part; France did not demand them; some of them were grossly against the will of France; that of 1812 with Russia was against the almost unanimous wish of the French, including ministers and marshals, army and citizens.

Though completely despotic, Napoleon's government was regular and systematic. Taxes were heavy but as government outlay was immense and made business, they were paid. No forced loans or confiscations of property; but he took what was of far more inestimable value, more than half the people's sons as conscripts, who died all over Europe by suffering, of march or battle, each with a marshal's baton in his mental vision.

The stoppage of external commerce stimulated domestic industry; the roads and canals built were covered with transports of goods. Produce of farm and workshop found a ready market. Beet root sugar took the place of the West India product. Chicory usurped the place of coffee. The rice fields of Italy must have been very profitable. Hard coin became scarce in the rest of Europe and in the United

States, but the French empire had coin. England exported much of her coin after suspension of coin payments, which lasted from 1798 to 1821, and America's and Russia's coin was drawn away by lack of sufficient tariff protection to cause manufacturers at home to keep their coin at home. Austria had little money except bad paper, and little export of manufactures to recruit its small supply, and Prussia was robbed to poverty by Napoleon. The enormous sums which Napoleon extorted from other peoples, were largely expended in France; many public works erected, which gave expansion to business.

In August, 1807, the French minister published an exceedingly glowing report of the splendor of French enterprise. Immense length of roads had been built or repaired; great highways had climbed over the Alps and Apennines; rivers made more navigable; new bridges spanned the rivers; Antwerp had become the maritime center; first-class war ships were on the Scheldt, which important river had been closed to commerce till the French came; fourteen large ships were there on the stocks; many more were finished and had gone down the river to Flushing, whose harbor was deepened to receive them; the harbors of Cherbourg, Dunkirk, Calais, Rochfort, and Marsailles were improved; every French conquest was a help to French enterprise.

But what could Napoleon do with these great ships? They were certain to be captured by the British if they left safe harbor. Napoleon could conscript peasants and soon make of them veteran soldiers. But peasant boys could not be transformed into skillful seamen without access to the sea.

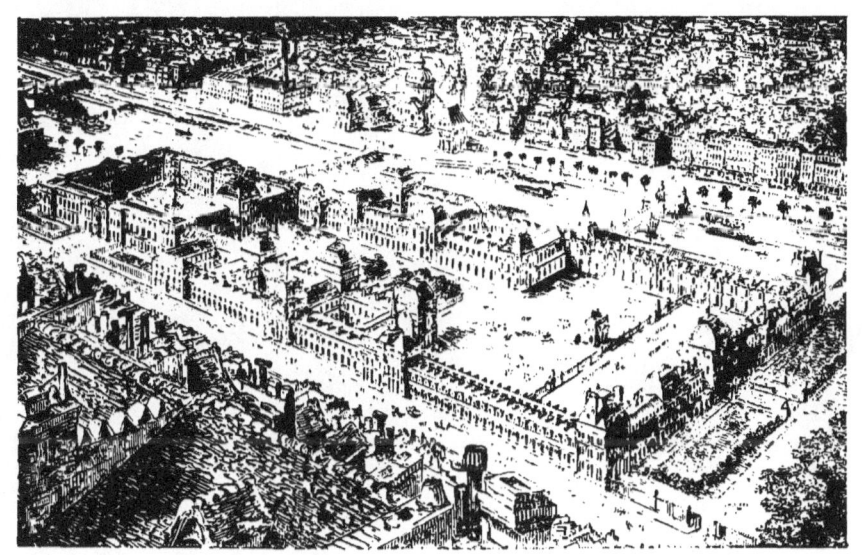

NAPOLEON'S PALACE OF THE TUILERIES AND LOUVRE.

ONE OF NAPOLEON'S PRISONS.

Many other objects were enumerated in that brilliant report. It is hardly surprising that its magnificence, close after the conquest of Prussia, the erection by Napoleon of the duchy of Warsaw, and the kingdom of Westphalia, and the monstrous cash robbery of Prussia, dazzled the French, though the plundered nations of Germany and Austria were not so content.

I do not here report the Napoleonic financial reports because they are unreliable.

Military spectacles and wonderful adulation greeted Napoleon on his return from Prussia. Yet he had, in eight months, drawn 240,000 conscripts, or more than the whole number of young Frenchmen who reached the military age in twelve months!

By magnificent reports and display, Napoleon was gilding the fetters of French liberty.

It is surprising that, down to a considerable later period, no French government had ever limited by law the period of imprisonment before trial. Few laws are more important. So great a safeguard to liberty had always been omitted. The *habeas corpus* writ is eminently British and American. Each French faction, on reaching power, wished to consign its opponents to prison. *Imprisonment.*

Napoleon established eight state prisons. So despotic was he that an order signed by him or by his Privy Council was sufficient to consign any person to rigorous imprisonment for any length of time. And this was not an idle power; it was used. It is not strange, then, that the opponents of Napoleon were silent. The inquisitions of his vigilant police were sure to detect any opponent. His spies under the Minister of Police, another set under Duroc, and a third system under himself, and each spying on the other, were ubiquitous.

In eight and one-fourth years, from September 24, 1805, to November 11, 1813, the number of conscripts decreed was 2,113,000, beside the voluntary enlistments, and beside the great army of 1804; amounting altogether to about 2,750,000 men and boys; departmental guards and levy *en masse* of 1814 not included. Yet so thorough was his despotism that all these levies were furnished. The slavish, fettered press was largely devoted to glorifying him and publishing his decrees. Little other political news was allowed to them. No Frenchman, once liable to the conscription, could hold any public office, exercise any public right, receive any legacy or inherit any property, without certificate that he had obeyed and was legally exempt — in actual service, discharged, or not required. Those who failed to join the army when drawn, were deprived of all civil rights, treated as deserters, were dressed and fed as convicts, and made to labor without pay on the public works. The horrors of this punishment were afterward much increased. Thus Napoleon procured the men who perished in his aggressive campaigns.

Napoleon's school system, his "University," was a measure to secure his own control of education, which he made military. Voluntary schools were not prohibited, and at one time about 400 existed, but he so oppressed them that most of them were closed. The most promising boys were put into special military schools, but all schools were military. Mathematics

French Schools.

and common branches only were studied in the lower schools. Everything was done to make of the boys good soldiers and unquestioning subjects. Napoleon's schools were not for enlightenment, but to make of the rising generation fit tools for despotism.

He had instituted a catechism in 1806, which taught obedience and almost worship of himself. Among its answers were:—"Because God, by loading our Emperor with gifts both in peace and war, has established him our sovereign and His own image on the earth," [1] and that "Those who fail in their duties toward our Emperor will render themselves worthy of eternal damnation." *Catechism.*

Napoleon controlled his servile Senate; the Legislative body was submissive; the Tribunate destroyed. He had genius for despotism. He so securely bound France, Germany, Prussia, Italy, Naples, Switzerland, Holland, Belgium and the Tyrol and Venice that submission was imperative. His reign threatened return of the dark ages. Already like coming events they "cast their shadows before" over all the Continent. Outside of the United States and the British empire not a free press existed. Even enlightened Germany, noble, freedom-loving Switzerland, enterprising Holland, or brave old Italy, could not publish a book without censorship, and Napoleon's censorship meant much. Napoleon admired Charlmagne, and it was the civilization of Charlemagne's Ninth century that he desired a thousand years later in the Nineteenth. *Despotism.*

[1] For this blasphemy see "Catechism of the Empire," 1806.

This great catastrophe had come to the French because their Revolution had not recognized nor sought equal liberty and equal *justice* and *humanity* to every person alike before the law.

Theirs was not a republican democracy from 1789 to 1800; it was simply strife of parties and persons, each of whom wished to wrong, to oppress the other. Had they recognized the vital principle of all real republican democracy, equal rights and equal protection of every person by the law; every one allowed and protected in his own opinions, person, career, and property, then there could have been no "Reign of Terror," no destroying men for their opinions, no Marat, no Danton, no Robespierre. It was violation of the most vital principles of real republican democracy that made the bloodshed of that frightful period possible. The moment that a democracy begins to tyrannize, that moment it ceases to be democracy. A democratic government must protect against license, it must not use license.

Real republican democracy cannot punish for political opinion. If it attempts to do so it changes its character. That the French Revolution did punish for political opinion is proof that it was not a republican democracy. Sometimes it was mob; sometimes oligarchy; sometimes both; Robespierre, the Terror, was despotism; to these, all real democrats and republicans are utterly opposed.

Many writers have confounded these principles. Let us see the truth. Mob rule is not real democracy; it is the oligarchy of only the men who compose the mob. Mob rule is not republicanism; a real republic is guaranteed, protected liberty without license, ruled only by the people in strictly orderly manner, and entirely respectful to every person's liberty and prosperity. Republican democracy is liberty, but is never license.

An oligarchy may be aristocratic or may be canaille, it may be powdered and perfumed silk-clad gentry, or it may be the dirtiest mob of savages, and yet if it be rule of the few it is oligarchy. Mobs are always but a few persons of the nation. If a mob rules it is then oligarchy — one of the furthest removes from real republican or real democratic rule.

Britain, now almost a republic, a democracy with monarchial forms, was then a monarchial oligarchy. The French Revolution was a rabble oligarchy. Both countries are greatly changed. Both have since then vastly advanced in civilized enlightment, in place of the semi-dark enlightenment of that bloody period.

Napoleon's despotism had not come from real democracy, but from oligarchy most marked. That he could consolidate such despotism was owing to the spirit of the times; so many an oligarchial Frenchman wished to compel everybody to his own opinion, a very anti-republican sentiment. Napoleon consolidated this very spirit by the spectacle of France, the aggregate French, ruling many states; thousands of Frenchmen personally ruling abroad; while the peoples who were down, were kept down by strong police, military and despotic practices.

All that France needed to make her Revolution a republican-democratic success was republicans and democrats. Lacking these she was never then a democracy.

The authors of Napoleon's accession to power, of

his despotism, were practically monarchists; they who favored the rule of the few or of one; they were not the few democratic-republicans, for these must need favor equal rights, equal civil protection, equal remedies in the law.

In March, 1808, by a *Senatus consultum*, Napoleon re-established nobility, hereditary and entailed. The odious system by which accident of birth and not ability or merit is rewarded, was again fastened upon France, that had struggled and suffered so much to rid herself of this burden.

Oppressive Nobility.

Napoleon had long sought the favor of the nobodies of the old noblesse. He had established a court of strict etiquette, where various trifling and absurd forms were practiced, and where even Cambaceres[1] had excited public derision by his ridiculous dress and new manners. Old noblesse and parvenues were bowing and grinning together in his ante-chambers, and making silly speeches to each other and speaking and acting adulation to the man who covered all Europe with mourning and suffering.

Napoleon robbed the Germans and Italians to endow these new, gold-plated receivers of stolen goods, and so increased the hatred of the robbed to him and to his bandit system. For these creatures about $450,000 were yearly abstracted from little Hanover alone, a single example of how royally Napoleon supplied these creatures at honest men's expense. The old noblesse thronged his court; the oldest and perhaps the most decayed from the parent stock, was

---

[1] "Senators" said Cambaceres, " You are no longer obscure plebeians or simple citizens. I, myself, am no longer citizen Cambaceres . . . I am a prince, your most serene highness and my most serene person," &c.

proud to become maid of honor and kneel to lace the Empress' shoe, an office which a plebeian might have deemed to be a degradation.

Napoleon tried to unite the two sets, but each knowing what miserable shams were the other, were at first disinclined to unite, though money caused some marriages. Napoleon's court was certainly tending to become like that of an Asiatic despot.

Every Frenchman was practically under guardianship by Napoleon. Liberty did not exist.

In Bavaria some of the privileges of nobility disappeared; nobles were required to help bear the burdens of the state, and common people were allowed to be eligible to public offices. The old, aristocratic assembly gave place to deputies of the country. Baden, also, abolished the exclusive privileges of nobles to hold office. <small>Bavaria.</small>

The pope was dissatisfied because the Code Napoleon, which permitted divorce, had been applied to the kingdom of Italy where it took the place of the Concordat which had made the Catholic the religion of the state. <small>Italy. 1807-8.</small>

Napoleon was displeased with the pope for his refusal to divorce Jerome Bonaparte from his American wife, which Napoleon's imperial decree soon after did, so that Jerome could marry a princess of Wurtemberg.

The French troops going to Naples seized Ancona. The pope was affronted. Napoleon pretended that he occupied Ancona as protector of the Holy See. He demanded that the pope close his ports to the English and his state to refugees.

Though Joseph Bonaparte had been made king of Naples by Napoleon, the pope claimed ancient "feudal rights" over Naples. The pope wanted a hand in politics and longed for its revenues.

Napoleon reminded him that it was only in times of ignorance that popes assumed the right to dispose of crowns. The quarrel was bitter. Napoleon took possession of about one-third of the "States of the Church" and united it to the kingdom of Italy, April, 1808.

"There is no necessity that the pope should be sovereign of Rome; the most holy popes were not so," said Bonaparte.

Secret societies were formed in Italy against Napoleon [Carbonari]. These societies formed in the interest of priestcraft and absolutism, afterward went to the other extreme of liberalism and patriotic service, to free Italy from French, Austrian, and domestic despotism.

XV

Spain.

SPAIN had lost Louisiana; had lost Trinidad; had lost her six million francs a month; had lost her commerce and her colonies; had thrown away her navy at Trafalgar; all for Napoleon; all for no reward whatever; all because Napoleon was grasping; all because Spain's king, Charles IV, was too weak, too degenerate, too foolish to resist. Never did country more need good, wise rulers, and she had a semi-fool.

He saw Napoleon hawking Spain's Balearic Islands in the market for his own exclusive benefit, and allowed the insult. Spanish Bourbons, the Inquisition, and ignorant, and intolerant churchmen had smothered Spanish patriotism; had kept its people unenlightened. Good men were not gone; they were suppressed. They were without opportunity under that frivolous king and court.

The alliance of St. Idlefonso, very foolishly made by this foolish king in 1796, made worse in 1801, and still worse by addition in 1803, was extremely disastrous to Spain. Still the nation adhered to the half-imbecile king who had made that alliance, instead of declaring him unfit to reign and setting him aside as they had done with his wholly idiotic older brother, whose place he occupied.

Spain's navy, a part of her army, and her treasure had been freely used by Napoleon in his own wars, with no compensation whatever to Spain. The foolish king had been deluded into signing a treaty in 1796, offensive and defensive with France. This was the whole origin of the long, sad, terrible involving of Spain with Napoleon. He never missed a chance to further entangle the worthless king.

He had ruined the Spanish navy at Trafalgar. He had required Charles to furnish him Spanish troops to serve in the north of Europe against any and all his own enemies. He required Charles to pay in Spanish silver dollars 72,000,000 francs a year to aid Napoleon's wars. This was a very large sum then, equal to much more now. Yet Charles and Spain had not a single real interest in common with Napoleon; had great interests on the other side. So Spain fought, and sacrificed against its own free commerce; against access to its transatlantic colonies, against its own peace. Because Spain was united with Napoleon, his enemy, Britain, with its great navy, found itself reluctantly compelled to cut off commerce and communication between Spain and its great possessions, including all South America, (except Brazil and Guiana), all Mexico, all Central America, Cuba, and other West Indies. All this because the king was not a manly man and Napoleon was a tyrant.

Still Spain adhered to the half-imbecile who adhered to the great destroyer of Spanish interests and humiliator of just Spanish pride. The king was merely the figure-head of the government, the real ruler was Manual Godoy, the queen's favorite, who was morally of little better character than the bad royal pair themselves. Singularly enough the king was a warm friend of his wife's favorite. Godoy had been taken from the Guards and made " Prince de la Paix," by her special favor, and by sufferance of both was allowed to manage state affairs.

It is wrong to charge God with intending Charles for a king. He would hardly send so bad a man to fill so great a place. He would hardly be likely to place at the head of a great nation a person who lacks manhood. Such examples as that of Charles lay heredity open to the suspicion that God does not favor it; that he never instituted it at all.

Had Godoy ruled entirely unfettered by the unworthy royal pair, the government would at least have had some little vigor and some patriotism. Bad as was the favorite, he was better than the king and queen. He regretted the vassalage of Spain to Napoleon; he wished to break it. When, in 1806, Napoleon moved his army against Prussia, Godoy hoped that the time had come to act, while Prussia and Russia should keep Napoleon and his troops busy at long distance from Spain. Godoy called a large Spanish force to arms. Napoleon, at Jena, heard this news. He resolved to dethrone the worthless king and queen; to rule Spain himself. To strengthen himself in the north and to weaken Godoy, he called for 16,000 of those Spanish troops. The crushing defeat of the Prussians alarmed Godoy; the cowardly king of that brave nation had no courage to refuse. So 16,000 of the best troops of Spain marched to Napoleon in Poland and fought the Russians and Prussians.

After Napoleon had made peace with Russia and Prussia at Tilsit, in 1807, he arrogantly demanded of the regent of Portugal, with whom France had no quarrel: —

1. To exclude British vessels from Portugal. *Portugal. 1807.*
2. To arrest all British subjects in Portugal.
3. To plunder them of their property.

Napoleon meanly warred not only on unoffending nations, but on private individuals, and plundered private property of non-belligerents, a great depravity even in war.

Little Portugal indignantly refused. It would exclude British vessels, but would not violate its hospitality to strangers in Portugal, nor degrade itself to become the robber of private property of its guests. This honorable reply of the regency did not abate Napoleon's bandit avarice. He knew that it was in the power of the regency to obtain a large sum by robbery of the British merchants in Portugal.

Napoleon assembled an army at Bayonne, near Spain, ostensibly against Portugal By treaty of March 19, 1804, Bonaparte had wrung from Portugal 16,000,000 francs, for which extortion he restored to her the right to open her ports during the war between France and England, and recognized Portugal's neutrality. Portugal had kept this treaty; we see now how he broke his faith pledged in that treaty.[1]

"The emperor for all reply declared war on Portugal,"[2] and ordered General Junot at Bayonne, to march immediately.[3]

The Portuguese envoy, Lima, at Paris, asked delay. Napoleon violently addressed him publicly before the diplomats : — [4]

> "If Portugal does not do what I wish the House of Braganza wil not reign two months." "I will no longer tolerate an English ambassador in Europe : I will declare war on any power that receives one after two months." "The English declare they will no longer respect neutrals at sea; I will no longer recognize them on land."[5]

Had a real statesman ruled Spain, unfettered by the imbecility and corruption of royalty, he might probably have secured to Spain the greatest obtainable prosperity by uniting, in 1804, in full concert with Great Britain, and before Trafalgar, placing a strong allied army on the Pyrenees frontier. Then instead of being driven from the seas by the British, she would have kept open her own vast colonial trade and preserved her American colonies and home treasure for her own defense. Then Napoleon could not

---

[1] Metternich Memoirs ii, 394.   [2] Ibid.
[3] Napoleon to Champigny; also to Clarke, October 12, 1807.
[4] October 15, 1807.   [5] Metternich to Stadion, October 6, 1807.

have taken the whole grand army against Austria in
1805 or against Prussia in 1806, and Russia could
have had time to bring up its army before he reached
Austria and perhaps before Napoleon could have
raised sufficient forces to both protect France on the
Spanish frontier and attack Ulm in Bavaria at the
same time.

But the miserable Charles IV, instead of manly
resistance, made a new treaty with Napoleon, October 27, 1807, by which he conspired against his
neighbor state, Portugal, with which he was at peace,
that it was to be divided into three parts, and despoiled. By the terms of this crime of bandit conspiracy, the southern one-third was to be donated to
Godoy as a principality. The northern third was to
be given to the baby king of "Etruria" (Tuscany)
in exchange for Tuscany for Napoleon. The remaining part of this rich plunder was to remain in sequestration for future disposal.

Twenty-eight thousand French troops were to be
permitted to march through Spain to Portugal.[1]
Spain was to furnish the same number.[1] Natural
obstacles rendered Spanish co-operation necessary
for the French to reach Portugal at all.

Feeble Charles IV was to receive the tinsel title,
"Emperor of the Two Americas," and this too at a
time when the miserable fellow could not send a single sail toward America without its probable capture
by British cruisers.

For one-third of still unconquered Portugal, this
degenerate creature [2] traded to Napoleon, who did not
own a foot of Portugal, the kingdom of his infant

---

[1] Napier i, 20.   [2] Rotteck Algemeine Weltgeschichte, 183.

grandson, Tuscany.¹ Charles' daughter Louise, unworthy child of unworthy sire, had reigned badly in Etruria, in the name of her baby son. To make her late boy husband, Louis, king of Etruria, Charles had embezzled and traded to Napoleon Spain's extremely valuable Louisiana, which was all of the present United States between the Mississippi and the Rocky Mountains, and south of Canada, except Texas. And then Louis had been only a puppet of Napoleon till his death, in 1804. French officers, directed by Napoleon, had ruled Etruria, often without even consulting Louis. Louise had proved as utterly incapable as her husband had been, and as bigoted, ignorant, and illiberal as Charles, her father.

The French took entire possession of Etruria, December 10, 1807, and Louise went home to Spain, wickedly hoping that Portugal would be conquered by the blood of good, brave men, and despoiled by her father and Napoleon, and one-third of it be fated to her own misgovernment.²

The French army entered Spain without waiting for the Conspiracy treaty to be signed. The French and Spanish army under Junot entered Portugal.

Portugal. 1808. That country was not prepared for this sudden, unprovoked invasion. It had confided in its own peaceful intentions. It had not expected unprovoked attack. A British naval officer proposed to the Prince Regent the alternatives, to surrender the Portuguese fleet to English keeping, or to use it to convey the regent and his friends to Brazil. The latter was accepted. Junot arrived and saw the fleet leaving the port of

¹ Rotteck.   ² Lanfrey.

Lisbon. It carried much treasure that Napoleon had hoped to plunder. Napoleon levied on Portugal for 100,000,000 francs, beside 6,000,000 francs for Junot, who also raised 5,000,000 francs for himself.[1]

Junot disbanded part of the Portuguese army, took 5,000 to serve with himself and sent the rest as so much plunder to France, to serve in the French army, and Napoleon proclaimed that the royal House of Portugal had ceased to reign. Portugal was conquered; but Napoleon, who freely broke solemn pledges, did not keep his word with the foolish Charles of Spain. Instead of dividing the plunder as they had agreed, he almost wholly excluded the Spanish from Portugal. The incapable and dark-minded Louise was not to further darken one-third of Portugal. In his desire for absolute power Napoleon paused at no treachery; he committed any perfidy or any violence; he caused any amount of suffering; committed any outrage; he wanted obedience and obedience only everywhere. No government, no system of government was sacred from his destroying hands. He would have conquered America as willingly as Portugal; he would have plundered it as readily as he robbed Prussia had he controlled the sea passage. For six years no nation but Britain had resisted his will, and not been crushed or beaten.

Had it been his fleets instead of those of Britain that conquered at Trafalgar and elsewhere completely, then all the world must have fallen under his power. He would have swept every sail from the seas except those of France and his allies; would have crossed the British Channel with an army; would probably

[1] Schlosser viii, 43.

have sent another across the Atlantic as he sent the army of the Rhine to St. Domingo, in the short time that the peace of 1802 allowed his armies to cross the seas.

Had he destroyed the British navy or driven it from the ocean as completely as it had beaten his navy, then the Danish, the Swedish, and all other navies, both war and commercial, would have been in his colossal power.

The world today hardly realizes how much it owes to Nelson and Collingwood's great victory of Trafalgar; the most important victory of the century, in its consequences to all the world. Trafalgar was the world's defense.

Napoleon concentrated another army on the border of Spain. He promised that it should not enter Spain without the king's consent. As usual he violated his promise.

Prince Ferdinand, heir to the Spanish crown, was weak, cunning, and ignorant. What else could be expected from his parentage? He was controlled by the priest, Canon Escoiquiz, who managed his affairs. Because Ferdinand hated France, many Spaniards liked him. Dissensions broke out at Madrid between the weak son and the weak father. Both feared Napoleon. The Spanish learned with astonishment, by royal proclamation, that the son had conspired against the father's throne. Ferdinand was arrested. He confessed in a humble but indefinite letter; he implored forgiveness. Charles pardoned him in public, Nov. 5, 1807, but carried on a scandalous trial of his accessories, as though accomplices must bear all

Ferdinand of Spain.

the punishment of their principals. Ferdinand had secretly written to Napoleon, soliciting a marriage alliance with the Bonaparte family. Napoleon thought of Lucian's daughter; but Lucian gave it no encouragement. Ferdinand received no answer.

Charles wrote to Napoleon asking him "to aid me with your knowledge and advice." [Oct. 29, 1807.]

Napoleon took advantage of these dissensions. Here was what he chose to regard as a call for assistance; just what he wanted. Fifty-three thousand French troops entered Spain in December, 1807.[1] Murat came in February, 1808; he took possession of Spanish fortresses; he approached Madrid; Napoleon had ordered him to use kind words.

The Spanish people were aroused, alarmed, indignant. Godoy saw that Napoleon had swindled him; he saw the great danger; he advised the royal depravities, Charles and his wife, Maria Louise, to fly to the south and thence to America. This was precisely what Napoleon desired, as it would give him a pretext to declare the throne vacated, and to seize upon Spain, as he was seizing Portugal.

By a great mistake of policy Napoleon had resolved to make a Bonaparte king of Spain. He might have continued to rule Spain as he had ruled it for a long time, through its own feeble and base hereditary Bourbon sovereign.[2] When Spain was thus in his power it was his fatal error to ask for more. The populace grew daily more excited. They at least did not wish for a Bonaparte; they resolved to prevent the great aggression Seeing that royalty apparently

Spain, 1808.

[1] Napier.   [2] Thiers Cons et Empire, iii, 19.

intended to fly, they took measures to prevent it. They watched the king's palace at Madrid; they guarded every avenue of royal running away. Everybody blamed Godoy; fury was excited against him. The faults of his royal mistress and of her husband were charged to him, the favorite.

An insurrection broke out March 18, 1808. The mob stormed Godoy's palace. He secreted himself in a loft. When, afterward, he attempted to escape, the people seized him; they wished to lynch him; but the queen did not sacrifice her favorite; the royal pair rescued him. But to keep him from the fury of the people they were compelled to send him, bruised and bleeding as he was, to the safety of a prison. As soon as practicable, they had him removed from the city and sent to Napoleon at Bayonne, on the French border. Possession of this man who could rule the Spanish king and queen, was a great prize to Napoleon.

The cowardly king was terribly frightened. When Godoy was gone his fears were so great, his own mind so small, his dependence on the absent favorite so complete, his inability to rule so utter, that in a frenzy he abdicated his crown to his son, March 10, as Ferdinand VII. A few days later Charles gathered his small wits, and sent to the approaching Murat a protest that his abdication was forced. Ferdinand maintained himself against his father and was proclaimed king, March 20, 1808. Murat, with French troop, arrived March 23. The next day, Ferdinand VII made solemn entry as king, into Madrid. Murat did not recognize Ferdinand as king, but used his means for discord. Ferdinand, all in the dark as to

Napoleon's intentions, and acting perversely against good advice, left the government to a Junta, with his uncle, Don Antonio, as president, and Murat as a member, and went toward France as far as Vittoria, whence he sent a letter to Napoleon complaining of his treatment, and asking the emperor's intentions. Napoleon's answer expressed a wish to be better acquainted with the particulars of the abdication. "I desire to talk with you on this point," he wrote. All along Ferdinand's route the people manifested opposition to his journey toward France, for the peasants were wiser than their prince. At Vittoria they cut the traces of his horses to prevent his proceeding further. They knew the treacherous character of Napoleon. Despite all remonstrances, with headstrong weakness, Ferdinand went to meet the great deceiver at Bayonne, in France. His fate was decided; he had lost the crown of Spain; it was the old story of the spider and the fly.

Charles and Maria Louise, invited, also came into Napoleon's trap at Bayonne.

With them all in his power, Napoleon was ready now to reveal his treachery. He declared his intentions thus:—

"Your Bourbons have never served me except against their will. They have always been ready to betray me. The regeneration of Spain is impossible in their hands; they will be always, in spite of themselves, the support of ancient abuses. My part is decided. The revolution must be accomplished. Spain will not lose a village."

He offered to Ferdinand that same Etruria, if he would cede his claims on Spain to Napoleon. Ferdinand refused. Had he accepted of Etruria in the most solemn compact, it would have been liable to be taken from him at any time by Napoleon, the treaty breaker.

Charles and his queen were received at Bayonne with royal flatteries. The French courtiers, and the princes knelt and kissed their hands. Charles, the foolish, still thought that he would have it all his own way. He commanded Ferdinand to give him a renunciation of the Spanish crown. Ferdinand peremptorily refused. The worthless ex-king rose, furious, blustering; he brandished his cane over Ferdinand's head; he arrogantly cried:—

"I will have you treated like the rebel emigrants, as an unnatural son, who wished to snatch away my life and my crown."

Ferdinand offered to obey his father if Charles would govern Spain without the advice of ministers whom his people detested. This of course meant the removal of Godoy from all influence.

Instead of decent, reasonable language, the unworthy Charles answered by severe reproaches. Reproaches seldom convince. Each day the quarrel grew more bitter. Each day further from agreement.

Then Ferdinand proposed to submit the decision to the Spanish Cortes. But this course the foolishness of Charles had obstructed. He had already committed the supreme folly and treason against himself and his own kingdom of investing the French marshal, Murat, Napoleon's own brother-in-law, with supreme power in the Spanish government as president of the governing Junta, and lieutenant-general of Spain! Idiocy could hardly have gone further.

Thus, in time of profound peace between France and Spain, Napoleon had, by fraud, by the greatest trickery, by gross treachery, got possession of several Spanish fortresses, of the capital, of the king, and now of the government de facto of Spain!

Without opportunity for Spaniards to defend, their government had fallen into the power of a stranger.

Now came frightful news from Madrid. The spirited Spanish people were not tame and treasonable like their royalty. A bloody insurrection occurred at the capital. The journey to Bayonne; their royalty in the hands of Napoleon in France, perhaps really prisoners; the advent of the French army; Murat at the head of Spain's Supreme Junta; excited, alarmed, angered, and then infuriated the proud Spanish people.

The French army were boys, newly conscripted. It was not the grand army. The Spaniards saw them with contempt. They compared them unfavorably with hardy Spaniards. The world was yet to learn what boys could do at Wagram, Bautsen, Lutsen, and Dresden.

May 2, a close carriage was supposed to be taking away Don Antonio whom Ferdinand had charged with the presidency of the Junta, where Charles had appointed Murat. They feared he was being abducted by some trick of Napoleon. The crowd objected. They used violent language. This not availing they cut the traces; a French officer was assaulted. The revolt quickly spread through the streets, the mob attacked the French hospital; the invalids defended. French troops hastened in from their camp outside the city. The fighting was severe. After dark peasants fired on the French sentinels. The revolt was quelled, but 400 French had fallen. The Spanish dead were less than 120.[1]

Murat ordered a military commission to try the Spanish taken prisoners during the melee. This

[1] Napier i, 25

commission condemned them to death. Spanish officials remonstrated, and Murat forbade the executions.[1] Yet forty Spaniards were shot by the French. It was charged that a French colonel put forty-five more prisoners to death.[1] This bloody affair rang through Spain. In eight days Spain was all in revolt.[2] Murders, pillage, cruelties, occurred where were French troops or French partisans.[2] The Madrid affair was the Spanish people's declaration of war. It was a great war, and was destined to last for seven years with varying fortunes. Napoleon had never before fought a people: till now he had made war on sovereigns, on governments, on systems. Mark the difference.

Four days after this bloody revolt, persecuted by Napoleon's threats, Ferdinand's courage gave way, and he resigned royalty to Charles, May 6, and renounced his further rights to Napoleon, May 10 [1808].[3]

But the miserable Charles had already [May 5] ceded to Napoleon all his rights to the throne of Spain and the Indies, with the single condition that the prince whom Napoleon should place on the throne should be independent, and the Roman Catholic should continue the only religion of Spain. Charles, his queen, the royal family, and Godoy received from Napoleon large estates and income in France, where they remained unable to escape for several years. Ferdinand was kept a prisoner in France.

Napoleon had got into Spain by fraud. His army entered as friends; he asked for strong places to guard his line for the conquest, plunder, and division of peaceful, unoffending Portugal. He was grace-

---

[1] Napier i, 25.   [2] Thiers iii, 19.   [3] Schlosser, Napier, Thiers.

fully given possession as a friend, by his co-conspirators of the Portugal crime, Charles and Godoy. He also pretended that he entered to keep out the foreign enemy, the British; he was himself the foreign enemy. His whole proceeding was deep, dark treachery. We shall see whether his great treachery prospered, whether it was any exception to the sound maxim that "Honesty is the best policy," as well as the best principle.

Said Napoleon, August 24, 1808: —

"Do you know why I made a change in Spain? Because I want to secure complete tranquility; because since the famous proclamation at the time of the campaign in Prussia, the miserable Prince de la Paix (Godoy) himself had, what no one would believe, increased the army by 50,000 men; because Spain, instead of putting her capital in the navy which I required to force England to peace,— she became daily more and more inpracticable,— spent it all in reinforcing the army, which could be used against me. I cannot blame them; I was too strong for them. And then the throne was occupied by Bourbons; they are my personal enemies. They and I cannot occupy thrones at the same time in Europe." [1]

Napoleon recalled his brother Joseph from Naples and made him king of Spain. He made Murat king of Naples, vice Joseph promoted. He gave Murat's duchy of Cleves and Berg, in 1809, to Napoleon Louis, reputed son of Louis Bonaparte, king of Holland, and his compelled wife, Hortense, daughter of Empress Josephine. It must be mentioned as part of history that many persons believed that Napoleon was father of this boy.

Treating with contempt the remonstrances of the Council of Castile against the validity of extorted concessions, he compelled from them forms of choice of Joseph as king. The Junta and municipality of

[1] Metternich Memoirs iii, 462.

Madrid concurred. The Cardinal Primate, a Bourbon, and first cousin to Charles IV, promoted it.

Napoleon summoned to meet him at Bayonne some of the principal Spanish subjects, to be present at the making of a constitution for Spain. Ninety-one persons of distinction obeyed this arbitrary mandate. At their first meeting they acknowledged Joseph as king, June 15, 1808.

This constitution, given by Bonaparte, July 7, 1808, left great power to the king. The ministers were to be responsible for execution of laws and of the king's commands. From 30 to 60 persons of distinction were to be a Council of State. Twenty-four selected from that body, and from official departments, were to be a Senate. The Cortes should be 150 members; one-third spiritual and temporal peers named by the government, and two-thirds the representatives of provinces, universities, principal towns and merchants.

The assembly should be held once at least in three years; dissolved by the king at discretion. All deliberations to be private; and no votes or opinions to be published by any one. Inadequate means were provided for removal of bad ministers. The civil code was to be made uniform. Personal liberty was to be respected, and no person to be confined without a warrant stating the reason. These various parts were to be promulgated within four years.

Napoleon cared little for the people; he believed that Spain was subdued; royalty was easily conquered; but an earnest people are not easily subdued. Spain was braver than its king

Probably the Spanish had no great love for the

Bourbons who had misruled and then betrayed them. But they had national pride; they did not like foreigners: they abhorred foreign rule. Napoleon nominated Joseph as king, June 6. That very day the Junta of Seville proclaimed Ferdinand VII, chose a council, declared war, and assumed the lead in the struggle. At many places the people rose in arms. At Cadiz they took five French ships of the line. A supply of arms and a multitude of Spanish prisoners released by the British, arrived. The arms were a present from England.

In July Joseph arrived at Madrid and was there proclaimed king. His only claims rested on fraud and force; his only hope on the French army. The millions of Spaniards had not consented.

Joseph required of the Council of Castile the oath of allegiance. This body, till now servile, remonstrated. The Spanish people were at war on the great fraud.

General Solano, marching home to Cadiz, from the Portugal invasion, was ordered by the "Supreme Junta of Seville" to assume hostility against the French. He refused and was murdered; a mania of assassination ran through Spain; at many places Spaniards and Frenchmen were murdered. The bloody priest, Canon Calvo of Madrid, went to Valencia, collected fanatics and massacred French residents, and menaced the Spanish Junta till he was seized and strangled with about 200 of his fanatics.

In each province Juntas were formed and war organized. Although Biscay and the Castiles were menaced by the presence of 50,000 French soldiers, the peasants began war. The French must keep together in large bodies. Monks and priests persuaded the ignorant that the church was in danger; "they fanaticized the mass of patriots;" monks and friars were leaders and instigators of tumult and barbarity.[1] The mildness of the religion of Jesus was wanting.

Smuggling "has always been carried on in Spain to an incredible extent," says Napier, "in consequence of monopolies and restrictions."[1] The French system would end this; so the smugglers became insurgents. Even the most ignorant knew that Napoleon had insulted Spain; they believed that Godoy caused the troubles; they believed that Ferdinand would like to redress them. Little they knew Ferdinand's mean disposition. He was like his degenerate parents.

Sir Walter Scott says : —

"The government of Spain, a worn out despotism, lodged in the hands of a family of the lowest degree of intellect, was one of the worst in Europe : and the state of the nobility, speaking in general (for there were noble exceptions), seemed scarce less degraded. The education of the nobility was committed to the priests, who took care to give them no light beyond Catholic bigotry. The customs of the country introduced them to premature indulgences, and they ceased to be children without arriving at the strength or the intellect of youth. The middle classes, inhabitants of towns, and those who followed the learned professions, had not been so generally subjected to the same withering influence of superstition and luxury. In many instances they had acquired good education, and were superior to bigotry. The lower classes . . . . were little interested by the imperfections of the government, for the system, though execrable, did not immediately affect their comforts. They lay too low for personal oppression, and as the expenses of the state were supplied from the American provinces, the Spanish peasants were strangers, in a measure, to the exactions of the tax gatherers.[2]

While the upper and the lower classes were generally ignorant, the middle class was intelligent, yet as

[1] Napier Peninsular War, i, 32.   [2] Scott's Life of Napoleon.

late as 1860 three-fourths of the population were unable to read.[1]

WAR IN SPAIN, 1808.

Beside militia, the Spanish army was about 97,000 men: 15,000 of them were in Holstein, under Napoleon; 20,000 were the army intended to aid to conquer and divide Portugal; 11,000 were Swiss; the rest were distributed about Spain.

In August Spain was delighted by the arrival of Romana, who, by a masterly strategy, had succeeded in escaping from Napoleon's service in Holstein on the North Sea, with about 10,000 Spanish troops, and embarking in English vessels adroitly, had come to fight against Napoleon in Spain.

The French attacked Valencia and were repulsed. In the battle of Rio Seco the Spanish army under Blake was terribly beaten with loss of between 5,000 and 6,000 killed and wounded, and the French captured great stores of muskets, clothing and ammunition.

The French army in Spain were about 70,000 men for duty, and 10,000 sick. It held good strategetical points; it was French, Swiss, Poles, and Portuguese, most of them raw levy. Twenty-three thousand more came in June, and 20,000 more were in reserve on the border of France.

In February 12,000 French had advanced to Barcelona, while Charles was king. Barcelona, with its wealth, its commerce, its strong fortress and its good harbor, was of great importance.

[1] Chambers' Cyclopedia.

On the very day that the new king, Joseph, entered his capital, — July 20, — the Spanish were victorious at Baylen, over Dupont, one of the best French generals, whom they compelled to surrender, with 17,000 men, and to add, also, Vedel's corps of 6,000, all on the promised condition of being sent back to France.[1] The Spanish shamefully broke the terms of this submission;[2] they abused and murdered some; they assassinated 80 French officers; they showed themselves undeserving of such successes, and fortune withdrew its favors. The surest way to make an enemy fight desperately is to abuse his prisoners; besides being grossly inhumane, it is the sure means to aid an enemy. Treat prisoners well and your enemy will the more readily surrender to be prisoners.

<small>Baylen. July 20, 1808.</small>

This heavy blow so alarmed Joseph that he seized the crown jewels, plundered the treasury and robbed the palaces of valuable portables and fled to Burgos; a disgraceful beginning to a reign.

The occupation of Madrid, however, does not have the same effect on the nation as would that of Paris on France, because Spain is made up of several provinces, once separate, and Biscay, Galicia, Catalonia, Andalusia, Valencia, and lesser districts have each their capital and defensive center.

Joseph feared that the whole country was about to fall upon him. Yet, says British Napier: —

"The French troops, instead of being sent to France, were maltreated, and numbers of them murdered in cold blood . . . . all who survived the march to Cadiz . . . . were cast into the hulks . . . . suffering so that few of them ever again saw France."[3]

The Spaniards certainly developed more cruelty

[1] Napier i, App. 512. [2] Napier i, 33. [3] Peninsular War, 1, 73.

than courage; more violence than intrepidity; more personal hatred of the French than enthusiasm for their own cause.[1] They were making but little of really efficient preparations for defense. Yet Joseph hardly felt safe when behind the Ebro with 57,000 French troops. Thus in August, 1808, Joseph had lost all Spain except Barcelona and the little country between Burgos and France. Thus was Napoleon's army defeated by a loosely-arranged, ill-managed, almost hap-hazard rising of turbid violence, fanatic hate, and inflamed patriotism. The terrible seige of Saragossa resulted in the defeat of the French after they had once got possession of nearly half of the city; but it left the town of nearly 50,000 inhabitants almost in ruins. [August 14, 1808.]

The character of Spain was unfavorable to the operations of the French. The Spanish acted much in small parties, cutting off supplies and foragers. Napoleon's system of supporting his troops by robbing the people was difficult in this country where they could move only in large parties.

The victory of Baylen cheered all Europe; it encouraged the Spanish; it gave them confidence; it damaged the prestige of French troops; it nerved England to send aid to Spain. Napoleon was making war on a people till now his ally. From 1799 Spain had seconded his efforts against other nations; many Spaniards fought for him against Austria, England, Russia, and Prussia. For him Spain had lost its commerce; its strong navy; the lives of its soldiers and sailors; and its national pride had been mortified. What bounds to his aggression would be set by a man who could thus attack an always

[1] Napier i, 33.

friendly power? No nation, no country could be safe from his rapacity. The conscience of Europe was aroused against him. Bonaparte's war was a great injustice; it was a great blunder; without it he ruled Spain through the feeble king; with it he lost control of Spain. He had thrown away his advantage; he could not force his rule; he had attacked the principle of nationality which it is both patriotic and natural to defend.

Spanish agents sent to England said, "Of men Spain has more than enough. Arms, ammunition, clothing it lacks." England sent them. The British war with Spain was ended, Spanish prisoners freed, clothed, regaled, and sent home to fight Napoleon's army. On news of the Bayonne transactions of Napoleon and Charles and Ferdinand, of its humiliation of Spanish royalty, Mexico and Spanish South America opened their ports to the British.[1]

Napoleon's sham king, Joseph, wrote to him, August 9, 1808, "I have not a single Spaniard left who is attached to my cause." He added, "If you wish it I will restore Ferdinand VII to them in your name, but retaining part of their territory as far as the Ebro," and he demanded back the throne of Naples which Napoleon had given to Murat.

The three Spanish armies of 19,000, 16,000, and 11,000 men were far from formidable; they were widely separated; councils were divided; so were the generals.[2]

Napoleon's servile Senate ordered 80,000 conscripts, and preparation for 80,000 more, though the last were called sixteen months before the legal time.

[1] Thiers iii, 68. [2] Napier i, 152.

Italy and Germany, too, must send their sons to suffer and die in Spain, although they had not the slightest quarrel with the Spanish. It was a cruel war, to no good purpose.

PORTUGAL, IN 1808.

Lisbon, containing all the civil, military, naval, and most of the commercial establishments of Portugal; the only fine harbor; one-quarter of the population; two-thirds of the wealth, was in the hands of France. Nine Russian ships of the line and a frigate were in the harbor, — a powerful aid to the French. Thus Portugal, without a defeat, without a battle, was a French capture, and Junot treated it as a prize, to be made the most of. He laid a heavy contribution to be collected in cash; he accepted British stolen or plundered goods, or royal property or church plate in payment. But it was found that runaway royalty had been as expert a plunderer as he, for it had carried off much of the church plate and bullion, and money drawn from the people.

Junot's police was effective, and Napier says that :—

"No act gave the Portuguese more offense than having the streets cleaned, and the wild dogs that infested them by thousands killed."[1]

Junot put Frenchmen into the lucrative Portuguese offices.

A Spanish army had invaded Portugal for conquest and plunder, at the same time with the French. A sudden revolt at Oporto expelled the French from that city. It formed a provincial government; many

[1] Napier's Peninsular War, i, 84.

other places followed. In both Portugal and Spain, the cruel French military executions, instead of overawing the insurgents, only excited them to greater vengeance.

At the revolt Junot disarmed the 6,600 Spanish troops at Lisbon, except 1,100, who escaped. But the revolt became general. The other 11,000 Spanish troops in Portugal were lost to the French. Junot's army effective was reduced below 30,000 men, of which 2,500 were already in hospital. The French made energetic marches, skirmishes and executions of peasants, but the revolt increased. The Portuguese did not, as the Spanish did, object to the aid of British troops. England sent 13,000. Sir Arthur Wellesley landed with them at Mondago Bay, advanced with real British energy, and gained the battle of Rolica, over the French, August 17, 1808. Re-inforced with British[1] and Portuguese, he took position near Vimeria, where August 21 he was attacked by Junot with 14,000 French. Wellesley defeated Junot. But as just then two other British generals arrived, each in turn taking command-in-chief, the pursuit of the defeated French was not well conducted. From this battle resulted the Convention of Cintra, August 30, 1808, by the terms of which the French army, now much reduced, was conveyed to France in British vessels, with their arms and baggage, and not forbidden to serve elsewhere. This convention, — an act of great wisdom on the part of both Wellesley and Junot, — was censured by the governments of both those able officers. The English ministry ordered inquiry, but kept the treaty. By it

[1] Wellesley's British are stated by W. Scott ii, 213, at 16,000; and by Thiers iii, 65, at 18,000, besides the Portuguese.

ARTHUR WELLESLEY
DUKE OF WELLINGTON.

England cleared Portugal of the French; by it Napoleon got back above 20,000 effective troops.

The Russian fleet in Lisbon harbor surrendered "in trust" not to be given back to Russia till peace, but the seamen and marines were sent to Russia at once.

At Erfurt, September 28, 1808, two emperors met to confederate in crime. Napoleon wished for closer union with the Czar. Each had his great projects for tyrannical conquest. Napoleon wanted dominion to Gibraltar; Alexander coveted Finland and Turkey. Their meeting was attended with great pomp: many princes were there. But Europe looked on disquieted. Great issues were believed to be at stake. They remained there till October 14.

Austria was arming; new levies were made and greater energy infused into the army. Napoleon protested. Austria kept up pleasant words and intercourse. But it was evident that Austria meant war. She was irritated by Napoleon's absorption of the Roman states and by his Spanish outrages. Napoleon demanded as proof of Austria's pacific intentions that she cease arming and recognize Joseph as king of Spain.

Prussia was still held by the French armies. Needing these troops in Spain, Napoleon agreed with the king of Prussia to fix at 140,000,000 francs, to be paid 6,000,000 a month, as the amount of robbery that the Prussians were still to pay to the French emperor. To please the Czar, Napoleon reduced this sum to 120,000,000 to be paid within three years, but he exacted the secret pledge of the Prussian king not to keep more than 42,000 soldiers and no militia for ten years, and in case of a German war Prussia was bound to furnish Napoleon with 16,000 Prussian men.

Napoleon pledged his word to evacuate all of Prussia except the three fortresses, Glogau, Stettin, and Custrin. It will be seen how badly he kept his pledged word. Napoleon said soon after:—

"I have asked for Stein's dismissal from the cabinet: without that the king of Prussia will not recover his states. I have sequestrated his property in Westphalia."

This threat indicates that Napoleon premeditated breaking his faith. The patriotic Von Stein resigned, but he continued to have great influence in Germany. Prussia having, on compulsion, signed the terms of this stupendous robbery of the Prussians, September 8, 1808, Frederick William at last again took possession of his diminished states, which he had lost in 1806 by his folly in making war before the Russians could come to his assistance.

In Germany Napoleon concentrated his available troops toward Austria, left Denmark, and withdrew 100,000 soldiers from Prussia, increased his army in Italy, and ordered Murat, king of Naples, to assemble an army to threaten Sicily.

Speeches and reports of the French ministers displayed the vast resources of France very impressively; the year's expenses below $150,000,000 all paid in metallic money; that France would feel no fresh burdens; that public works were progressing; inland commerce flourishing; and nearly a million of men in arms.

The Czar looked with secret satisfaction on the situation in Spain. Haunted by his own unholy desire to rob his neighbors, he saw that Spain might absorb so much of the resources and attention of Napoleon as to leave Russia free to annex Turkey's Roumania; he even hoped for Constantinople. But this last Napoleon utterly refused to permit. "The empire of the world is at Constantinople," he once said.

For peace on terms not stated and not as most historians state, on present possession, the two emperors united in addressing a demand to the British king, "preserving all powers which exist." Napoleon wrote it.[1] It was made in form both of threat and of appeal, adroitly to throw odium of refusal on England.

Napoleon and Alexander had agreed that France was to consent only to such a peace as should secure Sweden's Finland, and Turkey's Roumania to Russia; and Russia to consent only to one that would secure to France all her present possessions, and the crown of Spain to Joseph. If execution of this treaty produced war with Austria, then France and Russia were to join in mutual support.[2]

The French minister, Talleyrand, mentioned Napoleon's intention to be divorced, and said: — "His thoughts turn naturally toward the sisters of his ally and dearest friend." Alexander blushed; He was autocrat of all the Russias, but he was not all powerful with the females of his family; his mother strongly disliked Napoleon. Perhaps the Czar could not dispose of either of his two sisters. There might be difficulties. Napoleon and Alexander then discussed it.[3] The Czar would do what he could to gain his mother's and sister's consent.

The British ministry replied to the letter which

[1] Thiers III, 95.   [2] Ibid.   [3] Ibid.

the two emperors addressed to George III. They said that all the allies of Britain ought to have been admitted to the Erfurt negotiations, including the kings of Sweden, Sicily and Portugal regency, and the Spanish insurgents. The Czar answered that allies of Britain he would admit, but not the Spanish insurgents; he had recognized Joseph Bonaparte as king of Spain, and he was in alliance with Napoleon; he would treat on the basis of *uti possidetis*, or any basis for an honorable, just, and equal peace. Thiers says : —

> Having documents in their hands which proved that France would make no concessions to the Spanish insurgents, who were immensely popular in England it (the ministry) had nothing to fear from parliament so it made a peremptory declaration, offensive both to Russia and to France, to the effect that no peace was possible with two courts, one of which dethroned and kept as prisoners, the most legitimate kings, and the other of which suffered them to be treated unworthily for interested motives; that, moreover, the pacific proposals addressed to England were illusory, and devised for the purpose of disheartening the generous nations that had shaken off the oppressive yoke of France, and those who were yet preparing to do so ; that the negotiations were therefore to be considered as finally broken off, and that war should continue." [1]

The ministry feared that rumors of peace would chill the ardor for war of the Austrians and Spanish.

To this uncivil note by Canning, France replied with a proposal of the basis of present possession, each side to hold its conquests. But Canning broke off the correspondence; all chance of peace vanished. How can a war ever end if one side refuses to negotiate? It is a fearful responsibility to take. It was high crime in Canning and George.

Apparently Napoleon was, for once, sincere. The menacing aspect of Austria; the recent loss of Portu-

[1] State Papers.

gal; the secret societies of Germany, which threatened revolt at some unknown spot and moment; the commercial distresses of all Europe; the unexpected extent and obstinacy of the Spanish revolt, all indicate that it would have been more in the line of common sense and statesmanship if Canning had withheld his utterly useless recrimination, and ascertained to just what terms Napoleon would agree. France held in Spain only the strip north of the Ebro and a small part of Catalonia. The Spanish insurgents did not represent Ferdinand, whom Canning held to be king of Spain. True it would have been better to admit them. But their absence while really represented in part by their ally, England, ought not to have barred Canning from using any and all opportunity to seek peace. An attempt to negotiate at least was required by every principle of honor, interest and religion. To defy the vast power of the two emperors, the British ministry ought, at the very least, to have had a strong, thorough plan prepared for the Spanish war. But not a trace of any such plan is found! All British-Spanish war schemes were yet mere vague knight-errantry; visions without objective point! In this affair Canning exhibited astonishing lack of statesmanship. When Canning childishly committed the great political crime it is possible that Napoleon would have abandoned all Spain beyond the Ebro in exchange for peace; already Trafalgar had decided Britain's continued dominion on the seas; this was all that England could hope for from war, it is nearly all she obtained from six years longer of a great war, with all its risks, damage and vast expense; and the British national debt, if peace had followed, would today be immensely less than it is. At least Canning could have made this counter proposal : peace with Portugal free, and Spain for the Spaniards to the Ebro and the Aragon.

Napier says, at that time in Spain the many Juntas disagreed; the British provided much money, but those Spaniards into whose hands it came for public use, took it as donated to themselves; ignorance and pride, dissension and jealousy abounded among those who assumed to rule.[1]

"Only two months after the first burst of insurrection, corruption, intrigue and faction, even to the verge of civil war, were raging in the northern parts."[1]

In the south the Junta of Seville
"wasted their time in vain and frivolous disputes," and they "sacrificed the general welfare to views of private advantage and interest . . . . bestowed on their own creatures places of emolument." "Against this flagitious Junta also, the public indignation was rife."

They wanted to march the victorious army of Baylen against the Granadians. Of the many Juntas that of the Council of Castile had most influence. After much caviling, each Junta, with acute jealousy, intrigue and chicanery, named two deputies. These deputies met at Arunjuez, feebly organized, proclaimed Ferdinand VII, and assumed authority as the Supreme Junta. They called Spain to arms; they divided themselves into four sections for state departments and declared each section independent and all four of equal authority! So the ministry had no head. The need of a single general-in-chief was imperative. There were many aspirants for that place, but jealousies prevented filling it.

[1] Napier's Peninsular War.

October 6, 1808, came to Lisbon a new scheme; 30,000 British infantry and 5,000 cavalry, under command of Sir John Moore, were to try their fortunes in north Spain, where 67,000 French veterans were approaching; the plan to be arranged later with the Spanish generals. A campaign without a plan! A blunder of Castlereagh in the British ministry, second in folly only to Canning's refusal to treat for peace!

Moore was expected to organize a new army in a poor country; to provide transports over bad roads in the rainy season, and almost without money, while British money was lavished on inferior Spanish agents and intriguers; and all this when Moore was not informed of the number, location, situation, or value of either Spanish army, or with whom he was to act in concert! The British ministry had sent to the Spanish, $16,000,000,[1] and great supplies of ammunition and clothing, yet, says Napier:—

"Disunion, cupidity, incapacity in the high orders," and "the rulers grasping, improvident, boasting; the enemy powerful; the people insubordinate; the fighting men without arms or bread, when the British had sent 200,000 muskets," and
"found that to trust Spaniards in war was to lean on a broken reed."[1]

The Junta ordered a levy of 500,000 men. Only about 100,000 responded.[2] These were divided into three armies; the right under Palafox, the center under Castanos, the left under Blake.

Napoleon arrived again at Bayonne, November 3, 1808. Five days later he entered Spain with a great army. November 9, Blake's center, the best army of Spain, 12,000 troops and 7,000 armed peasants,

[1] Napier i, 166.   [2] Ibid, 283.

was smashed at Gamoral, and all its ammunition and stores at Burgos taken by the French under Marshal Soult, who pitilessly sacked the town, destroyed much property, and seized a great quantity of wool owned by Spanish nobles.

Napoleon wrote : —

"The Infantado and Spanish great lords are sole proprietors of half the kingdom of Naples; and in this kingdom they are worth no less than 200,000,000 [francs]. They have beside possessions in Belgium and Italy, which I intend to sequestrate."

The next day, November 10, Marshal Victor knocked to pieces most of Blake's army at Espinosa, leaving Blake, out of 25,000 men, little more than a mob of 7,000, and many of these lost or threw away their arms. Victor took many prisoners but dispersed many more. Blake again attacked, thrashed, and reduced to 4,000 men he fled to the mountains. The north of Spain was prostrated, fertile Castile and Leon laid open to the enemy.

November 22, 40,000 Spaniards, commanded by Castanos, were defeated at Tudela by Marshal Lannes, who took several thousand prisoners, 30 cannon, and all their ammunition and baggage, and dispersed many more Spanish soldiers. Aragon, Navarre, and New Castile, were opened to Napoleon's armies.

The Junta cashiered Blake and Castanos, and made Romana chief commander. The Spaniards seemed to throw down their arms and run away, only to take arms again elsewhere.

Napoleon was advancing, November 30, 1808, on Madrid. But he was north of the Guadarama mountains, which formed a remarkable line of defense to the Spanish capital province. Its passes are strong places. He marched direct for the high Somo Pass.

It was the last day of chilly November, 1808, when the French reached its foot. They found it occupied by San Juan, with about 12,000 Spaniards. They were strongly posted, on the right and left of the pass, pictur-esquely rising in lines one behind an-
other, that the musket fire of all might cover the road through the pass. From the French position below the road ascended. Sixteen cannon in the mouth of the pass frowned down upon the invaders, and threatened death to the bold men who should dare to enter that road.

Remarkable combat in the clouds.

That last autumn night hung solemn, heavy, over the wild, lofty grandeur of the mountains. The Spaniards were in the clouds. Under cover of the night three French battalions crept up the awful steep and got into the clouds toward the Spanish right; three more French battalions toward the Spanish left. Up, higher and higher they climbed, and spread themselves over the mountain side. Daylight came and dimly lighted the aim of their muskets. Their rapid flashes were quickly answered by the fire of the Spaniards. It was a veritable fight in the clouds of heaven, as well as in the clouds of battle smoke. The French made no further progress. They owed it to the obscurity of the dense clouds that the Spaniards had not hurled them headlong down the steep. The place seemed impregnable. What could six battalions of French do against 12,000 Spaniards who hung upon the precipitous sides of the pass and held it so strongly? The clouds mixed with the smoke of exploding muskets hung more thick and lower down the steep. Down there more French battalions, with six guns at their head, stood below the gap of the pass. The sixteen Spanish cannon were loaded, and ready to open fire on the head of the column as soon as it should appear in view and in range. Napoleon's march to Madrid was there barred. He was hastening to seize Madrid before General Castanos could arrive to defend it. His object seemed foiled. He listened to the cloud-wrapped musketry. Its sound indicated no success. He rode forward and attentively examined the strange scene; he advanced almost to the mouth of the pass; he instantly decided. Somebody must die. Who? Some of those Polish lancers, the front ranks of the Polish cavalry of his guard. He ordered those bold, dark horsemen to charge up the steep road, to seize the Spanish batteries. Their ringing bugles sounded the charge. Up, away dashed that gallant cavalry. A great flash, a crash of thunders above them; a wild, sharp rushing of shot; a sound as if an avalanche had started down from its high place. Down leveled were riders and horses; the front ranks were crushed, gone; all the ranks were riddled; the surviving horsemen were in confusion.

Quickly they rallied. The cannon for a few moments were unloaded; on them rushed the Poles, in the smoke and vapor. As they passed, the Spanish infantry on each side fired their muskets and fled toward the summit; the Poles cut down the gunners, took the guns: the Spanish army were in flight, leaving ammunition and baggage. "This surprising exploit," says General Napier, "can hardly be paralleled in the annals of war." That the pass was not intrenched, and the road so obstructed as to be impassable by cavalry indicates incapacity in the Spanish general, San Juan. A few hours work of 1,000 men with pickaxes and shovels would have neutralized the efforts of Napoleon's cavalry. It was frequently his good fortune to meet incompetent enemies.

Madrid was in anarchy; multitudes of armed peasants there imagined themselves soldiers: the streets were barricaded, the houses pierced for musketry. The populace were very violent; murder was rife; popular violence had reached madness; vengeance had broken loose; bands of furies paraded the streets; broke open the houses; rang the bells incessantly; and made the city a very pandemonium. The resources left to defend Madrid were too small. The French cavalry appeared. Madrid was summoned to surrender. It refused. But the Junta fled from Aranjuez to Badajos. Madrid had never been fortified; now ramparts were improvised.

Napoleon himself arrived before Madrid, December 2. The attack soon began. The French took the northern and the eastern gates in a few hours. The resistance was most obstinate. Napoleon summoned them to surrender and so spare their capital the horrors of a general assault by a surrender. The Spanish troops, under Castellar, withdrew in the night. In the morning of December 4, Madrid surrendered. The French disarmed the citizens and arrested several great lords. Madrid was soon tranquil. Then several Bonapartist decrees made wholesome reforms; abolished feudal rights, the Inquisition, and customs duties between provinces, and reduced the number of convents. But these much-needed improvements, being brought by force, were hateful to Spanish prejudices and even prepared the way for a reaction in favor of the wicked Inquisition.

Marshal St. Cyr overran Catalonia which joins France. The battle of Cardeden, December 15, gave Barcelonia to the French.

The British ministry's instructions to Sir John Moore were without a plan. He was merely directed to form a plan with the Spanish authorities. The Spanish defeat was not yet known in England. They had lost the campaign, were scattered, almost dispersed. What could a small British army of less than 26,000 effective men do against Napoleon with 300,000 French.[1]

The Spanish were unreliable for help to Spain or even to give Moore reliable information; they were selfish, inefficient.[2] Before the British opened the prospect of three hundred miles of winter march, to gather up its scattered forces; three hundred miles more to reach the Ebro. There they hoped to concert action with several independent generals, with forces unconnected, their leaders jealous, quarrelsome; their men different in many important particulars from the British, and especially hating all foreigners. What a prospect! And this to fight Napoleon, the most rapid and decided of men; to meet, under this renowned leader, the most famous soldiers, the best disciplined army that had appeared in modern ages! And these too in overwhelming numbers! This was the task that George III's ministry had set to Moore's devoted little army. Stupendous error! No British ministry but George's

[1] Napier, Peninsula War.   [2] Moore's Journal.

ever committed the like. Any tradesman on the Strand could have told them better. Even George's pet son, the Duke of York, knew better; he said the widely divided Spanish armies were weak; the concentrated French were strong; that 60,000 men ought and could be furnished; that on arrival they might find the Spanish beaten, and unaided have to meet the French, just as happened. And this was in Spain where the long repressed people knew not how to control themselves now that the old government was gone; where the common people were in the hands of the priests and of very selfish incapables so dark-minded that they had recalled the Jesuits whom Catholic Charles III had expelled.

Moore wrote to Castlereagh, October 9, 1808: "The army is without equipment of any kind" to convey artillery, ammunition or food; and no magazines, on the route. Yet he was required to march against the French.

The Spanish, with singular inefficiency, did not even inform him of the nature of the country, or what their own armies were doing.[1] They gave him very little information, their reports made by country people were frequently much exaggerated.

Sir David Baird landed a British army at Coruna to co-operate with Moore. He, too, was left by the British ministry without money.[2] To him, too, the Spanish did not fairly represent the condition of their armies, and they gave him little correct information,[3] which was lacking because the country people "are so slow, so talkative, and so credulous."[4] It was Spanish assertion that Moore's army would be 80,000

[1] Sir D. Baird to Moore, December 9.   [2] Moore to Hope, October 22.
[3] Baird to Moore, November 23.   [4] Boothby to Moore, January 1, 1809.

men.[1] They were really 23,500 British, and about 6,000 Spanish, a difference of 50,500.

Moore wrote to the ministry, November 24: — "I am without a shilling of money." Yet Castlereagh had just given $240,000 to Romana's Spanish army, when Moore's British needed it to procure food and supplies![2] Moore's journal and letters show that the Spanish people gave him little aid, but led him into peril by their mistaken statements and boasting. But it was the incompetent ministry in England that divided the British army into Moore's and Baird's separate forces, to the great peril of both parts, and left them without money or suitable means of transport; that had no plan of campaign, that thus fore-ordained disaster.[3]

The bold Moore was a grand soldier. He marched across Portugal into Spain. He arrived at Salamanca when the Spanish had received several defeats and their little armies were scattered and demoralized, the campaign already lost.

Napoleon, with 40,000 French, advanced from Madrid to throw himself on the British rear. Moore retreated north to Sahagun at almost a right angle from Napoleon's approach. He had indifferent Spanish support. Moore hoped to strike Soult a hard blow in the north before he could be re-inforced. Moore was irritated by the Spanish apathy. He believed that they would not make strenuous effort, though the British were so active to aid them.

But the French were in such force that Moore must retreat. The retreat was frightful. In their destitution, in that strange country, pursued by the

[1] Stuart to Moore, November 20. [2] Moore to Fray, November 10.
[3] Napier i, 269-73.

French, harrassed, wearied, on bad roads, lacking proper information of the route, it was found impossible to maintain strict discipline. Soldiers left the road to depredate; others became drunk and were left behind;[1] transportation was deficient. Many men were lost from cold, fatigue and straggling. For want of carriages the sick were left and baggage abandoned. Soldiers pillaged houses and incensed the people. Food was hard to get. Napoleon abandoned the pursuit to Soult and wrote to Joseph:—
"Your kingdom appears to me almost at peace."

British demoralization was severe when they halted at Lago, January 9, 1809, exhausted by bad weather, want of food, and excess of strong liquors. They rested there three days and offered battle; but the French were not ready to fight. Then the long, weary march was painfully resumed. The suffering was severe. At last, January 11, 1809, Moore's struggling, weary army came in sight of the sea. The sight was disappointing. They had expected to find British ships waiting there to receive them. Not a sail was in sight in all that vast expanse. They prepared to defend themselves. Five days later the French attacked them. British ships were just arriving. The battle of Coruna was fought to gain embarkation. It was successful; the army was saved, but the heroic Moore, after his terrible struggle against so many and so formidable obstacles was about ending, was killed, and,

"We left him alone in his glory."[2]

[1] "Drunkenness here appeared in frightful colors." Alison iii, 105.

[2] The beautiful poem, "Burial of Sir John Moore," was published anonymously in 1817. It was by an, till then, unknown Irishman, Charles Wolfe, who died in 1823, aged 32.

Yet the minister, Canning, tried to calumniate the dead hero, because, with only part of an army which the ministry had divided in two, without money, without the necessary draft animals, without the needed aid from the Spanish, Moore, with less than 24,000 effective British troops, and 6,000 Spanish, had not been victorious over Napoleon with 300,000! Such were the bad government influences that British heroes had over them, for Moore and his officers were heroes. A storm scattered the ships that bore to England Moore's army. The troops landed at various ports to startle the honest Britishers by their ragged, worn appearance.

While the evacuation of Spain by the British was actually happening, Canning, at London, signed a convention with the Spanish rear-admiral, Apodaca, binding Britain to close concert with Spain against the French, and precluding any cession of Spanish territory by the prisoner, Ferdinand VII; to keep Spanish ships, and the French ships at Cadiz, from the French; that a treaty of commerce should be made. George III, at last, recommended increase of the British force in Spain; but a few days later brought the frightful news of suffering, toil, marching, and retiring from Spain. The British parliament voted money to Spain and Portugal. British officers disciplined Portuguese troops, but Spanish pride long repelled that kind of help.

Saragossa sustained a second terrible siege of sixty days, December 24, 1808, to February 21, 1809. A mass of human beings under Palafox were its defendners; behind its old convents, its high-walled houses, everywhere without outside windows; in its narrow, crooked streets. The siege was energetic, the defense desperate. The whole affair was extremely horrible, sickening on both sides; it far surpassed the bounds of heroism; it was revolting, more than brutal; too satanic for detailed description. The French advanced only from one old building wall to another. Many had miserably perished when, January 29, 1809, a general assault, long, fierce, terrific and deadly, carried its outer walls. Then it ought to have surrendered. Against an army of a civilized country, no one has a right to prolong a hopeless defense, especially when women, children and old men are constantly exposed to the most frightful horrors of worse than honorable war. Humanity can hardly consider that siege; infernal and of more than barbaric ferocity; as otherwise than dishonorable to both parties. The wild, frenzied leaders compelled the Spaniards to fight or perish on "a horrid array of gibbets, on which crowds of wretches were suspended because their courage sank."[1] The defense was not real, manly bravery, it was beastly, tiger-like, frenzied ferocity. Said Lannes, the French commander :—

"Every house has to be taken by storm . . . . the siege of Saragossa resembles in nothing, any war we have had . . . . in a word, Sire, it is a horrible war."

It was war step by step, house to house, story to story. Epidemic came and lent the French its revolting aid to diminish the numbers of the defenders. At last the Spanish offered to surrender on terms long before offered with the addition that they be allowed to march away with certain covered carriages and join the Spanish armies.[2] These terms, designed

[1] Napier.   [2] Ibid.

to cover plunder, were rejected by the French. The French artillery then destroyed the church of Saragossa's patron saint. This was a blow to the credulous fanatics. Pestilence raged with direful celerity, and swept off thousands of women, children, soldiers and citizens. Several of the fanatic chiefs were killed. Then the Spaniards offered to surrender the place and march away if the peasants should not be taken as prisoners, and, to add to the disgrace of those miserably dishonorable fighting priests in the town, if these bloody pretenders to the religion of the peace-teaching Christ "could have their full revenues" punctually; and this shameful condition was proposed, "at the particular request of the clergy." To stop the most frightful siege of modern ages if the ignorant, bigoted priests would not lose money! The proposal was so disgraceful, so utterly unlike what the respectable clergy of any nation would think of demanding, that the unbelieving French rejected it with indignation.[1] So the horrors went on. At last, in dire extremity, the survivors surrendered. The French gave honorable terms; religion and property were guaranteed.

Within Saragossa 54,000 human beings had perished; 6,000 corpses lay around in the streets and under ruins; 48,000 had fallen by disease; 50,000 corpses were thrown into the Ebro;[1] 16,000 sick were ready to perish.

Engaged in the defense had been 50,000 armed men. The French were about two-thirds that number, and in the heart of a hostile country. The French did not lose above 4,000 men.[1] With all the

[1] Napier.

advantages of a strong city, 50,000 armed Spaniards were besieged and beaten by 35,000 Frenchmen. Was this heroism? Why did not the 50,000 Spaniards, at the first, meet and defeat the 35,000 French in a battle and have no siege at all? Yet the unsuccessful, revolting, sickening defense has been greatly extolled as heroism! Saragossa is not creditable to Spain nor to humanity. It was not the act of the better Spanish, but of fanatic frenzy, of the infuriated, ignorant. Spain has very many brighter pages than this. It is not manly heroism that could think of priests' revenues while thousands of their kindred, women and helpless children were frightfully perishing before their eyes. Napier says that Palafox, their nominal leader : —

"Can claim little credit for his conduct. For more than a month preceding the surrender he never came forth from a vaulted building which was impervious to shells . . . . where . . . . there is too much reason to believe he, and others of both sexes, lived in a state of sensuality."

XVI

AMERICA.

IT was navy that America needed, but Jefferson's Congress of 1808 gave it army for which it had no need, authorized 100,000 militia. For what could militia be used? England insulted us only at sea and abroad. Land soldiers against ships! Raw militia in America to protect vessels at sea! How could they ever meet to fight? The $5,000,000 thus wasted would have doubled our navy. A hundred thousand militia and seven new regiments of regular army and but 1,272 more seamen for our navy! Twenty-five insignificant little gun floats in our harbors to protect several thousands of miles of sea coast. The new regiments brought in four new brigadier-generals of poor material, two of whom afterward dishonored our arms. These imbecile ideas of Jefferson sent a laugh of derision through America. They are still amusing. Navy officers laughed, the people smiled broadly, and sailors roared; but Jefferson was really serious. Some of his followers opposed a navy because, they said, it made executive patronage. It was deplorable for the President to appoint a navy captain, but laudable for him to make brigadier-generals. But it was Jefferson's partisans who got the new army commissions; that was different.

In the elections of 1808 Madison, Monroe, and De Witt Clinton wanted the presidency. Jefferson chose the least capable, the most unsuitable, Madison; and his party, as usual, acquiesced. The Federalists supported for president, C. C. Pinckney of South Carolina, and for vice-president, Rufus King.

In 1808, merchants of Hull, Manchester, Liverpool, and London petitioned the British government for repeal of the odious Orders in Council. Lord Erskine, Henry Brougham, Mr. A. Baring, and other Whigs vigorously advocated the repeal, called the Orders unconstitutional and repugnant to law of nations as they really were. It was in vain. The Tory parliament passed an act affirming them, and fixed the tax on neutral vessels.

Jefferson's conciliatory words in his first term won

increase to his party, but embargo made great clamor in the North, and new opposition from business quarters. Congress gave $1,000,000 to fortify harbors; $852,000 to build 188 more useless gun floats; $1,000,000 for the 100,000 militia, and ordered seven regiments of 6,600 regular army. Small boats versus British ships of the line! Militia versus British frigates! Such was Jefferson's defensive policy.

Business men, merchants, seamen, asked permission to arm their vessels and defend them. Jefferson refused it. There was no heroism in his policy.

George III's folly provoked this embargo; Jefferson's greater folly laid it. Napoleon's Berlin Decree insulted, injured America but Jefferson's embargo aided Napoleon who wronged and opposed all commerce. The embargo pleased Napoleon.

Then came the patriotic uprising of Spain in 1808, against Napoleon Britain ceased its war on Spain and revoked its Orders in Council so far as the Spanish trade. Then opened again for trade, Spain, Portugal, Mexico, Cuba, South America, Central America. Brazil was already open. So were many other ports of the world: Canada, and all the world that is further south than France and Italy, — a vast field for trade. All the great whaling seas were open. Then Americans asked repeal of Jefferson's embargo, which forbade to sail abroad a single American ship. Jefferson refused; England taxed our ships and cargoes that were going to French dominions; he said tax is tribute, dependence; save our property and seamen by keeping them at home; let Europe have time to revise its conduct. This great trade, profitable and desirable, offered to America, rejected by Jefferson, was mostly taken by the British. Jefferson disliked the English; his embargo was made on purpose to damage England, to coerce her into relinquishing her restrictions on our trade, and her search and seizures, and Jefferson, by his short-sighted policy, rewarded his favorite enemy by all this rich commerce of which he deprived his own countrymen! Immense countries desired our vessels and our products of industry, but still Jefferson insisted that it remain unlawful for an American ship to sail the great seas of the world.

Jefferson offered repeal of the embargo in exchange for repeal of the Orders in Council, and the decrees of Berlin, Milan, and that of Bayonne, which ordered confiscation of every American ship in France or to arrive. Canning replied ironically, he could afford irony with Jefferson; Napoleon did not answer at all. Practically, Jefferson's offer to Napoleon amounted to a proposal to make war on England if Napoleon would repeal his decrees and England should not revoke the Orders.[1]

Our envoy to France, Armstrong, wrote to Jefferson that the embargo was not felt in France, and was forgotten in England. Armstrong wanted armed commerce instead of embargo. Sensible Armstrong! It would be more respectable, more manly, more likely to command respect abroad. He said: — "It is believed that we cannot do much and will not do what little we can."

At home, opposition to embargo became more intense. Embargo hurt the North and Maryland, and Delaware, far more than it did England or France. It was war against American industry in favor of its foreign rivals.

[1] Jefferson's instructions to our envoys, Pinckney and Armstrong.

But embargo was frequently evaded. Ships would sail; commerce is a part of civilization; it would assert itself. Jefferson tried force. He sent General Wilkinson, — the officer who had acted dishonorably in the Burr treason affair in the South, — with part of the new army to Lake Champlain, to act against New York and Vermont trade with our neighbor, Canada. He sent his little gun floats against trade from our eastern ports. Lest Britain should tax our ships passing her to go to France, Jefferson's armed cruisers chased, captured, and made prize of our vessels off our own ports.

Canning's reply to Jefferson was that the embargo was not impartial; since France had been the first aggressor it ought to be against France alone : nor could Britain buy off an improper hostile measure by the concession asked, if made really to benefit France, against which the Orders were originally aimed. And if embargo was merely municipal as said, what connection had it with Britain's retaliation against her enemies? The Berlin Decree attempted to overthrow British power and commerce. Europe was induced or compelled to join in it. American embargo unintentionally, but unfortunately aided the Continental System just when that aid was most conducive to its success, now unlikely. The Orders were to retaliate on that system. He denied British hostility to the United States. Without deprecating the embargo as hostility, he said he was anxious to remove that inconvenience to the Americans. This experiment might teach that Britain is not so dependent on American trade as to court it.

Jefferson's efforts to stop by force the evasions of

the embargo caused bloody encounters and then treason indictments. But Judge Livingstone decided that no resistence to law, however extensive or violent, is treason if overthrow of the government is not its object. Juries, too, were averse to convicting, so treason charges had little effect. Jefferson's power was not equal to his intent.

A special British envoy, Mr. Rose, arrived January 13, 1808. He was authorized to settle the Chesapeake affair. He said he could not do that until the President's proclamation which ordered British armed vessels out of American waters should be withdrawn. Our government was willing that this withdrawal and the reparation should bear the same date; it also insisted on including a settlement of the impressment question. Mr. Rose declined all this and he returned to England. Canning made a great error by not making the Chesapeake reparation even without a treaty, to remove the irritation made and continued by it.

The embargo act had offered the bribe that the President could suspend its operations against either belligerent that should withdraw its oppressive edicts toward neutrals, but like most other leading measures of Jefferson's presidency, it made miserable failure. Jefferson's policy withheld idle sailors and idle vessels from the Spanish trade to the great damage of the liberal Spanish patriots when besieged in Cadiz, certainly an un-American policy.

As we find much to admire in the career of William Pitt before 1793 and monstrous faults beginning that year, so of Jefferson prior to and from 1807. His oppressive embargo irritated the opposition to use refractory language, and these rash words in turn encouraged the British government to persist in its injurious regulations.

Of the terrible effects of the embargo in America, Jefferson's great biographer, warm admirer, and strong partisan, Mr. Randall, writing forty years later, in cool effrontery says: —

> "That measure (the embargo) unquestionably bore with severity on the interests of every great class. The farmer lost his markets, and had to pay enormously increased prices for such imported articles as he used. The merchant lost his trade, the mariner his occupation.... It was a period of financial embarrassments, — a time for economies, — an occasion for those commercial stop-laws which constitutions do not permit."[1]

And then of its still more direful effects on the helpless poor of England, Randall adds in a spirit of cruel exultation: —

> "Her (England's) annual exports to the United States had already reached about $50,000,000. This money was paid for the labor of innumerable artisans and it kept a multitude of manufacturing establishments in operation. Her exports and the imports received in return gave employment to an important branch of England's merchant marine. These several interests did not merely depend on the occupation thus given for profits or for surplus earnings, but to a considerable extent for the actual materials for subsistance. If the artisans of England were thrown out of employment they did not disappear like a speck among a population overstocked with an unsalable surplus of food. In thirty-six hours after the manufacturing establishment stopped one-half of its hands began to feel the pangs of hunger. A week or a fortnight brought the most provident of them to the same pass. The English operative, bred all his life exclusively to one kind of labor, could not, like an American, turn his hand readily to another. If he could there was no unfilled place where he might step in, as in America, and acquire a ready subsistence for his family. From the United States the cessation of commerce called forth grumblings on full stomachs, — from England it would soon draw out a shriek of starvation from a class."[1]

[1] Life of Jefferson.

But it was not the British people but the government of George III that committed the offenses against us. The British people did not then as they do now, choose the House of Commons which now rules the government. It is a spirit far from being above criticism that could thus cruelly destroy the vast value of American commerce in order to hurt the feelings of the obtuse George III, it could not destroy his personal comfort nor that of his favorite minister, Perceval, both already hardened by long years of wide-spread human suffering caused, in part, by them. For what else was the embargo? It struck at the real aggressors only through "the destruction of that class," the common English, who were powerless to prevent, and no more responsible for, the Orders in Council and the impressments, than was Jefferson himself, but were themselves defenseless victims of press gangs. Jefferson's provocation was from the British government; his retaliation was on the British people; it was also on the Americans.

Widely different are war between governments and war against a people. Napoleon's early wars in Italy were conflicts between governments; whoever won the people acquiesced; so were his wars of 1805 and 1809 with Austria; his war of 1812 was against both Russia and its people. However the American and British governments may differ, there ought never to be a war between these kindred peoples. Wars between peoples are much the worst of wars.

But Jefferson overreached himself; his embargo gave to English vessels much business and its profits that, without embargo, Americans would have had. British vessels even appeared in Napoleon's ports, pretending to be Americans, fabricated ship papers were extensively used. Customs officers in many ports tried not to detect these practices.

For what must England depend on America? For wheat? Cattle? Hemp? No: Russia, Poland, the Levant, India were glad to supply these things. For Timber? Naval stores? No, for Norway, Sweden, Russia were eager to furnish these articles. For sugar? Rice? Fruits? Tobacco? The British colonies sent these. Coal? Iron? America did not produce coal and iron: England had these at home in abundance. Fish? Oil? England had great fisheries while embargo almost destroyed ours. Embargo flung away our privilege of carrying these articles from other lands to England. Cotton? Yes, England wanted our cotton. Three months after embargo was laid, the British parliament passed an act, March 25, 1808, to require neutral vessels to take British license and pay transit duties. This was requiring tribute. It was unjustifiable. It would be $6,500 on a cargo of $43,500 worth of cotton, beside other fees of about $2,000; or about $13,000 on an American cargo of 400 hogsheads of tobacco. Many neutral vessels, many that were American, took such British licenses and British protection. With better reason Britain opened its West India ports to our vessels, that without clearances, illegally escaped the embargo of our ports.

Jefferson wrote to General Dearborn, August 9, 1808, that insurrection was threatened in Boston if importation of flour was stopped, and said he, "the next post will stop it." The resistance was such that he advised Governor Tompkins of New York to send militia where Jefferson had sent regulars, to the Canadian frontier. "Military force became necessary to support the authority of the revenue officers in several of our eastern ports and gunboats were sent into those ports for that purpose,"[1] as against an enemy.

The embago appears to have been as strictly enforced against France as against England, though France pretended to except Americans from the effects of the Decrees of Berlin and Milan until several months after the embargo existed. Jefferson long believed this fraudulent pretense of Napoleon was true. He wrote to Eppes, September 20, 1808:—

"His (Bonaparte's) beginning now for the first time to condemn our vessels augurs nothing friendly."

Strange, indeed, if France had remained "friendly" when its trade with us was embargoed. But Napoleon had, all along, sequestrated our vessels and cargoes ready for confiscation. It was only March, 1808, that he issued his Bayonne Decree to seize and confiscate every American vessel in France and all that should arrive.

Great Britain had the greatest commercial fleets the world had ever seen. Its navy had almost swept from the ocean its massive enemies and rivals by its victories at Trafalgar and its many other conquests upon and beyond the seas; supply ports were open to it in many parts of the world; yet it was the conceited opinion of Jefferson and his violent partisans, particularly in Virginia, that England could not subsist without American trade, while, in fact, England could obtain elsewhere all she needed of supplies, with the profits of the carrying trade beside. Jeffer-

[1] Randall iii, 262.

son's fatuitous flinging to her our carrying trade abroad, from foreign countries to England and Europe was making the British an ungracious present of much of our rich business, to the injury of America and the British poor working class.

Jefferson's majority in Congress felt warlike; it authorized him to equip our four frigates carrying but 144 guns in all. Great Britain had a navy more than a hundred times greater than ours.

The opposition held that embargo is unconstitutional. Talk of disunion was heard; it seems to have been mere talk. Jefferson and Madison had both once held that a state may nullify the acts of the General Government. Jefferson was the author[1] of the Kentucky nullifications resolutions of 1798, and Madison those a little later by Virginia. This was now bitterly retorted on them. Yet eight legislatures, those of New Hampshire, Pennsylvania, Ohio, Kentucky, Virginia, and North and South Carolina, resolved for the embargo. The whole country was agitated, embittered; everybody was angry; incubus was upon all business. Party spirit was oppressive, rampant; its spite did not die out for many a year.

January, 1809, Congress threatened to make the embargo more strict. Then appeared danger of civil war; the country was aflame. Congress, still more excited, passed an act calling together the new Congress in May, to repeal embargo and accept war with England.

When Jefferson's war on our commerce began, many planters believed that injury to our vessels and cargoes could harm only the commercial men and trading parts of the country, not the soil cultivators;

[1] Jefferson's Works. Jefferson to Nicholas.

they looked with complacency on a seizure when the sufferer was a Boston or Baltimore merchant, but when their unsold cotton and tobacco crops lay on their hands unsalable, their feelings, their pocket interests were aroused; and when England put a 25 per cent tax on cotton reshipped from England, the South was aroused. England's heavy license tax on tobacco trade to Europe stirred the Southern pocket to its depths. The Jefferson party were willing to ruin all of New York and Philadelphia's rich trade abroad in order to distress British workmen, because the British king and ministry over whom British workmen had little or no more control than had the slaves on Jefferson's plantation, had taxed cotton and tobacco, had prevented its free market in Europe. These plantation men called for war. "Want of revenue, want of ships, want of objects of attack, destruction of commerce, danger to our liberties from standing armies, are nothing but disguises for want of patriotism and contemptible cowardice," was the somewhat mixed declaration of Williams of South Carolina, in Congress, while he blindly opposed having an American navy, and declaimed that he would like to burn our few war ships, but he wanted war in America to free cotton from tax in England! This is a specimen of the logic of many partisans of those times.

When Joseph Story, the great lawyer, a Democrat, wanted fifty fast sailing frigates to swarm on many seas and keep thrice that number of British war ships busy to watch them, scarcely a member south of Delaware sustained his proposal, and Williams declaimed that if the rights of Americans were only so to be saved he was for abandoning them at once. Eager for war for cotton he was against defense of vessels or of manufactured goods, and he talked of "self-sacrifice of the South and selfishness of the North."

The bill to more strictly enforce the embargo passed the fatuitous Senate, December 21, 1808, by the decisive vote of twenty to seven. It aroused violent excitement in the commercial states : several customs collectors resigned ; newspapers appeared in mourning; resistance, even disunion were advocated ; town meetings protested ; they called upon state legislatures for relief. On the question of the powers of state and of the general governments both parties had reversed position. Jefferson's once "States Rights" party had now become the party of strong, central national rule ; the Federalists had become the States Right party.

The enforcing act passed finally, January 13, 1809. Collectors must, under its provisions, take charge of loading vessels, a really spy system, and allow no infractions of embargo. The president's power over trade was made despotic. Jefferson called on all state governors to hold ready militia to aid collectors; he was authorized to hire thirty more vessels to cruise against American commerce, to capture American vessels if found at sea on their own risk. Jefferson's policy was far more injurious to Americans than were the British Orders. Not a boat, not a baggage wagon, but might be seized on complaint of any informer who might be tempted by the Act's offer of half the goods and half of a fine of four times their value ! Dwelling-houses might be searched for evidence of contraband goods. Even trade between town and town in the same state was infringed. To this astonishing extent had these Jefferson men, so lately ultra advocates of local rule and against central power, become extreme oppressors of States, and of local business and trade.

The eastern states were now lost to Jefferson's party. In February, 1809, Massachusetts' General Court declared the enforcing act "unjust, oppressive, unconstitutional, and not legally binding," and advised resort to state courts to prevent its execution. Business men threatened the impeders of business with counter suits in state courts.

Napoleon's Berlin Decree was but revival of a decree of the French Directory of 1798 which Washington and John Adams had regarded as an act of war against America. The Massachusetts' legislature spoke out February 3, 1809: —

"Let Congress repeal the embargo, annul the convention with France, forbid all commercial intercourse with French dominions, arm our public and private ships, and unfurl the republican banner against the imperial standard. This done, the English Orders would cease to operate."

Petitions against embargo flooded that General Court. A bill was passed to prohibit search of dwellings without sworn warrants, but the Jefferson acting governor, Lincoln, vetoed it. Another Lincoln, collector of Boston, resigned rather than enforce the act. Many collectors resigned.

The commandant of the Boston harbor fort received government orders from Washington to allow no vessel to pass. All the vessels had their flags at half-mast. The excitement was very great.

In Congress were bitter debates. The able John Randolph of Virginia saw clearer than Jefferson; he warned the president to beware of measures so dangerous.

Governor Lincoln selected militia in Massachusetts to aid to enforce embargo. This act was illegal; to military officers belonged the making of all details; so Lincoln had the mortification of failure.

The Henry excitement was a great stir made over a rumor that the tough old soldier governor of Canada, James Craig, whose rule was so singular that England recalled him, had sent one John Henry to Boston to arrange with and comfort the disaffected; that neutrality of the eastern states in the embargo struggle was to be rewarded by England with free commerce. These rumors seem to have been ill-founded, but they were paraded for effect, and, three years later, in February, 1812, Mr. Madison gave Henry $50,000 of government's money for Henry's papers, which proved nothing after all. Jefferson's two accounts of the matter, one written in 1809, the other in 1825, differ.[1]

It was in 1809 that senator John Quincy Adams got his great fright and hurried to Washington with the story that Massachusetts would forcibly resist the embargo and dissolve the Union, and call in British aid, a charge re-produced twenty years later to obtain Jefferson partisan support for his election as president. But Jefferson was disinclined to believe this. He wrote that this would be the last state to really dissolve the Union, so dependent was it on the other states.

Governor Trumbull of Connecticut declined to detach state militia to aid embargo, as Jefferson's

[1] Jefferson to Monroe, Jan. 27, 1809; Randall's Jefferson iii, 293.

circular required. He believed it to be illegal to so use the militia, and the legislature took the same ground, and this attempt of a president to command state militia failed, because it was an attempt to usurp unlawful powers.

Russia, offended at Napoleon's assuming so much northern sway; at his hasty marriage with an Austrian; at his increase of Warsaw; at his refusal to ratify the Polish treaty; and pressed by Napoleon's many Russian enemies, was kept quiet, though restive, by her own great effort to rob Turkey of Roumania. How long could it last?

Russia argued that all Americans were not smugglers; some were lawful traders; that Russia would admit those that were lawful; that deprived of British trade she desired to retain that of the Americans; but here again Jefferson and Madison appeared as enemies to American interests; their embargoes and non-intercourse acts forbade American vessels to be abroad, in Russia or elsewhere! It was Jefferson theory *vs.* common sense.

For neutral trade it was true that the Americans were constantly running the embargo in spite of Jefferson; and great numbers of American vessels staid abroad to keep out of the ruinous grasp of Jefferson's unfriendly acts. But the existence of the embargo furnished Napoleon the argument that they could not be lawful American traders in Russia when it was unlawful for an American ship to be anywhere abroad. So Jefferson's influence was against Russia, and against American trade with Russia. Just so in case of Sweden.

The English ministry would not allow an American vessel to pass without paying British navigation fees or taking a British cargo. Napoleon seized American vessels or compelled them to give him one-half their cargo; thus between Jefferson, who would keep American ships to rot at the wharves, and King George, who made them pay high British license, and Napoleon, who seized one-half their cargo, and perhaps the whole, and the ship too, American commerce had a hard trial for existence. Yet with all these enemies the owners who kept their vessels abroad were finding lucrative commerce in many places.

In 1809 England wanted bread. It needed naval stores. It then allowed all vessels, even of enemies, to bring these essentials. They ran out of Boston, New York, Charleston, and other American ports, chased, perhaps, by Jefferson's small, inefficient war vessels, eluded the embargo, and were welcomed by hungry men in England to whom they brought American food, for which they perhaps received British goods, landed them at a second good profit in Russia, and brought back to England cargoes of Russian naval stores, which the British so much needed that they were ready to pay a good price. All these articles paid duty which fell really on the consumer in Britain in the enhanced price. At that time vessels entered the Thames from Russia, Holland, Belgium, and Hanse Towns, nations at war with England. But in 1810 British vessels entered France, under those licenses which Napoleon sold to enrich himself, with indigo, cochineal, dyes, fish, leather, and other articles which Napolean invited them to bribe him to allow. They were required to take away part cargo of silks or other French goods. But Manchester goods and Birmingham iron ware, coffee, and sugar he still forbade entry to the empire. French silks were prohibited in England; so these vessels, compelled to carry them in part cargo to the British coast, committed them to smugglers; great inconvenience to little profit.

Georgians were selling their cotton regardless of the embargo when a new British Order in Council, December 21, 1808, prohibited re-export of cotton and all American products from England, instead of the British heavy duties on every pound. This act struck directly at the American planters. No longer could they reach the continent by way of English markets. Now the lately harmonious Jefferson party were becoming divided. Then came a political panic. The alarm spread to Congress; a plan was started to repeal the embargo in June and then have war with England; but the excitement became wild. A motion to repeal it from March 15, against all but British and French, passed the strongly Jeffersonian House, February 3, although Congress had just passed an act calling an extra session of Congress in June, "for repealing the embargo in June and resuming and maintaining by force our right of navigation." Jefferson wrote:—

"I thought Congress had taken their ground firmly for continuing the embargo till June and then war. But a sudden and unaccountable revolution in opinion took place the last week, chiefly among the New England and New York members, and in a kind of panic they voted the repeal of the embargo, and by such a majority as gave all reason to believe that they would not agree either to war or non-intercourse."[1]

The embargo had broken down March 9, by its

[1] Jefferson's Works.

own weight. Jefferson was mortified. He accused of producing the panic a member of his own party, Judge Story of Salem, Massachusetts, who was a member but a few days to fill a vacancy. In our Congress few or none have accomplished so great result from so short membership. Congress passed acts that the new Congress should meet in May; that the act forbidding imports of certain English goods is repealed; that exports to France and Britain are prohibited, and all imports after May 20; this act to expire at the end of that session, but the president might extend the time for the act to go into effect. If either France or Britain enabled the president to proclaim that it had ceased to violate our commerce, then this act should cease toward that nation and its trade be open, but remain closed against either that should persist. It authorized the president to equip vessels for defense.

Early in 1808, the legislatures of New England, elected by the Jefferson party before the embargo folly (except Connecticut), four of the Middle States, and North and South Carolina, asked Jefferson to be a candidate for a third term of four years, but he declined. A congressional caucus, January 22, 1808, nominated for president, James Madison of Virginia; for vice-president, George Clinton of New York. Monroe, a better statesman than Madison, was disappointed that he was not selected for president. It was a great mistake; but Jefferson was able to name the man for nomination by his party, and he preferred Madison. The Federalists' candidates were: for president, Charles C. Pinckney of South Carolina; for vice-president, Rufus King. The election of

November, 1808, gave Madison 122 electoral votes to 47 for Pinckney.

Jefferson left the presidency March 4, 1809, after eight years' rule. His administration had been in several remarkable respects diametrically opposite to the favorite theories on which he had been first elected, and, still more remarkable, his devoted party had followed his reversal of their cherished opinions. He tried to govern too much; he was unwilling to let citizens rule their own affairs. His avowed sentiments pledged him to a strict construction of the Constitution, and to local, reserved States Rights of everything not specially granted to the general government in defined terms. When Monroe and Livingston, — wiser than he, — without law or instructions from him, bought Louisiana, he accepted the wise act, although he believed it violated the Constitution. But they, not he, are entitled to the credit of this great act of statesmanship. His embargo acts were not only extremely unwise, but his attempts to override state laws and private rights in his principle of embargo, and his mode of attempting to enforce it, were arbitrary, despotic, in defiance of the interests of citizens and the real legal power of the president, and he was repeatedly doing what courts held as illegal. Prior to 1801, Jefferson decidedly professed extreme regard for the right of men to exercise each his own judgment in his own personal affairs; but his embargo was to the very extreme opposed to any such just liberty. It was rushed through the House at dead of night, in secret session, and never was American commercial act more worthy of darkness, mental, moral and political darkness, and midnight secrecy.

The boldest Federalist would never have dared to carry centralized power to so very alarming and really dangerous extreme. He so far passed their ideas of arbitrary central power that they fought him from the ground that he had occupied till he became president, a great lesson of how the ins and outs of power change a man's actions. Few persons really know what they would do if intrusted with power. Old "States Rights" Jefferson men now were advocating implicit central obedience; old central power Federalists were now loudly declaiming state and local rights. With Jefferson went out the panic-stricken Congress. The surplus of $17,000,000, — a great sum in those days, — with which Jefferson had entered on embargo, was gone. Jefferson's second term had not been honorable, creditable or advantageous to Americans. It was bad statesmanship badly executed. Men who may claim to be his disciples should state whether they mean of Jefferson before, or the changed Jefferson after he became president, or such claim is unintelligible.

In a full suit of clothes of American make, Madison took the official oath as president.

Embargo had helped to start home manufacture. A well-adjusted tariff would have done it better.

Madison, an irresolute man, called to his cabinet three weak men: Robert Smith became Secretary of State; Dr. Eustis, War; Paul Hamilton, Navy; the outlook was not good. But the able Switz, Albert Gallatin was Secretary of the Treasury. The cabinet contained only these four places.

In the United States, embargo made exit March 9, 1809; Congress repealed it; forbade our vessels to sail or to engage in any foreign commerce, and excluded British and French vessels from entering our ports after May 20, 1809, on penalty of confiscation. Few French vessels could reach America without capture by British cruisers, it was folly, only an irritation to Napoleon to pass this act to forbid them, it provoked him to heavy retaliation in the next year.

Many American vessels, avoiding the unfriendly embargo of Jefferson were already abroad where they remained, took British cargoes of colonial products to England, with British licenses, sometimes at their own account, oftener on account of British, Dutch, Russian, Danish, or Hanse merchants, put to sea, under British convoy if it was necessary, entered north Europe ports, sometimes French ports, as neutrals, pretended they had not been to England, obtained credence from local officers willing to be deceived, and landed cargoes.

When Congress passed this absurd prohibition of American commerce, Holland itself was not blockaded; it was not until seven weeks later, April 26, 1809, when the ministry had heard of the new act of Congress, that they declared Holland in blockade.[1] In May they suspended this blockade for a time, to suit the Erskine affair.

Official returns named above 4,000 men impressed by the British since the French war began, of which not a fifth were British subjects.

[1] Lyman's Diplomacy, 277.

"The American consul at London estimated the number of impressments during the war at nearly three times the amount of names returned."[1]

Randall[2] says:—

"Our minister in England believed that it was more to destroy our rivalry in commerce and navigation than to directly affect France, that the Orders in Council had been issued."

This is doubtful. But if so then Jefferson and Congress gave most efficient aid to George III's hostile design, for embargo hurt our commerce far more than the British damaged it.

Mr. Erskine, a frank, honorable man, came as British envoy. British Whigs in parliament had attacked so vehemently the Orders in Council, that in April, 1809, the ministry so modified them as to open to Americans the Baltic, the German ocean, part of Italy, and the Dutch colonies. This gave Americans free access to Russian and Swedish ports, even against Napoleon's bitter opposition. British ships arriving in Russian waters had been seized by Russia, to gratify the vengeful Napoleon. Then British merchants employed great numbers of American vessels in their trade with Russia, because of the great risk that the Czar would continue to confiscate British ships. This trade was very profitable to Americans.

Southern planters' unsalable crops had accumulated; their money was gone, their credit lost, very emphatic dullness had settled on their farms, even Jefferson's own plantation was now suffering from loss of tobacco market. Still they had not fully learned that there are intimate relations between farming and freighting, that successful farming requires open transportation.

[1] Randall's Life of Jefferson.   [2] Ibid.

The British basis given to Mr. Erskine was: —

1. The actual exclusion of British and French war vessels from our waters to be equal.

2. England would renew the disavowal of the Chesapeake affair, restore the three men.

3. She would reserve the right to claim seamen deserters of British birth.

4. America to disavow Captain Barron's retention of British deserters and his denial of it, and any consequent outrages.

5. American agents not to encourage British army or navy desertions.

6. As the subject of desertion would require act of Congress, England would waive disavowals for the past, if America would accept as reparation the return of the three men; and Britain would add, as "spontaneous generosity," provisions for the widows and orphans.

Berkley, the cause of the Chesapeake affair, had been promptly recalled, but lately he had received another employment, so Canning would permit no further mark of displeasure against him.

Canning offered to remove effect of the Orders in Council of January and November, 1807, from Americans on these conditions: —

1. The repeal as to Britain but the maintaining as to France and countries which adopted its decrees, all existing non-intercourse acts, and exclusion of their war ships.

2. America to renounce all trade with colonies of belligerents not allowed in time of peace.

3. British war ships to be allowed to enforce by

captures American non-intercourse with France and her allies. If accepted these terms might be practiced before treaty.

Mr. Erskine offered the Chesapeake reparation with "provisions for the unfortunate sufferers," thus exceeding his "spontaneous generosity" instructions.

President Madison accepted, with a growl that punishment of Captain Berkley "would best comport with what was due from his Britannic Majesty to his own honor." Madison ought not to have sent, nor Erskine to have received, this useless remark.

Erskine announced the ministry's intention to send an envoy to settle all disputes, and to withdraw the original Orders in Council, persuaded that the president would proclaim renewal of intercourse. The subject of colonial trade was passed over as of little consequence, no American commerce being allowed with French colonies. The capture condition was omitted because America could not so far renounce rights of sovereignty over its vessels, and the Americans in the unlawful French traffic would not be likely to claim protection from our country lest their embargo bonds be enforced. Mr. Erskine engaged that the odious Orders in Council should be withdrawn, June 10, 1809. This agreement was published. President Madison suspended the non-intercourse act of March, 1809, so far as Britain was concerned. This news was received in our seaports with lively joy. Federalists exulted that it exhibited the extreme moderation and equity of Britain, and that Jefferson's obstinacy and French proclivities had prevented earlier agreement. They exalted Madison for the time. Some Jefferson Republicans exulted in the belief that this agreement was proof that England felt the embargo, and that it was a good measure; others disliked any agreement with George III, and feared the anger of Napoleon.

The business effect was great; many hundreds of our vessels put to sea; business sprang into active life; again American energy had an open field for exercise. Again our sails would be on every sea.

April 12, 1809. Britain so modified the Orders in Council that only France, Holland, and north Italy were blockaded; all the rest of the world was now free from British blockade, except the French colonies on which blockade was now placed, making it for their interest to be taken by Britain which could give them better market than France.

Napoleon was depredating on American vessels, forty-eight had been condemned by his prize courts within two years, and many more captures were pending confiscation.

Southern Republicans warmly opposed allowing any American trade with Hayti, because it was a free negro country; they voted it down in Congress, but it was very quietly resumed on expiration of its prohibition and has been continued ever since.

Madison advised Congress to "protect and foster" manufactures lately began; he laid up Jefferson's gun craft, discharged the militia from liability to be called.

Canning repudiated the Erskine arrangement, as not authorized, illusory. He took special exception to Madison's remark about Berkley, the British king must be the judge of what "comports with his own honor." Everybody was sorry, all but the French faction. Useless words had done harm. The British ministry protected for a short time the American property so suddenly shipped. Madison withdrew his proclamation leaving in full force the Act which prohibited imports and entry of any British or French vessel.

Mr. Jackson came to succeed Mr. Erskine. Madison was displeased that he brought no "Explanations," and very properly refused to allow Canning's colonial trade prohibition, or to permit British cruisers to aid American non-intercourse with France by capture of our ships that should break our law. Jackson said the capture of most of the French colonies, close blockade of the rest, and British release of so much of Europe from blockade rendered these conditions of comparative indifference, and he was not instructed to re-propose them, he was ready to receive proposals. Our Secretary of State, Smith, suggested the suspension of both the Orders in Council and the non-importation Act, pending full negotiations. Jackson proposed to refer this condition to the ministry. Smith and Jackson got into a war of words, rather puerile, and broke off the negotiations, for which neither of them was competent. Jackson charged that Smith knew before signing that Erskine exceeded his instructions. Smith denied it. Jackson repeated it. Madison, angry, refused further correspondence with Jackson and he went home.

American ship owners now asked only to be let alone. But Southern planters, missing their markets, now called for such protection as they had derided for commerce; with the bravado of those times they clamored for war with England.

The only war act of Congress in 1810 was the

giving of $5,000 for torpedo experiments to Robert Fulton, of whose steamboats four were in use on the Hudson and three elsewhere.

The non-intercourse Act of March 9, 1809, expired May 1, 1810. Congress authorized the president, if either Britain or France should revoke its unfriendly edicts, to revive the non-importation Act against the other only, and let fall all but exclusion of British and French war ships.

Less than $4,000,000 were in the American treasury when 1810 came in, against $17,000,000 when embargo began, in 1807. Embargo had greatly damaged commerce, but had aided home manufactures. Prior to embargo the United States had but 15 cotton mills, of 8,000 spindles; by 1810, 62 mills were running 31,000 spindles, and many mills were being built. Bed tickings were 55 to 90 cents a yard; stripes and checks, 30 to 45; gingham, 40 to 50 cents; shirting and sheeting, 35 to 75 cents. Wool and linen were household manufactures, made with simple wheel and loom. Calico was not American, it came from abroad.

Now our commerce was to take care of itself. Napoleon would allow no trade with his allies which was not shared by France. He caused seizure of American vessels in large number in Spain, in Holland where his own brother, King Louis, resisted this iniquity; and in Denmark, Hamburg, Naples, and Baltic ports. One pretext was that American and British vessels brought British goods with forged papers, representing them as American goods. Such evasions existed, but Napoleon made no discrimination, but willfully plundered a vast amount of really

American property, regularly imported. He said our government had made great seizures of French vessels under the absurd embargo. Our minister, Armstrong, showed that this pretext was false, but it made no difference to him that Jefferson's seizures were but four little French vessels; that was enough; he would retaliate; he took hundreds of our vessels. Says Thiers : —

"He had, indeed, confiscated a great number of them, and in their rich cargoes he found means of supplying his treasury almost as abundant as those which were yielded by the war contributions imposed on conquered countries."[1]

His Rambouillett Decree, dated in March, issued in May, 1810, ordered the sale of 132 vessels and cargoes, valued at $8,000,000, and also of all American vessels that should enter any port occupied by French!

His third pretext was the non-intercourse act of March 9, 1809. But strangely enough, his Rambouillet Decree was not actually issued until that law had expired by its own limit. The bare fact was that Napoleon wished to commit the robbery for the sake of the plunder. So bad pretexts served him. He professed willingness to respect American rights if America "would resist British tyranny, compel the British ministry to retract the Orders in Council, or declare war" against England.[1] But as his word could not be trusted his profession was of but little worth.

[1] Con. et Emp. viii, 358.

XVII

AUSTRIA and France were preparing to collide early in 1809. The condition of Europe recalled Napoleon from Spain. He left Joseph as his lieutenant. The resolute will of Napoleon gone, the French army, no longer a compact body, massive, terrible, became several bodies. After deducting 58,000 sick in hospitals, and 25,000 stragglers, and small details, 240,000 were in the field.[1]

Austria was arming. That alarmed Napoleon. France was not satisfied. It was uneasy. France did not like the Spanish war. It had no cause of quarrel with Spain. France wanted rest. Financial difficulties existed. Paris criticized his errors. He wanted a new conscription. The public funds fell to 80. He bought in 62,000,000 rentes to keep the price from going still lower. Negotiations went on abroad. The fifth coalition was forming against France. Now ordinary French funds were short. For a long time he had obtained great sums by robbery of foreign countries. The French budget for general expenses for 1806-7 fell a little below 900,000,000 francs.[2] It was the same as in 1807-8-9, the armies being paid from the "Army Treasury," namely, the great robbery of other nations. January 1, 1809, 300,000,000 francs were in this separate army treasury, of which Austria had been robbed of 20,000,000 and Prussia of 280,000,000. From this bandit fund the French treasury proper borrowed 84,000,000.[2]

Napoleon demanded of Poland, Saxony, Bavaria, Baden, and Wurtemberg, about 113,000 troops against

[1] Napier, 282.   [2] Thiers.

Austria, and obtained probably 100,000. Of Jerome Bonaparte's Westphalia, and of Louis Bonaparte's Holland he demanded 20,000 each.[1] Yet neither of these countries had any cause against Austria, they must simply fight for Bonaparte in his own private quarrel.

Austria counted on about 300,000 active troops, and 200,000 reserves, and the Hungarian volunteers.[2] Napoleon, though he had immense armies himself, insisted that Austria must disarm. But the war spirit was aroused in Austria; even the militia were being drilled.

Russia was busy trying to rob Sweden of Finland. Turkey, under Mahmoud, suspected the real fact that Napoleon had promised her Roumania to Russia. So Turkey threw away the French alliance and made peace with the British, and hated Napoleon and the French.

Fifty thousand Austrians were to aid the Tyrol and threaten Italy; 10,000 were to act against the French in Dalmatia; 40,000 toward Warsaw to hold in check the Poles and Saxons, and to watch Russia; and 200,000 were to form the great army under Archduke Charles, in Bohemia and upper Austria. The reserves would cover Vienna. The Emperor, Francis I of Austria, aware by painful experience, that he was not a capable man, had called the Archduke Charles to the head of Austrian war affairs.

Of this war Sir Walter Scott says: —

"This breach of friendship appears, certainly, to have been sought by Austria, without any of those plausible reasons of complaint, on which nations generally are desirous to bottom their quarrels. She

[1] Thiers.   [2] Thiers iii, 172.

did not allege with respect to herself or her dominions, that France had, by any recent aggression, given her cause of offense "

What was the cause of the war? Nothing. Austria was tired of being apprehensive of France. She had, for ages, been the rival; she hoped to be the superior; she meant to be, at least, the equal of France; she had been badly beaten in the war of 1805; she wished to gain vengeance, to recover prestige.

Austria's attack was a great mistake; it was inopportune. Had she a year earlier thrown her whole force upon the flank and rear of Napoleon, when, checked and weakened, he stood in front of the Russians after Eylau, then, in all human probability, Napoleon could have been thrown back, defeated, upon the Rhine, followed, as in 1814, by allied Russian, Austrian, Prussian, Swedish, and perhaps German, armies. But Austria had let that great opportunity pass. In fifteen years Austria had lost Belgium, Suabia, Lombardy, the Tyrol, and Dalmatia, and had gained and lost Venice.

Austria began war against France, April 9, 1809, but war was not declared at all.[1]

With 140,000 men [2] in five divisions, Archduke Charles invaded Bavaria. The Tyrol, led by an innkeeper, Andreas Hofer, rose in revolt in favor of Austria. Peasants attacked its Bavarian garrisons.

Napoleon's army was always distinguished for celerity. It already protected Germany. Davoust was at Ratisbon; Lannes at Augsburg; Massena at Ulm. Berthier commanded the French till Napoleon should arrive; By April 17 he had spread the 140,-

[1] Thiers, iii, 180.　　[2] Ibid iii, 182.

000 French over twenty-five leagues, with one center at Ratisbon and another at Augsburg, in danger of being cut in two by the Austrians. Such was the dangerous effect of the absence of the great master of concentration.

Charles was a tactician. But when he was ready to strike direct from Bohemia on the single corps of 60,000 French under Davoust at Ratisbon, before they should be reinforced, he was compelled by an order from Vienna to turn back, and enter Bavaria only by crossing the Inn at Branau. This change cost several days of extremely valuable time beside the serious mischief of the change of the field plan. Still with this embarassment, he nearly succeeded, April 17, in getting between Davoust and Massena who was many leagues away at Augsburg. Charles took Landshut and pushed his columns forward toward Ratisbon, Neustadt, and Kelheim where were the important points, the lower bridges over the Danube. Immense stake depended on his celerity; but he only moved from two to three leagues a day. Possession of those bridges would render him master of both banks of the Danube. His left occupied Munich, the capital of Bavaria, whose king fled to Napoleon.

Napoleon's center was the Bavarian troops at Ingoldstadt. Davoust at Ratisbon was not only in danger of being separated from all supports, but 40,000 more Austrians were marching down from the northeast, from Bohemia, on him. Swift, energetic Austrian movements might surround and place him in a situation like Mack's at Ulm in 1805.

The Tyrolese expelled the Bavarian troops from

the Tyrol, and took about 6,000 of them prisoners. Austria had thus recovered the Tyrol which in 1805 Napoleon had torn from Austria and given to Bavaria, his ally.

Such was the dangerous situation for France when, April 17, Napoleon arrived at Donauworth. A great commander like Sir John Moore, in unfettered Austrian command, would soon have decided the great campaign against the French, by able marching.

Germany was deeply stirred with hope for the defeat of Napoleon. The Prussians were greatly exasperated. Napoleon was using the money of which he had robbed them, to make war on Austria. Could the Prussian patriots, Stein, Scharnhorst, and Blücher, have been at the head of Prussian affairs, and untrammelled by an incapable king, all northern Germany might have risen against this foreign despoiler of Prussia, and carried the war from Germany into France. Then, as through his whole career, Napoleon owed much of his success to the fact that almost every country of Europe was badly handicapped by its incapable sovereign, who impeded the free exercise of the nation's power.

Quickly Napoleon saw and set about remedying Berthier's great blunder. Was there still time? Would not the Austrians be upon Davoust before he could extricate his corps? Napoleon sent orders to Davoust to retreat toward the Bavarians; to Massena to hasten forward his corps with utmost speed to concentrate the army. The fate of the French right, the fortunes of the campaign, perhaps the result of the great war appeared to hang, trembling, on the vigorous celerity of the Austrians in crushing Da-

voust quickly. Abensberg was the vital point.
Should Charles move quickly forward in strong force
and occupy Abensberg, he would bar the French from
concentrating. He could reach that point more
easily than Ratisbon; he was nearer to it than Davoust. This would throw Davoust back on Ratisbon,
where he would be caught between Charles and the
two Austrian corps coming from Bohemia; thus his
60,000 French would be trapped by 140,000 Austrians. But celerity is a lesson that few military men
ever learn. So is concentration; so is vigor. These
are the three great points of Napoleon's system;
these are the military principles by which he subjugated so many nations. Instead of marching quickly
in force on the vital point, — Abensberg, — or of
striking Davoust hard with overwhelming force,
Charles divided his concentrated force. He sent
Archduke Louis with perhaps 15,000 men, a fourth
of Davoust's numbers, to Abensberg, and with about
25,000, less than one-half, Charles moved on Ratisbon, to face Davoust's 60,000. But Davoust used
celerity. Leaving 3,000 men at Ratisbon, he was
almost to Neustadt by April 19. Strong detachments
met and made a bloody combat at Thann, where each
side lost about 3,000 men. It was Davoust that
reached Abensberg. Massena's advance met and defeated 5,000 Austrian cavalry at Plaffenhosen. Napoleon had so far concentrated in a front thirty miles
broad; the Austrians were separated on forty-eight
miles front, with twelve miles space between unoccupied, and still two Austrian corps were out of supporting distance, north of the Danube. On the 20th
of April, the Austrians had halted near Abensberg,

not expecting attack. But the swift-moving French were upon them; and an Austrian defeat opened up the gap in their front; their left was beyond supporting distance. They lost about 8,000 men, a total of nearly 14,000 in two days.[1] Next day the French pressed upon the separated Austrian left under Archduke Louis, defeated that slow-moving noble, captured Landshut, which he lacked energy to protect although it contained immense Austrian military stores, just what Napoleon desired for use. But the Austrian general, Hiller, had made a very desperate fight, and retired only when he had lost nearly 6,000 men, 25 cannon, 600 ammunition wagons, and a valuable pontoon train. Several other combats occurred. The Austrians fought well. But too often separation placed them at disadvantage. Charles took Ratisbon and made prisoners of the 3,000 French that Davoust had left there. Napoleon, advancing from Landshut, met the Austrians near the Laber, and Marshal Ney fought his desperate battle of Eckmuhl, April 22, from which came his title, Duke of Eckmuhl. The Austrian left was again defeated and thrown back toward Ratisbon. Charles then withdrew his whole army to the north of the Danube at Ratisbon,[2] except the corps of Hiller. When Napoleon arrived, April 17, the Austrians ought by concentration, vigor and celerity to have quickly defeated the French, but as they disregarded those great military principles, and Napoleon observed them, he had in six days recovered from his bad position, taken or disabled nearly 60,000 Austrians, captured above 100 cannon[3] and thrown back, beaten and disheartened, the great

[1] Thiers iii, 191.   [2] Ibid.   [3] Ibid 198

Austrian army, and opened the way to Vienna, except the obstacle of Hiller's corps.

Defeated in Bavaria, the Austrians were victorious in Italy over Prince Eugene, whose French army they defeated and drove across the Adige. The Tyrolese had swept the enemy from their mountains, but the Bavarians now re-occupied part of that country. That mountain war was very fierce, energetic, as religious and mountain war is apt to be; it was, however, Catholic Tyrol against Catholic Bavaria, though France aided the invading Bavarians.

An Austrian army under command of Prince Ferdinand invaded Poland. Its 35,000 men defeated Napoleon's friendly Poles and took their capital. Napoleon's lieutenants were doing badly. Ferdinand tried to engage Prussia in the war for north German liberation. The Prussian and German people were ready, eager, ardent. All Germany, three-fourths of the world beside, desired the overthrow of Napoleon's power. Not a people of Europe except the French and part of the Italians and Poles were friendly to him. He had exasperated the world by his arbitrary outrages.

The numerous and influential secret society, the Tugenbund, organized for German liberation, and liberty, and good government, pervaded Germany. Many Prussians were members. Von Stein was its head. Germans were enthusiastic for liberty, were restive under Napoleon's oppressive rule. They were embittered against his gigantic cash robberies; his great levies of supplies; "his Continental System"; his war against the world's trade; his compelling Germans to serve as his soldiers in wars with countries against which Germany had no quarrel or complaint; and frequently to fight against those to whom they were friends, compelled to lose their lives or be crippled for life in battle for Napoleon when they would rather have fought against him. He was a great oppressor of Germany. In many cases, like that of Baden, he had enabled its own little princes to be only more tyrannical and exacting. Napoleon still held several Prussian fortresses taken in 1806. He had drained the country of money by the enormous sums he compelled Prussia to pay him, which the incapable Prussian king had not guarded against when he appointed the feeble-minded old Kalreuth to make the peace of 1807, at Tilsit. It was for lack of a king that was capable of great resolution that Prussia was kept from joining all her forces with the Austrian 35,000 that had just overrun Poland, for the liberation of all north Germany and Prussia. Several ebulitions appeared. Major Schill, Captain Katt, and the Duke of Brunswick each led a movement. They had chivalrous adventures which threw contempt on Napoleon's Westphalia military authorities: Schill made a dashing, partisan ride for many leagues through the country, threatened strong Magdeburg, held dismantled Stralsund for several days, and was at last killed in an assault made by Dutch and Danes, only after he had given great alarm to the French agents and officials. But the prestige of Napoleon was too strong for Germany to rise without the aid of the burdensome Prussian king. Napoleon's success in Bavaria compelled Ferdinand to relinquish Poland and retire into Austria, but he invaded Saxony and captured several important cities.

The Russians who were to aid Napoleon against Austria, came very slowly toward Cracow. They did not wish to hasten. They would have liked better to fight Napoleon.

Napoleon decided to move on Vienna. It was such a march as a general well might decline. On his left flank, though north of the Danube, was the army of Charles, defeated, but still formidable. Napoleon was on the south side of that river. On his right was the Tyrol, up in arms against him. His line of communications would be in utmost danger. But, after sending orders to Bernadotte, who commanded the Saxons at Dresden, to move at once forward; to Poniatowski in Poland, to enter Gallicia; to Eugene in Italy, to advance, Napoleon moved on, April 26, for the Inn and for Vienna.

Charles sent proposals to exchange prisoners, and suggesting peace, April 28, but this dispatch was not seasonably received. Hiller's Austrian corps, still south of the Danube, made gallant resistance at several points. At the Traun crossing, near Linz, a desperately contested battle between Hiller and Massena, with heavy loss on both sides, was an Austrian defeat, May 3, 1809. The battle-ground presented a frightful spectacle. "Dead and half-burnt men lay, by hundreds, in the streets; mutilated and burnt limbs obstructed the way at every step. It was impossible to ride through the streets covered with ruins and horses," is the testimony of an eye witness. Had not Napoleon possessed great inherent, brutal, cruel inhumanity, these revolting sights must have diminished his love of war.

Charles' slow army did not arrive to defend Vienna.

Napoleon took it after a bombardment, May 13, with its immense arsenal of war stores and 400 cannon. Massena had taken 50 cannon on the road. Vienna supplied all that the French army needed. Napoleon's celerity had again won a great result.

Napoleon's success sent Archduke John's Austrian army in Italy hurrying home, pursued by Eugene's Italian army, which inflicted severe disasters; Trieste, Laybach, the whole Austrian frontier, were taken by these Italians, who drove John's army into Hungary where it was useless. This ruined Austrian hopes in the Tyrol; its bloody revolt was a failure. The Bavarians re-took Innspruck, May 19.

With eager eyes all the world looked on. Tremendous interests were at stake. Defeat of Charles would now leave Austria in the dust; Napoleon still to dictate Germany; defeat of Napoleon, decisive, would rouse all Germany and probably excite Prussia to throw its military might, aided by the patriotic enthusiasm of Germany, down upon his broken lines. Napoleon was wagering his throne against decisive defeat. He must advance. But the Vienna bridge was destroyed. Yet he must cross the Danube to reach Charles. The Austrians had left vast bridge materials. Pretending to begin a bridge two miles above Vienna, one was prepared ten miles below, by way of two small islands, to Lobau island, which was separated only by a narrow stream from Charles and the north bank. Strangely enough Charles did not oppose this act, though his army was present on the ridge perhaps a mile back from Lobau; 80,000 men, with 300 cannon. May 21, two pontoon bridges were

Battle of Lobau.

quickly thrown across this narrow stream and the French columns began crossing. Still more strange Charles did not oppose the crossing. Mid-way between the villages of Esling and Aspern, each half a mile from the river, over the main bridge poured the columns of Napoleon, upon the plain. These villages formed bastions for each French flank. It is remarkable that Charles did not hold these villages, and still more singular that he had not constructed a strong line of heavy earthwork on their entire front, along the bank of the river, where the Austrians could have fought under strong protection, while the invaders were entirely exposed to the Austrian fire. Even small advantages are not to be disdained at the beginning of a battle, and here was a great advantage neglected. About 50,000 of Napoleon's mongrel army drawn from many nations, were in position between the two villages when the Austrians made a tremendous attack. Around the two villages, which considerably strengthened the French position, the fighting was dreadful, furious; both sides fought with frightful energy and destruction. The enormous losses did not dishearten them. As great numbers fell, still greater numbers fought on. The fast-crossing French hurried into the appalling harvest of death. New Austrian forces came up and added to stupendous horror. Night came on indecisive battle. Amid the multitude of the dying and the dead, both armies, in the darkness, prepared for greater battle on the morrow.

In the gloom of night, both parties were reinforced; the invaders were 70,000 beside Davoust's 30,000 more at hand ready to cross, against probably 100,-

000 Austrians. Long before the morning sun had begun to lighten the field, the sanguinary conflict re-commenced. Long the battle raged, desperate, terrible, doubtful. A great charge ordered by Napoleon, made by Lannes, was frightfully devastated by the Austrians whose center receded before it so that the front and both flanks at once of the charging columns were exposed to Austria's deadly semi-circle of fast flashing fire. His progress arrested, his men mowed down by Austrian batteries at half-musket shot distance, he could neither deploy nor return the awful fire to advantage. The day was being lost. The Austrians saw a gap in Napoleon's right; into it they bravely charged; they pierced it; the day was won; Napoleon was beaten. Checked, shattered, dispirited, his army retreated across the bridges to Lobau. It was none to soon, for the bridges were giving way under the pressure of the rapidly rising river and the timbers and boats laden with stones which the Austrians sent down the current against them. As the invaders retreated, the Austrian cannon wheeled in concentric circles round their diminishing numbers and made bloody destruction by their continuously crashing fire. The bloody-handed Marshal Lannes, who had commanded the French in the frightfully revolting siege of Saragossa, a few months before, which had caused the deplorable misery, and horrible death of 54,000 Spanish men, women, and helpless children, now received his death wound at Aspern. It was not till all night had dragged its long hours of continued destruction that the defeated Napoleon again had his torn and shattered army back into Lobau island, and the avenging Austrian cannon

ceased to thunder, and the wearied victors sank to sleep by the side of their guns. Napoleon was fairly beaten and driven from the field in a great battle. At Eylau, in 1807, he had been beaten, but not driven from the field. But this battle of Aspern was not decisive. It left Napoleon able to fight again.

The loss on both sides was enormous, its real numbers uncertain. The Austrian official report was 4,287 killed, and 16,300 wounded; 20,587 in all. Napoleon's report was absurdly unreliable. His loss was probably much larger than the Austrians'. Probably 50,000 men were killed or disabled on both sides.

Driven into Lobau, Napoleon's retreat was impracticable; the Danube had swollen; the bridge to the south shore was swept away; he was penned up in Lobau; his artillery ammunition was almost gone; provisions were lacking. It was the opinion of the bravest marshals that it was best to retire to the south bank if means could be found. But Napoleon said, "Shall we abandon the wounded? Shall 20,000 brave men add to the trophies of the enemy?"

Charles had ordered the Archduke John, who commanded the Austrian army of Italy, to march to the Danube at Linz. Had John obeyed like a good soldier, and arrived promptly at Linz, he could now have held the south bank, barred the way for reinforcements to reach Napoleon, and the invader would have been lost.

Again princely incompetency spared Napoleon. John was a high hereditary noble; he did not think it was necessary for him to obey, so he had marched his army to Hungary, where it was useless. And John was not removed from command! At Linz

John's army and Kollowgrath's corps, would have been about 60,000 men, to aid to prevent Napoleon's escape to the south bank; to prevent supply of food from reaching him; to cut his line of communications with France. His disobedience deprived Austria of the fruits of its terrible victory. Within two days Napoleon re-established the lost bridges to the south bank. For forty-three days the two armies remained in their positions. With rapidity Lobau was made a great fortified camp.

The Tyrolese rose again and poured in great force down their mountains and glens, and animated by the spirit of the dark ages, for it was against progress that these superstitious men warred, they drove away the 6,000 Bavarian garrison at Innspruck, with loss of half its numbers. The Tyrolese belonged rather to the ninth than to the nineteenth century. Hofer and Speckbacker were regarded by their countrymen as saviors of liberty, which certainly they were not.

Napoleon levied on Germany additional troops to destroy their own country's hopes.

An Austrian invasion of Franconia was successful.

Again John disobeyed orders with fatal result, and exposed his army, where Eugene overtook and defeated it at Raab. And yet John being a high prince, was allowed to command, at the peril of Austria, while guilty of disobedience, for which the best general would have been removed and punished.

The military forces of Napoleon were still immense. Eugene's Italian army arrived, May 26, and more than made up for Napoleon's loss at Aspern. Napoleon openly built four bridges to the south shore. Secretly he prepared three ready to be thrown across to the north or Austrian shore. He built a line of works facing the Austrians and mounted it with 120 heavy guns brought from Vienna. He made ostensible attempts to prepare for crossing at Nussdorf and Spitz.

July 2, 1809, Napoleon's other armies began to arrive. Bernadotte came with the Saxon army; then appeared Vandamme with Germans from Wurtemberg, Suabia, and the Rhine; Wrede with the Bavarians lately fighting in the Tyrol; Macdonald and Broussier from the south; Marmont from far off Dalmatia; then the Italian veterans of Eugene who had just again chased the wretched John to Hungary. By evening of July 4, Napoleon had 180,000[1] men assembled in Lobau, an island not more than two and a half miles long and one and three-fourths wide.

The Austrians had erected immense field works, extending through Aspern and Esling to the Danube, and placed on them 150 heavy cannon. Charles ought to have strongly intrenched the whole shore opposite the whole length of Lobau, so as to cover every possible crossing, as Wellington, Sherman or Lee would have done. His earthworks were too limited. The great Austrian army, largely increased, was about a league in rear. Charles ought to have concentrated all the available force of the empire to the front in trenches. One hundred and forty thousand Austrians awaited the attack. Napoleon's 900[2] cannon were to oppose 700 Austrian guns.[3] The Austrian corps, as usual, were separated; Napoleon's, as usual, were concentrated. Austrian stores captured at Vienna supplied the needs of Napoleon's

[1] Napoleon's statement.   [2] Alison iii, 245.   [3] Thiers.

army. Charles ordered up the recusant John, who, with 36,000 men was at Presburg, watching, across the river, Eugene's deserted camp, unaware that Eugene's Italians were already at Lobau. John moved slowly, sulkily. He wanted to keep his separate command.

At last Napoleon was ready. The battle of Wagram opened July 5, 1809. A demonstration at the great bridge, and a false attempt there to place a bridge to their shore drew Austrian attention. **Battle of Wagram.** A hundred French cannon there opened fire on the Austrians, who were deceived. Their batteries thundered back a terrible fire on that spot; both shores were lines of cannon flames; the night was ablaze with the tremendous flashing. The secret bridges were quickly thrown across at another spot. By three o'clock, A.M., Napoleon's armies were crossing. A terrible tempest was raging; rain fell in torrents; nature's lightnings flashed bright amid the blaze of cannon; heaven's artillery loudly answered the thundering crash of heavy guns; the blaze of a whole village added to the lurid scenic wildness where Napoleon's 900 cannon flung their screaming, shrieking death missiles, and the immense Austrian batteries answered back in the night's Plutonian, fiery gloom, with crash after crash like the tremendous impingement of colliding worlds.

Great was the surprise of the Austrians when daylight showed not a man across the Aspern bridge, but Napoleon's great army across further down, and ready for the great battle that should humiliate either Austria or Napoleon. The Austrians saw their own position turned; their short, heavy intrenchments, intended to bar the passage, useless. This could not have occurred if they had strongly fortified the whole distance in front of Lobau.

They fell back a mile on the plateau of Wagram, a position chosen with care, leaving their great intrenchments. Strangely Charles had neglected to intrench Wagram plateau itself. Picks and shovels may be as valuable as cannon in war.

The necessity of guarding against a crossing at distant places, had drawn strong detachments from the Austrians, so just at Wagram Napoleon's army, no doubt, out-numbered them.

Then was a day of terrible battle with varying fortunes, but rather favorable to the Austrians. They gained great advantage on their right, and when Napoleon made a great effort to break their center, they repulsed him with French disorder. Charles had again ordered John to join him, but John had not arrived. When night came the battle was still undecided. Both armies rested and slept on the bloody field.

The next day, on that front of nine miles, 300,000 men with 1,100[1] cannon, were ready to renew the awful conflict. The Austrians began the great attack; they defeated Napoleon's left; they hoped to give him a general defeat; it was imminent. Now Napoleon made the greatest efforts against the Austrian left. John's army was needed and intensely hoped for to decide a great victory for Austria; still John did not appear. Charles sent to him the most urgent orders to hasten. Nothing would hasten that hereditary commander. How different had the brave Hiller commanded John's corps! Charles made important

[1] Thiers.

movements on his left which he hoped John would come up and aid. The great folly of trusting high commands to princes was strongly apparent. Had John been other than a high noble he would long ago have been replaced by a general who would obey orders. Napoleon was in desperate straits, and an Austrian army was kept back by this hereditary prince from coming to his overthrow!

Seeing that a great disaster and defeat threatened him, Napoleon ordered a great, a desperate charge on the Austria center. On this rested his own safety. It was bravely, heroically executed by Macdonald. It was near failing; it barely succeeded. John's arrival would have been Napoleon's ruin.

At last the Austrians retired, with no rout, no great loss of prisoners. They formed in good order on a line of heights not far away. Night and John came together. He came up in rear of Napoleon's right; just the place to do immense damage; to reverse the fortunes of the day; to strike a panic into the French now in the disorder of victory; to overthrow Napoleon's army and his throne at a single blow.

But this hereditary commander, born to be a general, not qualified to be a corporal, with his great corps of fresh troops, having the opportunity to attempt what Blücher did at Waterloo, and what any man whose claim to command is not birth but merit would have done, halted, faced about, retreated.

The Austrian accounts show their loss in killed and wounded as above 23,000. They lost nine cannon and took eleven. They took 7,000 prisoners and twelve eagles. Savary, who was with Napoleon, says the number of prisoners on each side was about equal.

Another battle followed at Znaym. It ended with an armistice, July 12, 1809.

During this truce one-third of the Austrian monarchy was in Napoleon's power. He immediately compelled an enormous payment of money to him by the part of Austria that he occupied, a monstrous burden especially when money was scarce and of high value in Austria. He required that all the vast expenses of his great army from April 1 to October should be drawn from the conquered provinces.

Peace negotiations lasted till October 14, when by the treaty of Vienna, Austria was compelled to give to the Confederation of the Rhine many square miles of territory, with 3,500,000 inhabitants; and to Napoleon, Salzberg, parts of Carinthia and Croatia, Carniola, Trieste, Istria, and other ground, making the Save the Austrian boundary. These provinces, with Dalmatia, Venetian Istria, and Ragusa, Napoleon formed into a new state, called Illyria. Austria was compelled to cede West Gallicia and part of East Gallicia to Warsaw, and part of East Gallicia, with 400,000 people, to Russia, although the Russian army had moved with unwilling slowness to aid Napoleon against Austria.

The Emperor Francis I resigned as Grand Master of the Teutonic Knights; he acknowledged all changes made or to be made in Italy, Spain, and Portugal; he joined, without reserve, Napoleon's "Continental System" to exclude all English goods; and he agreed to pay to Napoleon 85,000,000 francs additional to the large sums the French had already extorted from the Austrians;[1] and he bound himself

[1] Thiers iii, 326.

not to keep his army above 150,000 men till a maritime peace.

Napoleon considered a plan of separating the three dominions of Francis I, Austria, Hungary, and Bohemia, each with a separate sovereign. Metternich wrote, April 25, 1809:—

"The division of Europe into powers of which the strongest should not have more than three or four million of subjects has for some time been Napoleon's plan."

Austria had done magnificent fighting. With all his talents, Napoleon had barely succeeded; any other general would have failed. Had the Austrians been as well commanded, they would have won overwhelming victory. The reason that the common Austrians fought better at Aspern and Wagram than in former French wars since 1789 is that they had sympathized with the French attempts for liberty, and believed it could be had with good government and safety and security, as it is in America and Great Britain, but now had learned that there was nothing either democratic or republican in Napoleon's government, nor justice nor equity in his character. They had ceased to admire him as the common people's representative; they now saw in him the grasping, avaricious tyrant, the war-mad disturber, the devastator of German and Austrian prosperity; the destroyer of their quiet, safety, and happiness; the incendiary of their homes. They fought the man who burned their houses; who robbed them of their food and crops for his army's forage, who invaded their country; who laid waste their farms; who filled their land with mourning for their slain; who made war-cripples of their sons and brothers; who showed no disposition to give peace to distressed Europe so long as he should live.

When the French evacuated Vienna they ruthlessly blew up the fortifications of that beautiful city, a gross and useless breach of faith after war was over.

XVIII.

In England, in 1809, a new trouble appeared. An enormous sum of money, 19,300,000 sterling had disappeared from the Admiralty board and the St. Domingo fund. Who had taken this $90,000,000?

And yet another trouble. The Duke of York, George III's pet son, was commander-in-chief of the British army. It is a fact; that noble army of gallant men was thus handicapped. The duke's mistress, Mrs. Clarke, had been, with the duke's knowledge, taking bribes for military promotions. Sir Arthur Wellesley, afterward the duke of Wellington, wrote:—

"The love letters have created a terrible impression .... people are outrageous in the country on account of the immorality of his life, which makes no impression in town .... There has appeared in the last two days a general system of swindling, applicable to all the offices of the State, in which Mrs. Clarke has been most active, and a great gainer. These transactions, which have deservedly created so much indignation, have been carried on by the scum of the earth." [1]

The worthless duke of York resigned.

Perceval moved for leave to bring in a bill to prevent brokerage of offices. The Commons decided to inquire into the East India patronage. "Sale of writerships and cadetships were found to be so

[1] Wellington's Supplementary Dispatches vi, 567, 575.

enormous."[1] Castlereagh, head of the War Office, "had been dabbling in the dirt of this market . . . . bartering an Indian writership for a seat in parliament for his friend, Lord Clancarty . . . . Castlereagh admitted the facts and acknowledged the offenses."[1] Yet he was kept in the ministry. Perceval, too, just when he had been so afraid that members would travel on Sunday that he changed the day of the meeting of parliament from Monday to Thursday, had been trading for a seat for Dr. Dick to vote to screen the king's pet son.[1]

The ministry had long felt the incapacity of Castlereagh as War Secretary, but they had been too afraid of hurting his feelings to remove him! They let him go on and prepare the great Walcheren folly. George III did nothing; his reasons for not acting seem to have been that as the guilt of Castlereagh had been detected, it would damage him to be dismissed!

The Walcheren folly of 1809 was remarkable. Among the very best soldiers of Europe are the British. They are brave, skillful, and enduring. But George III's cabinets were singularly deficient in practicable ability; they too much resembled the king. The course of the ministry threw very undeserved discredit on the army. From the beginning of war by Pitt in 1793 to 1812, the king and cabinet had never given the army a fair chance anywhere in Europe. When they sent it at all, they always handicapped it by fewness of numbers, as in Naples under "Maida" Stewart in 1805; or by both smallness of numbers and lack of support and supply, as in Portugal and Spain under Moore and Wellington;

[1] Miss Martineau I, 282, History England.

or by a bad commander and general mismanagement, as in the Walcheren expedition of 1809.

Instead of a swift, strong expedition to the Elbe at the critical moment, Antwerp was aimed at by a tardy, ill-timed, grand, showy affair, at enormous cost, with "A commander known to have owed his appointment to royal favor,"[1] as an ultra friend to George III admits, to seek dockyards to destroy and ships to burn or bring away. Another distinguished friend to George says : — [2]

"Yet, weighed with the difficulty and danger of an attack on them, the object of destroying them seems to have been very inadequate. Admitting that Buonaparte might succeed in building ships in the Scheldt, or elsewhere, there was no possibility, in the existing state of the world, that he could have been able to get sailors to man them, unless, at least, modern seamen could have been bred on dry land."

If such an expedition was to go, then most of all it would require the utmost ability in its commander. Yet George gave the command to his favorite, the Earl of Chatham, brother of William Pitt, whom, if possible, he exceeded as a bad manager. This new commander, says George's great friend Scott : —

"Was remarkable for a spirit of inactivity and procrastination, the consequences of which had been felt in all the public offices which he held and which therefore were likely to be peculiarly fatal in an expedition requiring the utmost celerity and promptitude of action."

This so-called "secret" expedition was paraded with the utmost ostentation : —

"During the three days on which it ran down the English shore every height was covered with people .... all England seemed to have collected on the coast."[3]

This is the way that the ministry kept the important secret. Its destination was to be concealed,

[1] Alison iii, 268.   [2] Sir Walter Scott's Napoleon, 53.
[3] C. Knight vii, 293.

yet an order issued during embarkation mentioned the "burgomaster," an office peculiar to the low countries." It was the most stupendous expedition that Great Britain had ever sent abroad. It was very magnificent, very costly. It carried 39,143 soldiers; an immense number of sailors and marines; at least four thousand cannon, and 9,000 horses. Besides one hundred and sixty transports and other vessels, here sailed thirty-seven of those monstrous floating war castles, called ships of the line, now disappeared from the seas; and five 44 and 50 gun ships and 18 frigates. Ancient Rome or Greece never saw its equal. The renowned Spanish Armada of 1588 was far inferior in strength. But this display was ill-timed, it looked like a triumph, but a triumph better follow than precede battle. Too late it was discovered that boats for landing were deficient in numbers. The Austrian war was ended. The armistice for peace was July 12. Wagram had been lost July 6. It was not till July 28 that the first British division sailed for Walcheren. It was too late to affect the Austrian campaign, or to rouse Germany; now nobody in Germany thought of rising against Napoleon. The crisis had passed; the golden opportunity was gone. Twenty days after Wagram, eighteen days after armistice, several weeks too late, 20,000 men landed at Walcheren. Even then, had Chatham acted with military promptness, and pushed forward vigorously to Antwerp, it must have fallen into his hands. Extensively as the ministry had advertised that this "secret" expedition was coming, yet so completely had Napoleon denuded the country of troops to fight the Austrians, that Antwerp, garrisoned by but 3,000

MADE A BLIND BEGGAR BY WALCHEREN.

half-invalid troops,[1] could not have held out against a much less force had a general like Sir John Moore commanded. Chatham captured Middleburg, invested Flushing, and occupied Batz, the key to both channels of the river Scheldt, and two-thirds of the way from where they had landed to Antwerp. The French vessels had gone from Flushing up the river. The English squadron neglected to pursue; Chatham was too slow. Good officers of experience advised rushing at once for Antwerp, but the incompetent Chatham would attack Flushing first. It consumed a fortnight to prepare for that, though had Antwerp fallen Flushing would have surrendered without a shot. Napoleon afterward said to O'Meara that if a few thousand men had landed at Wilhemstad and marched direct to Antwerp, it might have been taken by a *coup-de-main*. But the quick advance was not made. Time was wasted besieging Flushing. It was bombarded and it surrendered, August 16, with only 4,500 defenders. Nineteen days were gone. The French had strengthened two intermediate places and were now in the way. Then the continued occupation of Walcheren to seal up the great port of Antwerp was contemplated. But it was a terribly unhealthy spot; it was the sickly season; fevers prostrated the English by thousands; many died in Walcheren island; 12,863 were sent home sick.[2]

Fouché sent Bernadotte to Antwerp. He soon made it defensible, and gave the British ships such a cannonade that they left the river. Flushing was given up. Chatham's army and navy evacuated Walcheren and its waters, December 23, 1809. Thus

[1] Scott: Thiers.   [2] Parl. papers No. 24, Parl. debates xv, 23 April.

ended the great expedition, untimely sent, but which, had it been sent in season under an able commander, might have inflicted a severe blow on Napoleon's power.

Miss Martineau (English)[1] says: —

"When Walcheren was evacuated, December 23, nearly half the force sent out five months before were dead or missing; and of those who returned, 35,000 were admitted into the hospitals of England before the next first of June. Twenty millions sterling (almost $100,-000,000) were spent on the expedition. It was the purchase money of tens of thousands of deaths, and the ineffacable national disgrace."

To this remark I reply that it was not a disgrace to the honorable British people nor to their army or navy. Soldiers or seamen can hardly be expected to win renown if directed by incapacity at headquarters. The whole disgrace belongs alone to George III and his war minister, Castlereagh, and George's Chatham. Chatham was: —

"Totally destitute of the activity and decision requisite . . . . destitute of experience, unknown to fame."[2] "The military command was given, as the selection of the present cabinet had been, to Lord Chatham for no better reason than that he was a favorite with the king and queen. . . . . It was wholly a court appointment."[3]

This case illustrates the evil of heredity in affairs, and contrasts strongly with the better system in Victoria's reign of leaving affairs to be managed by an executive ministry not responsible to the crown. Even after the revolting misery of the enormous failure the court and ministry tried to shield Chatham, but outraged public opinion drove him to resign his place in George's cabinet. In September while the army and navy were intensely suffering at Walcheren, Canning insisted that Castlereagh be dismissed.

[1] History England i, 273. [2] Alison's Europe iii, 265.
[3] Martineau i, 271.

George was reluctant. Castlereagh controlled about thirty votes in parliament. Castlereagh discovered that the ministers had all along regarded him as incompetent; he resigned and challenged and fought and wounded Canning. The ministry was low in popular contempt. Canning too went out and with him that far better man, Huskinson.

A mournful jubilee of grief came October 25 for the beginning of the fiftieth year that Britain had been afflicted with George's reign. The unworthy king's pet son was just disgraced for crime, George was at mutual hatred with his other sons; his friends, the "Pittites," were quarrelling; George's government was in disgrace abroad and dishonor at home; the Walcheren misery, the royal thieveries, imbecilities, corruptions, had disgusted the British people; it was prayer for relief from George's miseries, not jubilee that was wanted. The best that could be said of George III was that he stood between the British and a dissolute successor, George, Prince of Wales, whom few or none loved, and whose vices and crimes the British feared. This had caused some unhealthy sympathy for the British king. For one day the people sang, rang the bells, feasted, had processions and illuminations, and deserters were pardoned. Never had a great people more need of a holiday; the times were the depth of British gloom; some good natured Britons, unable to find anything else in hard old George to admire, showed "respect to his length of days."

The Walcheren calamity broke up the ministry. The half-dead Duke of Portland retired and died. This ministry had come in, March 25, 1807, in disgrace; its existence was ignominious; it went out in public contempt.

December 1, 1809, after attempt at coalition with Whigs, a Tory ministry was formed, Perceval, Premier; Lord Wellesley, Foreign Office; Robert Jenkinson (Lord Liverpool),[1] War Office.

Perceval "was adverse to all the liberal doctrines of the age."[2] The British of today are not accountable for him for he belonged to an age now gone by in England.

The Walcheren alarm greatly aided Napoleon by enabling him to call out a great force of the National Guard (militia) for that occasion, and once out he kept them as permanent troops.[3] "England produces us an army of 80,000 men, whom we could not have procured otherwise," he wrote.

The Tyrol was not included in the armistice. Therefore during peace negotiations it continued to be the scene of desperate strife. After Aspern, Tyrolese had freed their mountains from invaders. But Wagram struck them with horror. Fresh French and Bavarian troops were sent to subdue them and the Austrians retired. The Tyrolese attacked these troops at the bridge of Laditch, August 4, and after a wild, romantic fight in the narrow defile, drove them back with a loss of 1,200 men. This successful outbreak aroused a general rising. Eight days later, in a general battle near Innspruck, they again defeated the invaders with great loss and disaster, and compelled them to retreat from the Tyrol to Salsburg. Again the Tyrol was free. Andreas Hofer formed a Tyrol government. Napoleon prepared to crush them.

---

[1] He had been Lord Hawksbury. [2] Alison iii, 271. [3] Thiers i, 317.

After gaining several advantages, Eugene offered amnesty for submission. Peace with Austria had been signed; there could be no hope of Austrian help. The Tyrol refused the peace. But early snows drove the peasants down from the mountains and made them more accessible. After considerable more severe fighting the revolt was crushed in blood. Many chiefs accepted amnesty; Hofer still resisted; he was captured January 5, 1810. Napoleon ordered that this patriot be tried by court-martial and shot, which was done at Mantua. It was cruel and contrary to the laws of war, it was practically assassination by Napoleon's orders, like the German case of Palm, the book-seller.

In July, 1809, an English expedition, by great enterprise, captured the last French possessions in St. Domingo. Martinique was taken in February, 1809. These were important British successes. Zante and Cephalonia, islands near Turkey, were freed from French rule by British force.

Papal affairs excited Europe. French troops occupied Rome, February 2, 1808. In April Napoleon's imperial decree united four papal provinces with the "Kingdom of Italy." In Rome the French took control of the posts, the press, and the taxes, and incorporated the pope's troops with the French. An alliance, offensive and defensive, the pope had refused. May 17, 1809, Napoleon, then in Austria, decreed that the states of the pope are reunited with the French empire. By "reunited" he referred to the fact that these states were given to the pope a thousand years before by Charlemagne, whose gift Napoleon claimed to rescind. Napoleon held that the pope should be above the contest and affairs of politics; that he should be a spiritual power only, with a liberal yearly income of 2,000,000 francs which this decree assigned him, and independent of all quarrels of secular governments. Yet he himself tried to rule the pope. Napoleon decreed Rome to be a free imperial city. To this decree, published at Rome, July 11, 1808, Pius VII responded by a bull of excommunication, not mentioning Napoleon by name, but against all authors or accomplices of the act. It prohibited any one from holding it as authority for any attack on the person of Napoleon or of his adherents. The French stopped the pope's couriers who were carrying his protests to foreign countries. The pope pretended to be a prisoner, but he formed a new guard after his guards were merged with the French. The French disarmed it, and threatened his secretary. Napoleon proclaimed abolition of the Inquisition, of entails, of convents, and of church jurisdictions, that he would change nothing in the Church, its dogmas or its rites.[1] The lower class and priests were indignant; the better class not well satisfied with either pope or emperor.[1] At night, July 5, 1809, the French general, Radet, entered the Quirinal, which had just been broken open, and in respectful manner asked the pope to renounce his temporal sovereignty. Pius VII declined. A carriage was in waiting, the pope was conducted to France. He remained at Savona in France above three years, carefully watched but not imprisoned. Napoleon had made a great blunder. His rash act shocked the Catholics. The pope at Rome was a less interesting

[1] Thiers iii, 330.

man than the pope regarded as a state prisoner in France. The pope's excommunication bull was widely distributed in Spain to irritate against the emperor.

Rome felt the great change. That ancient city awoke to modern life. Great works, half obscured by the ruins of fourteen centuries, were cleared and again seen in their beauty. The code Napoleon, the conscription, the "Continental System," were introduced in vigor. The emperor decreed Rome the second city of the empire.

England and Turkey made a treaty of peace, January 5, 1809. Now British goods were sent into Turkey, and thence into Hungary and Austria, finding a valuable market. Americans entered this valuable trade only as they eluded Jefferson's embargo and non-intercourse acts. Those who obeyed the absurd Jefferson law missed this good business ; many of those who disobeyed obtained great profits.

George III's ministry sent a strong British and Sicilian force, too late, as usual, which they wasted in tardy, unseasonable moves against the French in Naples. It did not sail from Palermo till the Austrian Archduke John, with his army in whose aid it was sent, had been gone from Italy a month ! Such was the inefficient government Great Britain had to endure.

Several French war and merchant vessels were destroyed by the British near Genoa, October 30, 1809.

Wellesley landed at Lisbon, April 22, 1809, with 30,000 British soldiers.

Napoleon ordered Marshal Soult to enter Portugal. After many combats he defeated the Spanish under Romana and took Oporto by hard fighting. His troops sacked the city. With Oporto he took 197 cannon, great magazines of powder and thirty loaded British vessels. Soult governed at Oporto with firmness; he conciliated some of the Portuguese. But the Portuguese were so reluctant to fight for the invaders that "the odious spectacle was constantly exhibited of men marched in chains to re-inforce armies."[1] A conspiracy to make Soult king of Portugal came to nothing, though many French officers would have been glad thus to have escaped from serving Napoleon. But the Spanish and Portuguese closed Soult's line of communication with the French in Spain. He was isolated. Wellesley advanced against him. Soult tried to retreat. Wellesley came to Oporto and found him unprepared. A battle, May 12, 1809, defeated, compelled Soult to hasten to retreat. In his forced flight he abandoned cannon, baggage, even a part of the army money. He arrived in northwest Spain with great loss. Portugal was a second time freed from the French. It was decided British victory. The track of Soult's retreat was marked by burning villages, set on fire by both French and British,[2] — both lawless. The British commander wrote of the British troops : —

"There is not an outrage of any description which has not been committed on a people who have uniformly received us as friends " . who . . "have plundered the country terribly."[3]

War at best is very cruel; it causes frightful suffering, but when thus aggravated by outrages it is barbarity. The only sure way to avoid such cruelties, such shocking barbarities, is to avoid war. The

[1] Napier. [2] Theirs iii, 286.
[3] Wellesley to Castlereagh, May 31 and June 17, 1809.

persons who cause war are responsible for its enormities.

The French defeated the Spaniards in the battles of Cuidad Real and Medelin, March 1809. The little Spanish armies were much scattered and not united under any general head. Ill organized and badly provided they may have amounted to 153,000 men, that, with Wellesley's 42,000 made 195,000 total.[1] The French invaders probably were 300,000, but divided by a separate command being allowed to each marshal, and divided command always weakens an army. In the north were French military governments. As much as possible of the expense of this great military force was forcibly taken from the country according to Napoleon's systematic plan of general robbery. The loss of battles depressed Spanish spirit. Twenty-eight thousand heads of families enrolled themselves in a few days at Madrid as friendly to Joseph. Yet King Joseph was neither a statesman nor a good general. He was regarded coolly by the French and more coolly by his few submissive subjects. The marshals despised him; Napoleon constantly blamed and annoyed him; he lacked the spirit of his brother Lucien, to abandon the hopeless struggle and Napoleon's tyranny and leave the country, but he claimed of Napoleon a right to be restored as king of Naples where Murat now reigned. It was little gain to Napoleon that he made any of his family kings. As such each one was a failure. Only one, Louis, was worthy to rule, and Napoleon ruined the usefulness of Louis. Jerome and Joseph

[1] 26,000 British and Germans and the 16,000 Portuguese under British General Beresford.

lacked executive ability, Murat was fit only to lead cavalry under some other commander. Fettered by Napoleon's rapacity, Joseph and Louis could not use the milder, conciliatory policy. Napoleon wanted in Spain and Holland only strong, arbitrary rule. Those who have believed him in any degree disposed to favor republican government have singularly mistaken his despotic character. There was nothing republican or democratic in his disposition. His nature was absolutist.

Wellesley joined with Cuesta's Spanish army of 42,000 men. But lack of cordial, prompt and energetic Spanish support, the egotistical willfulness of Cuesta compelled Wellesley to receive battle instead of giving it. At Talavera, July 28, 1809, Wellesley gave the French a serious defeat; compelled their retreat, but could not improve the victory because of Cuesta's incapacity, and the failure of Spain to furnish needed supplies, even the necessary food. It was found that British need more to eat than do Spaniards, which facts soon after compelled Wellesley to retire, leaving many wounded to the French, who gave them courteous treatment.[1]

It was ominous to Napoleon that the British were proving so competent as soldiers. Talavera victory indicates what might have been done in Prussia if George's ministry had sent there 60,000 men under Wellesley or Beresford, when Napoleon had just received his terrible check from the Russians at Eylau, February 8, 1807. It was the British and Portuguese that had fairly and severely beaten the French at Talavera. The Spanish, though present, had given

[1] Napier. Thiers.

but little aid. Marshal Victor had chosen to attack without waiting for Soult, who was coming. Wellesley showed that he could repulse a superior force of the best troops of France, led by a veteran marshal; therefore it was a remarkable event in Napoleonic wars. Vain Cuesta, who might have aided Wellesley greatly, now met the French at Arzobispo, near Talavera, and had his army knocked to pieces, August 8, 1809, his artillery lost, 38,000 men dispersed. Five days later the French defeated another Spanish army reckoned at 35,000 men, under Venegas, at Almonevid. The Spanish were immensely losing by not supporting and cordially acting with Wellesley. England, justly proud of the soldierly qualities of Wellesley, made him Marquis of Wellington.

May, 1809, Marshal Suchet's defeat and dispersal of Blake's Spanish army, decided for French possession of Aragon for that year. Details of the many battles, sieges, marches, in Spain, are too much to state here. It was a harrassing system of warfare.

The shocking, terribly revolting siege of Gerona, resulted, December 12, 1809, in its surrender. The town was almost destroyed; its people and garrison starved. Nine thousand of them perished, of whom 4,000 were citizens. <small>Gerona. Dec. 12, 1809.</small> But 4,300 of its garrison were left to become prisoners. It had held out seven months; 180 cannon had battered it; 80,000 cannon balls had struck it; 2,000 bombs had aided the frightful destruction; 15,000 men had perished around its walls; thus this terrible siege had cost 24,000 lives; A single item in the vast destruction for which Napoleon alone is responsible for his attempt to place his incapable brother over a nation who hated the very name of Bonaparte. It was not France that made this war, it was Napoleon; the French people were opposed to the whole Spanish and Portuguese war. France was forced to it.

Napoleon's peninsular war was a very high crime. All the crimes committed by all the felons in all the prisons of Europe today, are far short in their atrocities and the human suffering caused to the immense magnitude of terrible distress; to the wholesale torments inflicted in this single war by the arrogant despotism of Napoleon's madness to rule or ruin. It was an unnecessary war; it was unprovoked; it was useless; it was very cruel. His cold blooded murder of the 4,000 prisoners at Acre, in 1799; his confessed murder of the 300 Russian soldiers, at Moscow, in 1812; his murder of the misguided patriot, Hofer, in 1809, were merciful compared with the useless and very cruel siege of Gerona, in 1809, or the destruction of the 54,000 Spanish men, women and children, in the siege of Saragossa, in 1808. If the perpetrator of a single murder deserves hanging or imprisonment for life, what does not the man deserve who, without provocation, without either insult or injury, wantonly invades, with a great army of above 323,000 men, a peaceful, friendly nation, for no other purpose than to arbitrarily, despotically rule it?

The French conquered the rich province of Andalusia by the total defeat of the southern Spanish army under Arezega, November 12, at Oceana after the British, unsupported, had retired to Portugal. The victors took 2,000 prisoners and 55 cannon. Joseph entered Cordova in triumph, January 17, 1810, and into Seville itself, February 17. The Spanish Supreme Junta retired to Cadiz which has the sea on three sides and is a strong position against land forces; 20,000 Spanish soldiers were there. Spanish guerilla warfare existed extensively. French soldiers must keep together or they were sure to be lost. Defeated in one spot the guerillas reappeared in another. The French were not safe unless in strong force. Napoleon was fighting a people. Some guerillas were in large, some in small parties. Soult proclaimed that he would treat them as banditti. They replied that they would execute two Frenchmen for every guerilla so punished. These threats were fulfilled on both sides. It was a murderous war; both sides were degenerating into savages. Bonaparte had made not only a crime, but a great blunder in attacking Spain. Before he began this dreadful war he ruled Spain through its miserable, worthless king, Charles IV, and his minister, Godoy, whom he compelled to give him vast sums of money and free use of Spain's navy and many Spanish soldiers for his French army. By the war Napoleon had greedily killed the goose that laid the golden eggs. Napoleon had expected to compel Spain to pay all the great costs of its own conquest, the pay, subsistence, clothing, everything of the invading French army. But so general was the hostility of the Spanish that the French army and Napoleon's new king, Joseph, must receive money from France or starve. The French robbed the Spanish people by contributions wherever practicable, but they were not answerable to Joseph, and he had neither power or much influence but that forced by the French arms, and the

French marshals disregarded him. "I am king of Spain only by your arms," he wrote to Napoleon, February 17, 1809. It was still true in 1810.

December, 1809, Wellington moved to near Almeida in Portugal. He improved at Torres Vedras and in front of Lisbon, those lines afterward so famous. Wellington's plans were well laid, but the division of the opponents of the French into three nationalities, British, Spanish, and Portuguese, was subject to all the usual difficulties of divided commands, and the irregularities of the Spanish; their several divided Juntas, their subdivided armies, their lack of discipline and united action, the vain pride of their leaders, their frittering away of force in separate commands, their unreliableness as allies greatly damaged their prospects.

Strange intrigues occurred. Napoleon wished to sound the British ministry respecting peace. Instead of going frankly about it, this important business was committed to intrigue. Labouchere, a Dutch banker, was sent to England as if on ordinary business, to be a mediator. He had no credentials. The British Minister of Foreign Affairs, Marquis Wellesley, expressed wish for peace if officially offered with definite disposals, but saw no utility in this clandestine affair, without authority or appearance of sincere desire for peace. If Napoleon was ready to treat why act slily as if ashamed of it?

Mr. Baring, speaking only for himself, suggested to Labouchere an arrangement to leave Malta to England, Sicily to its king Ferdinand who had never lost its possession, Spain to Ferdinand VII, giving as far as the Ebro to France. These terms were certainly not illiberal to Napoleon when he had never conquered or occupied a single foot of Sicily, had no need of Malta, and could hardly maintain his hold on Spain with 300,000 men.

England was willing to treat on either basis, viz: —
1. Possession before the war.
2. Present possession.
3. Reciprocal compensations.

Napoleon refused and let devastation go on. Labouchere's report showed to Napoleon that Spain was now the great point of contention. Well had it been for him had he yielded to the wishes of the French people and made peace on so favorable terms.

The price of sugar was made high by the prohibition of colonial goods, but France was now making beet sugar. British goods were forced high in price, but this stimulated French manufacture, and the French had the whole continent as a market for their silks, woolens, and cotton goods; they got cotton from the Levant, Naples, and Spain, and thus prohibitory protection was founding production in France and defying the Jefferson-Madison embargo policy.

At that moment the most prominent man in France next to Napoleon was Fouché, Minister of Police. Fouché was also secretly trying negotiations said to be unknown to Napoleon. He had sent to England, Ouvrard, a notorious speculator. Napoleon's intrigue discovered that of Fouché. The tricky emperor, enraged or pretending rage, dismissed the cunning minister and sent him to Italy. But Napoleon's intrigue was spoiled. This mean affair ended efforts between him and England for peace. Thenceforth they fought out the long war began in 1793, intermitted in 1801-2, recommenced in 1803 after intermission of fourteen months, and continued till 1814, and resumed for a "hundred days" in 1815, more than twenty-one years of war.

Fouché's plan comprised restoration of mutilated Spain to Bourbon Ferdinand of Spain, or if Joseph Bonaparte were retained as king of Spain then to give to Ferdinand a kingdom made of the Spanish colonies; and for Bourbon Louis, oldest brother of Louis XVI, a new kingdom to be made of the United States of America by French conquest.

Fouché reasoned thus: —

"The Americans are republicans; they had not aided Napoleon; they were hateful to the British ministry; Jefferson's and Madison's embargoes had embroiled them with both France and England; the French ought never to have aided their liberation; Napoleon, the correcter of faults, was to replace them under a European monarch; England must rejoice to see them checked in their ambition, punished for their revolt. Jefferson was chief of a party; that party was in power; Jefferson was a known admirer of France; he had lived in Paris; his party was friendly to the French; the southern states contained much French sentiment; it was only the commercial north that was more friendly to the British."

That Jefferson would have vigorously fought this scheme is undoubted, but that is not how Napoleon estimated friends of France; he believed them acquiescent. The existence of the American Republic was a constant menace to European restrictions. On the seizure of four French vessels for violation of our useless embargo folly, Napoleon had said to the American minister: —

"The extent of the loss is nothing: the honor of the flag is everything. You have laid hands upon vessels protected by my flag, and a single attempt would be sufficient to make me seize all the American marine if I could."[1]

Had it been the British ocean supremacy that was crushed at Trafalgar instead of that of Napoleon ; had not the powerful British navy held the ocean between France and America, only a small pretext may have been sufficient, — for his greatest wars were made on small provocations, — for Napoleon to have inundated America with troops of many nations, to destroy our liberties, not for a Bourbon, but for the only man for whom he ever worked, himself.

At that very time he was increasing his navy ; he had 42 ships of the line ; he expected to have 100 by 1812, which with frigates and corvettes could embark 150,000 troops ; and he had ordered that the great Antwerp docks be enlarged. For what could be all this vast expenditure? With 100 ships of the line, after Trafalgar, he could not hope to cope with Britain on the seas. What, then? Nobody ever saw his chances plainer than did Napoleon. Few ever equalled him in that faculty. His great chance, then, was peace with the coming George IV, the new regent, and conquests beyond seas. Remember he had said at Ulm : — " I want colonies, commerce."

The bad personal character of the coming George IV rather invited the scheme. Napoleon made the mistake of not crediting Britain with more conscience than he himself possessed.

[1] Thiers, Con. et Emp., vol. iii, tome 38, p. 358.

The Dutch have the honor of having been pioneers of religious and mental freedom. They had opulent free ports in the West Indies, South Africa,[1] South America, and in the East Indies with Trincomalee, the best harbor in the Indian ocean. Their commercial policy was most liberal, trade was least restricted. They became wealthy; their two per cent public bonds were sometimes above par. Even when champions of the seas, in 1674, they limited contraband, and allowed safety to neutrals. But when, in 1688, their Stadtholder, William of Orange, became king of Great Britain, they became its ally in detrimental wars against France by land, while their fleets were allowed to decline. Hence arose injurious factions. The Stadtholder party favored having armies and opposed naval expenditures. Their fleets continued to decline; they became weak at sea where they had before become wealthy. The patriot party now felt that Holland was deeply wronged by the great injury that England inflicted on their carrying trade, and by her insults to their flag; they longed to restore their maritime prosperity; they opposed having an army; they loved their country. This party were liberals.

In 1806 Napoleon required this "Batavian Republic" to ask for his brother Louis as their king. Holland could only submit. Napoleon made Louis king of Holland, in May, 1806. It was not the act of the Hollanders.

King Louis appears to have possessed a conscience. Napoleon was, therefore, displeased with him. Dutch prosperity depended largely on commerce. Louis

[1] Bancroft's U. S , v, 14.

had tried to soften the great hardships of Napoleon's continental blockade by not enforcing it with rigor. Importations were made of goods much needed for the common comfort of Holland and north Germany. Some little of the distress was thus alleviated. Louis seems to have been willing that his subjects should be comfortable even if this made some obscure English mechanic also comfortable. But to Napoleon this willingness that a British workman should have food and clothes was a political crime in Louis. The British must be starved into peace on his terms. George III was a bad king, so war must be made against food for British workmen's families! Few meaner principles have ever been admitted into war than this "Continental System" of starving both Europe and the British; a war of strength against weakness; a war as much on the women and helpless children as on the stubborn, hard old king. For actual comfort the continent needed the British market, and the British required the continental markets. Any bar to these beyond proper home labor protection is always impediment to the comfort of all but those who have wealth sufficient to buoy them above ordinary disadvantages. No other man in Europe ever so much warred against the common rights of labor as did Napoleon. He has been lauded as the head of European democracy; there was no democracy whatever in his rule; much farther from real republican democracy, which simply is the willing, harmonious union of all to guarantee and protect the individuals, each to do his honest, fair best for himself without ever injuring another in any way; and which must regulate the rights of all, by law equally applicable to all, so that none may trespass on another. Such is real democracy, republicanism. It did not exist in the French revolution's persecutions for opinion's sake. Marat, Danton, Robespierre, Napoleon were no more democrats than was the Emperor of Austria, less so than the Czar of Russia, who from 1801 to 1812 was inclined to be a liberal, still farther from democracy than even hard old George himself, who was the king of a nation then partially, now almost wholly republican in fact, though monarchial in form.

Great Britain was really and by far the freest country of Europe; perhaps Denmark ranked next; Napoleon who in 1802 returned to cruel slavery the St. Domingans after the slaves had freed themselves, was far less a liberal or a humane man than the Czar Alexander, who just then freed the serfs of the Baltic provinces of Russia. Napoleon's government was much less liberal than that of Austria under Joseph II and Leopold II from 1780 to 1792. The evils that Napoleon inflicted during the time that he controlled Poland, from 1807 to 1813, were more severe, more terrible than those inflicted in the same length of succeeding years after it fell into the power of Russia. It is the greatest mistake to suppose that Napoleon was either republican or democrat, or that he represented anything but despotism. The free press and free speech of America and British countries were utterly wanting wherever his power could reach; even Sweden under madcap Gustavus was better, freer governed. Yet the strange delusion was held then and for forty years later, by many Americans, that Napoleon struggled for the rights of men against despotism. Few assumptions could be less true. He did fight against several despots; but only with an arbitrary one man power. He never found a republic or a republican principle within his reach but that he destroyed it. The 1,000 year old republic of Venice, the 1,400 year old republic of Genoa, the grand old Swiss republic, all the new republics, France, Italy, Holland, he ruled by his own arbitrary will; and the will of Napoleon meant much, for seldom has the world seen such a meddler, who so much interfered in every department and every duty, and frequently hindered the good that they would. The so-called Italian Republic was no more a republic than imperial Germany of 1890, though Germany is far from being a republic.

In his conquests Napoleon oppressed labor by his wholesale plundering, by his terrible exactions of money and property. In France, Germany, Italy, Switzerland, and Holland, he robbed labor of the person of the laborer himself by conscripting him to fight and die abroad. He especially hated British labor and colonial labor. His prohibition of imports of British and colonial property was especially intended to mortify the dull George III and his immediate supporters by causing the utter poverty, distress, misery of British laborers. He could not expect to starve the hard old king nor his ministers, nor the ruling class then in England; it was the poor, the working people, those whose bread depended on employment, that he meant to starve. And this, too, is really the very class that Jefferson's embargo and Madison's non-intercourse Acts were to aid Napoleon to starve.[1]

[1] Ruf. King's statement.

King Louis had committed errors; he had re-established the old noblesse, granted new titles, formed an expensive new guard with marshals; given unearned pensions to nobles. Of these and of the smallness of the Dutch navy Napoleon complained. Louis had actually appointed Dutchmen instead of Frenchmen to Dutch offices! He had mistaken himself for a protector of his subjects instead of being a mere French agent; had favored Dutch trade and commerce instead of the caprice of Napoleon; he had omitted to entirely prevent Dutch trade; sugar, coffee, cotton, food was actually arriving in Holland, and ships were taking away return cargoes of Dutch produce. These facts angered the unjust Napoleon. It was "the Americans" at fault; "the Americans" must be robbed was Napoleon's idea. He pretended to believe that these American ships and goods were really English. Lost to sentiments of honor Napoleon demanded of Louis to repudiate two-thirds of the debt of Holland; to give to him fourteen ships of the line, seven frigates and seven brigs or corvettes fully armed and equipped; to give him an army of 25,000 Dutch; to treacherously seize American vessels that enter Holland; to practically abandon Dutch sovereignty by allowing French courts in Paris to settle Dutch prize cases; "to give up to him to be disposed of to his profit all American vessels that should enter the ports of Holland."[1] Great amounts of American property were in Holland; Napoleon wanted to grab them; their sale would produce him a large sum; he wanted to plunder the goods. He also demanded rigid exclusion of British

---

[1] Thiers Con. et Empire, tome 38, p. 368.

goods. Louis must retract his bad decrees favoring noblesse, and cancel the new titles and marshals which he had unwisely made.

Louis knew that the Americans had entered Dutch ports in peaceful commerce, with no hostile intentions toward France; that they had trusted to his honor and his laws for good faith, and his conscience, his honor, his sense of manliness revolted against the bandit demand of Napoleon. Louis did not wish to be the wholesale robber of quiet American and British merchants, like the great despoiler of non-combatants himself. Louis demurred.

Louis went to Paris, April 10, 1810. Wishing to avoid Napoleon's hospitality he accepted that of his mother, Letitia. "His first act was to demand a separation from his wife,"[2] Hortense, whom many believed to prefer Napoleon to her husband. The matter was so far hushed that it was agreed that they should continue to live separately without formal act of divorce.

March, 1810, Napoleon compelled Louis to cede to France the Dutch possessions west of the Rhine.

In Holland many ships eluded Napoleon's decrees; Denmark aided trade; Russia, greatly needing market for raw material, and requiring foreign goods, eluded his system and carried on a trade under the American flag, when Napoleon was trying to compel all Europe into his war against commerce.

The great natural avarice of Napoleon was excited by the rich stores of American and British property in Holland. Because King Louis would no further rob Americans in Holland, Napoleon decreed non-inter-

[1] "Historical Documents" iii, 156-57.

course with Holland. As Holland was already cut off from its own ocean commerce by the war with Britain, to now separate it from France, and to bar it from Europe as this decree would do, would stifle its trade, prostrate its business.

King Louis obtained revocation of this decree by promising a change; he would allow arrest of the American traders in Holland. Napoleon caused their arrests there and in the Hanse towns. He urged Denmark and Prussia to arrest their American traders. He said they were English who assumed to be Americans for protection as neutrals. If Americans, they have crossed the sea, he said, against American law (the embargo and non-intercourse laws), he would make no distinction. The treacherous emperor, true to his robber instincts, wished to decoy American and British traders, under pretense of safety, into his hands, that he might rob them. He proposed to Prussia :—

"Let them enter, and arrest them afterward: deliver the cargoes to me, and I will take them in part payment of the Prussian debt."[1]

Prussia, more honorable, did not accept that dishonesty, but admitted the traders to fair trade wherever Napoleon did not prevent it. October, 1810, Napoleon compelled Prussia to exclude American vessels. At this same time Napoleon was enriching himself and his favorites by sale of permits to trade.

"You require," said the Czar of Russia, "that I shall cut off my subjects from trade with England; that I shall prevent selling their wheat and naval stores, for which they can find no market but with English merchants; that I shall condemn them not to receive in exchange, sugar, coffee, and manufactures which they need; and you do not hesitate to bring your silk, cloth, wine, into England, and

[1] Thiers Con. et Emp., v. III, 359 360.

thence bring sugar and coffee which your laws so strictly exclude from all the rest of the continent. Be not then, so rigid to others, while so indulgent to yourself."[1]

In warring against commerce, Napoleon was really warring against mankind.

Spanish American Caracas and Buenos Ayres were in revolt. The British and American settlers proclaimed Florida independent. Mobile had a Spanish garrison. The insurgents asked American protection. Madison preferred to take possession under color of the Louisiana purchase. In 1811 Congress secretly passed an act to occupy both Floridas. The danger was too great that a foreign power would occupy them. Though extensively robbing Americans, Napoleon contrived to flatter Jefferson's party by saying he was ready to waive the Decrees of Berlin and Milan in the "special favor" of America, if America would cause England to respect our neutrality ; and by saying that France would not oppose our seizing Florida, nor object to independence of Spanish America. These Spanish colonies were beyond his own reach ; he was barred from them by the British navy, so it cost him no plunder to let Spain lose them.

The "American cargoes" which Napoleon required Louis to yield to him were largely claimed as Dutch property; some were really Dutch goods brought under the American flag, from Dutch colonies ; some really American, and some British and Dutch partnership property.

In place of these Louis tried to content his robber brother with prizes taken by privateers, but it was the "American cargoes" that Napoleon wanted to plunder ; he insisted on having them. I find in all

[1] Thiers' Cons. et Empire, t. 111, 359, 360.

his own letters and orders[1] on this subject that he calls this property "American."

Louis resisted the great crime. Napoleon filled the coasts and country with French agents; he even formed commissions of customs and military officers to summarily try persons accused of trade. Louis ordered discharge of all persons arrested for trade.[2] Napoleon meanly compelled the Dutch to give up to French vessels the Rhine navigation above Nimeguen.

These outrages made Louis very indignant. He tried to let the American property alone. He had tried to govern Holland for its people. This Napoleon would not permit; he ordered the French army to interfere. Disgusted with Napoleon Louis abdicated, July 3, 1810, in favor of Hortense's son, the boy, Napoleon Louis, with Hortense as regent. King Louis secretly fled from Holland to Austria. Napoleon had made this boy Grand Duke of Berg, vacated by Murat, but governed as a French province. The abdication and flight of Louis made a profound sensation in Europe.

Napoleon annexed Holland to France, July 9, 1810. French and Belgians ruled it. He confiscated the "American cargoes," he made them his own plunder.

By decree of August 5, 1810, Napoleon committed an astounding robbery. One-half of all goods already imported regularly, one-half of privateer's prizes, one-half of legal neutral cargoes were to be seized by surprise. English goods were to be confiscated in whole even though owned by his own subjects. He would license imports at 50% duty, but not of

Great robbery by Napoleon.

[1] Napoleon to Louis. [2] Thiers Con. et Empire, viii, 385.

English goods, sugar, or coffee (except Mocha), nor tobacco, dyes, rice, or produce of colonies. He now made his system of licenses general.

In Holland, Hamburg, Bremen, Pomerania, Prussia, Dantzic, in such German towns as Leipsic, Frankfort, in Switzerland, Italy, Venice, Genoa, Leghorn, Naples, were stores of such goods belonging to natives and to American and British merchants. These he plundered without law. Napoleon hurried off couriers to the German states, Prussia, Italy, Switzerland, Denmark, Sweden, Austria, and even to Russia, urging them to tax, to seize, to confiscate one-half or the whole of such goods, enrich their treasuries, inflict a blow on British commerce, and render future smuggling of little avail. Bavaria, Wurtemburg, Baden, and Saxony, controlled by Napoleon, quickly enforced this decree. Disregarding law and decency, Napoleon again robbed the neutral Free Cities, Hamburg, Bremen, and Lubec. He plundered Prussian Stettin and Custrin and Polish Dantzic, towns entitled to his special protection and which had French garrisons. In many places throughout central Europe he plundered the merchants of great values. He compelled every continental state except Russia, Turkey, and insurgent Spain and Portugal, and Austria which had no ports, to accept the decree of robbery of its own citizens and British merchants, and, especially in Holland, of Americans. Northern Spain, Germany, Holland, and Italy suffered severely from his robberies. He allowed 20% commission to his officers and soldiers to commit these depredations. Auction sales on his account were held in many places. He required that all English cotton goods and hardware be burned or destroyed.

This gigantic robbery brought Napoleon in 1810 $30,000,000 cash beside vast amounts of plundered goods some of which were American property.

He authorized that any vessel of any nation at sea might be taken by French privateers, unless it had a license stating where from, where to touch, and what its cargo. He tried to betray more American vessels into his ports in order to rob them by appearing to relax his coast guards. Such was the dangerous character with whom President Madison and Congress were coquetting. As France needed raw cotton and naval stores he now allowed vessels to go to England if they took French wheat, silks, cloth, or wine in exchange.

His French admirer, Thiers, naively says:—

"The whole system of commerce was thus regulated by decree,— that is, rendered almost impossible."

Bourrienne (French) says:—

"The speculation in licenses was carried to a scandalous extent only to enrich a few." "Smuggling on a small scale was punishable by death, whilst the government itself carried it on extensively. The same cause filled the treasury with money and the prisons with victims." "At Hamburg a poor man was threatened with death for smuggling a loaf of sugar, while perhaps Napoleon was signing a license to admit a million loaves."

"Murat and his officers smuggled at Naples." "The 'Continental System' was worthy only of ages of ignorance and barbarism, and, had it been admissible in theory was impracticable in practice." "Enormous quantities of English goods and colonial produce accumulated in Holstein .... and were smuggled."

Later Napoleon permitted importations at Hamburg at 33% duty, which in 1811 was 60,000,000 francs revenue.

"This system, however, embroiled us (France) with Sweden and Russia who could not endure that Napoleon should exact a strict blockade from them while himself distributing licenses in abundance."

"All nations under French influence were required to adopt it, and and at one time it covered all Europe but Spain and Turkey." "The continent was, nevertheless, inundated with articles of English make."

Holland's debt was so large that it called for 80,-000,000 francs a year. Napoleon repudiated two-thirds of the debt. Holland had large quantities of sugar, coffee, cotton, and indigo, worth less than the price in France, on these he put a 50% tax and duty for his own special profit.

He put Dutch members into the French Senate, Council, Corps Legislatif, and highest law courts, and fused its army and navy with those of France.

The war had lasted seven years without exchange of prisoners. Both sides held many. Some of them had been seven years captive. When the war suddenly began again, in 1803, many English were traveling in France. Napoleon arrested these innocent non-combatants and had cruelly held them all these years as prisoners of war. In April, 1810, Mr. Mackenzie, British agent, tried to effect an exchange. Napoleon demanded that the non-combatants should be included in exchange for French soldiers and sailors! Of course this would be very unfair. French soldiers and sailors might be at once put to fight England, while civilians would be of no military use. England, with justice, objected. But Napoleon, disregarding right and justice, insisted. Overcome by humanity, England gave way; consented to this gross injustice. But this did not satisfy the unjust emperor. The British held many thousands more French than France held of British prisoners. Then Napoleon insisted that the surplus French be given him for Germans, Spaniards, Portuguese, or others. But it was unreasonable to expect Britain to restore French soldiers to French armies in exchange for foreigners who owed England no service or allegiance, and who might perhaps as readily join the French ranks as the British. Then Mr. Mackenzie made the fair and liberal proposal to exchange for Napoleon's British prisoners, man for man, rank for rank of French, and when the number of British held by France were exhausted, to give likewise Frenchmen for any British allies in equal numbers. Napoleon would not consent to this humane offer, so the attempt to exchange failed. By his refusal of the simplest justice, he condemned 48,649 of his own brave soldiers, some of whom had already been prisoners for seven years, to four years longer of imprisonment in Great Britain, after they had too faithfully fought for him; and then it was not Napoleon, but his enemy, England, that, in 1814, freely liberated these captives. Napoleon did not clothe or feed his captives in British hands. The British sent the means of support to France for their men in Napoleon's mean hands![1]

He had conscripted these men from their homes; they had helped his power and conquest, and thus treacherously this man who lacked the noble principle of friendship and of fair dealing, left them to be detained, fed, clothed, or neglected by the nation whom it was his ardent desire to ruin, while he exacted British money to support British prisoners of war, in his hands.

Lack of real money troubled Great Britain. She suspended specie payments from February, 1797, till 1821, and used paper instead. Thus she temporarily enjoyed the advantage of apparent increase of her

[1] Alison iii, 394.

working capital to the amount of her displaced gold and silver, most of which was exported and practically sold. When peace came, in 1815, and she again desired to use coin, great distress followed from the heavy burden of having to re-purchase gold and silver abroad. The practical effect of the matter was equivalent to a loan to her for the intervening years, that had to be paid at peace, by great sacrifice and suffering.

The spring of 1810 was cold and wet; large imports of grain that cost £7,000,000 had to be made. In August, wheat was up to 116s. per quarter, about $3.50 per bushel. Then fine weather reduced it to 94s., 7d., or $2.45 a bushel, and ruined wheat dealers.

Confiscations of British goods in the Baltic ruined many merchants; losses in South America ruined many more. Credit collapsed. The crash began in July; several banks stopped in August; wild panic followed, fluctuations, losses, failure. "Besides stoppages and compositions equal in number to half the traders in the kingdom," the bankruptcies were numerous, 2,314 for 1810. Hunger of work-people, outcry for food, alarm against machinery, war on weaving frames, began the dark coming years. Paper money practically sank from about 2½ % to 13¾ % discount.

British expenditure, in 1809, was £89,522,000; in 1810 it was £85,243,620. The taxes were very heavy; the loans borrowed were large; the already great national debt was much increased. £174,765,620, or almost $870,000,000 was expended in two years. Of England's three allies, Austria had been defeated, crushed, disabled; Spain was overrun by the enemy ; and Portugal was prostrated. This frightful outlay of British money was a great disaster of itself. What victory could remunerate such a burden of debt as was laid on Britain? The figures were truly startling. How long could a population of less than 12,000,000 stand this tremendous outlay? It had, in two years, been about $75 apiece for every man, woman and child in all Great Britain. The terrible financial crash made it look as if the end was near. Britain had then stood above fifteen years of war, with less than two years of intermission, and still peace appeared no nearer. What could be the result? A terrible prospect threatened her.

America was threatening war. Russia was uneasy and was preparing for tremendous war, for a struggle so great that it will be ever memorable in history. The Peninsular war was to assume immense proportions. Germany was in a patriotic ferment. Austria was watching its opportunity. All Europe was approaching an impending gigantic collision of nations, a tremendous crash of armies, whose story will be told and received with wonder by many coming generations. In another volume we shall continue its great, eventful history through one of the most remarkable periods of the world's existence.

INDEX.

AMERICA admired France, 182. An American shot, 181. Assailed by Napoleon, 120. Americans robbed by Napoleon, 422-9. Army, 121, 181-2, 274, 347-8, 360. British aided Americans, 118, 183, 293. Employed American vessels, 369. British aggressions, 178, 180, 182, 260, 263, 273. Tax, 260, 271-5, 348, 355. Concessions, 184, 263, 268, 276, 363, 370. British blockades, 177; of West Indies, 185, 188, 263, 372. Impressments, 178, 182, 184, 189, 258, 36). Orders in Council, 188, 260, 272-5, 348, 363-72. "Search and Seizures," 177, 194, 256, 259. Americans employed British deserters, 179, 277.

Chesapeake affair, 257-9, 278, 371. *Citizenship*, 184-5.

Commerce (Am.), 46, 177, 193, 258, 262-3.

Congress against our trade, 181, 258, 261. New act, 269, 277, 357, 360. *No Trade Policy*, 180, 190, 261, 267, 270-5, 347, 358, 365-71; suspended, 372. renewed, 373.

Continental System, BERLIN DECREE, 186; MILAN DECREE, 271; BAYONNE DECREE, 275, 363; RAMBOUILLET DECREE, 375. Napoleon's *Licenses*, 363. His treachery, 188. Napoleon robbed Americans, 120, 260, 274-6, 372-5, 417, 422-9. Editors, 279.

EMBARGO, 46, 120, 190, 261-9, 280. Former, 277. Illegal, 280, 348, 369. Aids our enemy, 352-6. Force Law, 359; Massachusetts, 360; Connecticut, 361; repealed, 364, 407.

JEFFERSON,—his character, 264-7. His party, 179; opposed Washington, 190, 193, 278. Against trade, 190; against a navy, 181, 278; his libel suits, 193; betrays his professions, 193, 215, 264, 277. Admires France, 181-2, 262, 277. Wants to control judges, 265. Would extend slavery, 265. Against an army, 274-8. Wants war with Spain, 263; refused Spanish minister, 276. His "States Rights," 268, 357. Disliked Delaware, 263 He captures American vessels, 270, 359, 363. Harms Boston, 274; is rebuked by a court, 274; orders away British ships, 258, 277; loses America's best treaty chance, 189. Coercion, 277; keeps trouble open; Charges against him, 278. Starving policy, 279. Censures a court, 281. Despotic, 215, 359; for strong central power, 359. Exit, 366.

Money, 263, 347, 349, 367, 374.

Madison's plan, 180 190, ,367. Advises tariff protection, 372. Henry, 361.

Navy, 121, 181-2, 347-9. Williams, 274, 358. Frigates and gunfloats, 181, 274, 347-9, 358. Our four frigates, 357, 365.

Neutrality, 190, 256, 258, 260, 271.

Negotiations, 184; treaty, 185; rejected, 189; Washington's, 190; Jay, 258; Rose, 270, 352; Erskine, 369; Canning, 259, 350-1, 370. Jackson, 373. Canning's terms, 370; rejects treaty, 372. Non-intercourse enforced, 373.

Parties, 178, 183, 261-5, 270, 360, 371. Doctrines reversed, 307, 371.

Planters want war, 358-64, 373; think trade is robbery, 369; against *Hayti* trade, 372-3. Prices, 374. Population, 182.
Randolph, 180, 360. Revenue, 271. Russia favors American trade, 362.
Right of harbor, 258.
Slave power, 262, 273, 279. Judge Story, 365.
Trade, 177, 193, 260-3, 272, 362, 407. Trafalgar, 118.

AUSTRIA; coalition against Napoleon, 78-81. Emperor, 74, 87, 89, 96, 138. Exit German empire, 200. Finance, 95. Ministry and condition, 95-7. War of 1805, Ulm, 98. Four battles, 103-5.
Armies, 95, 98, 102, 137, 230, 337, 377-8. Austerlitz, 139. Presburg treaty, 160. Losses, 160. Charles rules, 165, 245; refuses war, 245. Austria arming, 329, 376. Charles, 377. War of 1809 with France, 376; Battles; of Thann, 381; Hiller's fight and Echmuhl, 382; in Italy, 383; of Traun, 385; John beaten, 386; Lobau, 386; John fails, 389-90; Wagram, 391; Peace, 395. Losses, 395. The Tyrol, 385-6, 390; Hofer, 404-5.
Bavaria, 97, 101, 137, 160, 303. Baden, 303. Belgium, 95.

BRITISH, Addington, 61. Alliances, 78, 81, 86, 88, 129, 211. Army, 250, 398.
Blockades, 177, 263. Burdens, 168, 173. Buenos Ayres robbed, 198, 246.
British in Egypt, 246; in Italy and South America, 198, 246; in Turkey, 246, 407; enter Spain, 328; expel the French from Portugal, 328.
Diplomacy, 194; Cintra, 194, 278, 328, 352; Napoleon and Fouché, 414. British terms, 79, 414.
Finance, 87, 173, 244, 430. Flogging, 174. Frauds, 82, 170, 210, 397.
Fox, 63, 89, 169, 171, 174-6, 184, 189, 194-9, 209.
George III, 30, 60, 75, 78, 82, 129, 155, 170-4, 188, 243-7, 258, 403. Prince George, 60, 415.
Impressments, 177, 194. System of, 258, 368. Enlistments, 173.
Maida battle, 197. Malta, 86.
Ministry, 61, 78, 82, 170. New, 169-74, 178. Canning, 171. Offer to America, 184-7. Ministry of 1806, 189, 194. On Catholics, 247. Threaten Turkey; Beaten, 246. Whigs dismissed, 248. Feeble government 1807, 248. Aids Sweden, 250. Perceval, 189, 249. Prussian treaty, 252. British opportunity, 134, 141, 243, 250, 410. Injured Denmark, 281-3. Refused Erfurt peace offer, 332. Bad ministry, 398. Castlereagh, 398, 403. New ministry (Perceval), 404. Naples affair, 407.
Navy, 93, 120, 163, 182. Its deserters, 163, 277.
Nelson, 70, 90, 122. TRAFALGAR, 110, 312, 340, 343.
Napoleon's peace intrigue of 1810, 414; British terms, 415. His treachery, 194.
ORDERS IN COUNCIL, 177, 188, 260, 272, 275, 348.
Parliament, 70, 249. Parties, 63, 166, 170, 404.
Pitt, William, 60, 75. Basis, 79, 83, 88, 98, 106, 129, 134, 136, 155, 168, 172.
Prisoners of War, 429. Outlook bad, 429-232.
Peninsular war, 74. Treasure frigates, 75, 90, 328, 340, 343, 407. Talavera, 410.

UNITED STATES AND EUROPE. 435

Royal scandals, 210, 397. Russia seizes British vessels, 369.
Taxes, 173. *Tax neutrals*, 260, 275, 348, 355, 366. Trade and peace with Turkey, 407.
Walcheren affair, 398. Whigs, 248, 260, 272, 348. Wellington, 408-10.
Cargoes, 180. *Christians*, 279. Coalitions, 67, 78, 81, 86, 88, 129, 211.
Court, Imperial, 59. *Courts, decisions* of, 30-2, 193, 274, 352.
Democracy, 179, 300. Denmark, 187, 281. Copenhagen outrage, 282. Denmark robbed, 285.
Editors, 279. Education, 298. Erfurt, 329. Equilibrium, 81.

FRANCE, and America, 118, 183. American robbery by Napoleon, 120, 260, 274-6, 372-5, 417. 422-29. Antwerp, 296. Armies, 77, 137, 211, 230, 300, 330, 378. Armistice, 228. Augereau's corps lost, 226. Austrian war of 1805, 138. Austrian war of 1809, 376, 385.
Battles: Aerstadt, 222. Austerlitz, 139. Arzibispo, 411. Baylen, 324. Coruna, 343. Eckmuhl, 382. Elchingen, 105. Eylau, 235. Friedland, 251. Camoral, 335. Gerona, 411. Golymin, 233. Gunsberg, 103. Haslach, 103. Heilsberg, 251. Jena, 213. Lobau, 386. Maida, 197. Oceana, 412. Pultusk, 231. Rio Seco, 323. Gamoral, Espinosa, Tudela and Somo Pass, 334-5. Talavera, 410. Trafalgar, 109. Traun, 385. Ulm, 103. Wagram, 391.
Bonaparte boy, 319, 426; family, 409; Joseph, king of Naples, 160; king of Spain, 319-21: fled, 324. lost Spain, 325-6; in despair, 409, 413. Louis, king of Holland, 419, 422. NAPOLEON, character of, 120-1, 202-5, 233, 295, 410, 412. Hates liberty, 121.
Bonaparte at *Boulogne*, 68, 77, 99. A Bonaparte peace, 293. At Erfurt, 331. Offers the British peace, 77.
Catechism of the empire, 198, 299.
Coalitions against Napoleon, 67, 86, 88, 96, 129, 150, 211.
Confederation of the Rhine, 69, 74, 199-204, 254. Commerce, 108. Concordat, 70.
CONTINENTAL SYSTEM, 186-7; Berlin decree, 187, 254; Milan decree, 271-2. Bayonne decree, 275, 291; Rambouillet decree, 375.
Conscriptions, 99, 100, 228, 244, 297-8, 317, 326, 376, 390, 404.
Constitution subverted, 293. Coronation, 71. Bad Imperial court, 302.
Despotism, 55-60, 182, 293, 303, 311, 410. Diplomacy with Prussia, 227; with England, 332. Divorce, 72, 303, 331.
Empire came, 57. D'Enghien, 55, 66. Eugene, 85, 161, 386, 390.
Eylau's gloom, 244; Napoleon after Eylau, 243, 250.
Fetes, 71, 161. France not a republic, 182. Fouché's plan to conquer America, 120, 415. French glory, 162, 297, 330. French Industries, 295-6, 415.
Josephine, 72. Judges dependent, 294.
Legion of Honor, 68. Linois beaten, 60.
Money affairs, 71, 74, 142, 153, 164, 295, 330, 376, 429. Moreau, 56. Murat, 167, 319.
NAPOLEON'S *ingratitude*, 121, 183. Navy, 77, 90, 163, 296, 417. Nobility, 165, 302.
Plots of Napoleon and Fouché in 1810, 414.
Plot against Napoleon, 54; plot by him, 56. His police and prisons, 297.

436   UNITED STATES AND EUROPE.

The *Press* of Europe, 293-8. French public works and thrift, 294-6, 330.
Prisoners of war, 429.
The *Pope* and Napoleon, 70-3, 303. Excommunication of Napoleon, 405. Captive, 405.
"*Protection*" and French business, 415.
Poland and Napoleon, 230, 234, 250, 254, 256, 376, 384.
Portuguese war, 74, 307, 316, 327-8, 310. Exit royalty, 311, 327. Conquest and revolt, 327. Soult, 407. Forced service, 408. Battle of Oporto, 408.
Prussia and Napoleon (see Prussia), Russia and Napoleon (see Russia).
Revolution versus kings, 294-300. Neither republic nor democracy, 300, 419.
Robbery in general of American and other merchants in (Holland) Europe, 422.
Robbery by Napoleon, 101; he robs Americans, 120, 201-2, 260, 294, 275-6, 372-5, 422-8. He robs Austrians, 295, 395. Everywhere, 293. Robs Germans, 225, 227, 302. Robs Hanse cities, 67, 202, 230, 245. Robs Hanover, 302. Robs Hesse, 226, 228. Robs Italians, 302. Robs Leipsic, 227. Robs Prussia, 225, 227, 228, 233, 292, 329. Robs Spaniards, 305, 336. Robs several countries, 422-8. Robs Wittenberg, 227.
Sale of Peoples by Napoleon, 176, 195, 210, 255, 292, 304.
Spanish aggressions of Napoleon, 74-7, 90, 210, 305, 310, 316. His Peninsular war a crime and useless, 413.
Sardinia and *Sicily*, 195, 293.
SYSTEM OF BATTLE OF NAPOLEON, 151. His strategy and Tactics, 100.
Genoa, 65, 69, 85.
Treachery of Napoleon, 120, 183, 194-205, 234, 245, 430; to Americans, 188; to Austrians, 165, 199, 206; to England, 194-5; to Prussia, 201-8, 330; to Spain, 311-12, 316, 318, 325; to French prisoners. 429; to Tuscany (Etruria), 292, 310.
Shipping, 90, 296; Trade lost, 295. French taxes, 295.
Germany, 69. Exit empire, 74, 86, 96, 133, 137, 199. Seizures, 201. Palm murdered, 206. Officials, 227. Robbed, 225-7, 290. Stein, 330; hate Napoleon, 201, 383. Schill and Katt, 384. Wants war, 380-6. Fesch is primate, 201.
Hanover, 67, 87, 128, 133, 176, 196, 255, 312.
Hanse towns, 67, 87; robbed, 202, 230, 245.
Hesse, 200-4, 226, 228.
Holland, 133, 160 (King Louis, 166), 184, 195, 254, 368, 374, 377. In 1810, 418.
Industries, Labor and Wages, 45. Inventions, 45. Iona, 405.
Ireland, 63, 82, 247.
Italy, 64, 80, 84-9, 137. Honorable British action, 166.
Malta, 86. *Manufactures*, 30, 45. Marriages, 72, 161.
Naples, 137, 160 (King Joseph, 160-6).
Parallel between Napoleon and Pitt, 155.
Peace sought by *Fox*, 194. Presburg peace, 157, 159, 162. Napoleon broke it, 165. Peace of *Tilsit*, 253, 292. Pichegru, 54.
Pope, The, 70-3, 303. Bull against Napoleon, 405. Captive in France, 405.
Postage and paper, 46. The *Press*, 279.

UNITED STATES AND EUROPE. 437

PRUSSIA, 67, 122-7, 131, 133. 141, 157, 174, 183, 200-9 (war 211), 213, 222, 226.
Prussian army, 126, 131, 140, 213-28, 233, 290. Arms, 207.
Battles of Aerstadt, 222. Jena, 213. Four battles, 251.
Confederation of Rhine, 69, 74, 199-204, 254.
Embargo by England, 176. Exemptions, 291.
Hanover, 133, 176.
King of Prussia, 122 (in 1806, 174), 124, 127, 129-33. Admits Russians, 131. Orders three armies, 131. Sentiment with Alexander, 127, 132. Anspach, 131. Ultimatum, 132. Civil to Russians, 176. Prussia insulted by Napoleon, 200-8. The king for war, 204, 207-8. Wants subsidy, 207. Ultimatum, 208. Wrongs Prussian army, 211. Bad policy, 212. Wrongs Saxony, 212. WAR, 211. Defeat, 214. Bad strategy, 216. Battle of Jena, 217; of Aerstadt, 222. Surrenders, 225, 226, 234. Officials, 227. Negotiates, 227, lets a fool decide, 253, 292. Reigns over a remnant, 254. Napoleon robs Prussia, 225-8, 292, 329.
Ministry and policy, 123, 128, Hardenberg, 128. Haugwitz, 128, 132, 144, 157. Forced treaty, 174-6.
Napoleon's treachery to Prussia, 176, 194, 200-4, 330.
North Germany and Prussia, 67, 86, 121, 200.
Patriots, 203. Population, 212. Prosperity, 126. Promotions (army), 211.
Prussia's *opportunity*, 202. Honorable action, 424.
Queen Luise of Prussia, 207.
Stein reforms, 290. Von Stein, 330, 380-3. Scharnhorst, 291.
Treaty with Napoleon, 144, 157; failed, 174; new treaty, 174.
Treaty with Great Britain, 252. Treaty of Tilsit, 253. Treaty with Sweden, 245.
TUGENBUND, 292, 383.

POLAND, 230, 234, 250. Warsaw, 254, 256, 376, 384.

PORTUGAL, Napoleon's demand, 307; cheated, 308; conspiracy of Napoleon and Charles IV, 309. War and plunder, 310. Revolt, 327.
Wellington came, defeated Junot; Cintra, 328.
Wellington again, 407. Soult takes Oporto, 407. British victory, Soult driven from Portugal, 408. Outrages, 408. Torres Vedras, 414.
Republics, 300. Rights of *Neutrals*, 178.

RUSSIA, 64-7, 78, 81-6, 131. 187. Treaty with Oubril, 194, 204-5, 211, 228, 231. War (1806), 228, 231, 234, 251.
Armies, 86, 127, 131, 137, 228.
Battles of Austerlitz, 139. Battle of Eylau, 235. Napoleon retreated, 243; beaten, he suspended the war, 245. Battle of Friedland, 251; of Heilsberg, 251; of Pultusk, 231. Four battles, 251. Raft and armistice, 252. Peace of *Tilsit*, 252. Ultimatum to England, 255. 2d treaty, 255. Mediation, 256. *Benningsen*, 231, 235, 251.
Character of *Alexander*, 65, 252. His terms in Oubril affair, 66.
Emperors at *Erfurt*, 329-30. Letter to English king, 331 (1808).
Russia and Prussia, 131, 211. Russia took spoils of Prussia, 254.
Russia and Turkey, 229, 239, 245, 255, 277, 329.

SAXONY, 200, 212, 227.
Sardinia and Sicily, 193-4, 293, 330.
SLAVERY, 25-44. Everywhere, 44. Import, 25, 27, 32, 36, 39, 41, 44. Judge Holt decides England free, 30; reversed. Bench (Mansfield) decision, 32. England and slavery, 26, 30, 43, 44. Friends Society, 36, 38. Indian slavery, 25, 31. Royalty supports slavery, 27, 31, 43. Debates on, 36. Hopper and Ridgly, 38. Slavery in territories, 34, 41. Tax on slave imports, 32, 34, 35. Oglethorpe, 28, Va., 26, 27, 30, 32. Slaveholders liked Napoleon, 178. England forbade American manufacturing, 30. New England on slavery, 26, 33, 36, 40. Slave soldiers in Revolutionary army, 33. Citizenship, 33. Anti-slavery societies, 34, 36. Fugitives, 38, 39. The slave trade, 40, 196. Jefferson wanted to extend slavery, 266. Madison wanted to make soldiers of slaves, 34.
Sovereigns, characters of, 65-6, 79, 81, 83, 204, 205.

SPAIN, alliance with France, 74, 305. Napoleon wrongs Spain, 210, 303; subsidy, 305. Losses, 305. Army, 323, 326. Finance, 335-41.
British distrust, 74. British aid, 326. Fleet, 90. Bourbons, 305-15. British Moore, 334, 344; Baird, 341; no plan, 335; British money, 235.
Charles IV, 77, 304, 306-8, 312; asks advice, 313; runs away, 313; resigns, 314; his quarrel, 316. Ceded crown to Napoleon, 316.
Ferdinand, 312-23.
French enter Spain, 310. *War* with Portugal, 310. Spain invaded, 313. Revolt and outrages, 313 24. Condition, 322. Constitution of Bayonne, 320. Murders, 321. Juntas, 321-34. Monks, 322. Smuggling, 322. What Scott says, 322. Romana, 323. *Battles* of Rio Seco, 323; Baylen, 324; French driven, 333; Napoleon comes, 335; *Battles* of Coruna, 343; Espinosa, Gamoral, Tudela and Somo Pass, 336; Cuidad Real, 409; Talavera, 410; Arabispo, 411; Horrible Gerona, 411; Oceana, 412.
Corruption, 324-5. *Cruel* crime against prisoners, 324. *Guerillas*, 413.
Godoy, 75, 210, 306-8, 314, 318.
Joseph Bonaparte, king, 319-29, 413. *Murat*, 314-16. Men shot, 317.
Saragossa (siege), 344.
Spanish *Slave Trade*, 25-32, 197.
Steam, 49. *Schools* and *Sunday-schools*, 46.
Sweden, 66-8, 86, 88, 159, 211, 284. King Gustavus IV, 66-8, 88, 133, 158. 211, 284. Exit, 286.
Switzerland, 160.
Trade, 46, 260.
Trafalgar, 109, 163. Tories, 171. Tilsit Peace, 253.
Turkey, 229, 245-6, 255, 377; and Servia, 286.
Tuscany, 292. Louise, 310. Seized, 310-15.
Tyrol, 380-3, 390, 404. Hofer murdered, 405.

Wages and Labor, 45. Sailor's wages, 262.
Watt, James, 51.
War between Peoples, 211, 354, 396. War between rulers, 201, 207, 220, 278.
Walcheren affair, 398.

www.ingramcontent.com/pod-product-compliance
Lightning Source LLC
Chambersburg PA
CBHW022111300426
44117CB00007B/666